PRAISE FOR *RETURN TO ORDER*

"*Return to Order* provides an interesting analysis of how the United States has departed from the spiritual, cultural, and economic precepts that supported the founding and the early history of our republic. It also sets forth valuable recommendations for restoring our society to its foundation of ordered liberty and traditional values."

— *The Honorable Edwin Meese III*
Former Attorney General of the United States

"This is a timely and important book as our nation faces one of the most critical challenges in its history. Overcoming the economic disaster America is facing cannot be solved simply through economic policy. Americans and their leaders must put in place policy that will restore values, work ethics, and, as the author points out so well, honor.... Restoring honor to our economic landscape will put the nation on the path to recovery."

— *Lt. Gen. Benjamin R. Mixon, USA (Ret.)*
Former Commanding General, United States Army Pacific

"The depth of knowledge and originality of Horvat's analysis, plus the scope and inspiration of his vision for a true solution to our current economic crisis, make *Return to Order* worthy of becoming the bedside book for those who believe America is worth fighting for."

— *Joseph M. Scheidler*
National Director, Pro-Life Action League

"By calling the reader to embrace the cardinal virtues of temperance, justice, prudence and fortitude, *Return to Order* suggests a practical pathway to avoid the economic and spiritual crises that are looming before us and, by means of religious conversion, reestablish a right order for human flourishing. I hope that this work will receive the attention it so deserves."

— *Most Rev. John C. Nienstedt*
Archbishop of Saint Paul and Minneapolis

"Horvat's fabulous analysis of our present crisis can and should be a most important instrument in reshaping the educational foundations of our youth, preparing them for leadership..."

— *David S. Miller*
Senior Vice President, US Bank

"John Horvat sounds a clarion call for a return to fiscal and moral sanity. A must read!"

— *Col. George E. "Bud" Day, USAF (Ret.)*
Medal of Honor recipient and former POW

"The central theme of frenetic intemperance is original, interesting, and compelling. The diagnosis of contemporary social maladies must focus on moral failings, and *Return to Order* rightly does so. Its insightful thesis deserves wide circulation and consideration."

— *Kevin E. Schmiesing, Ph.D.*
Research Fellow, Acton Institute for the Study of Religion and Liberty;
Book Review Editor, Journal of Markets & Morality

"Inside the chaos of our days, the book is a welcome beacon that helps us get our bearings and set us on the path to true order. It defines real leadership and calls all to virtue and trust in Providence. It is my fervent hope that this book will get the attention it deserves and that it will help bring about God's highest designs for the American people at this crossroads in history."

— *H.I.R.H. Prince Bertrand of Orleans-Braganza*
Prince Imperial of Brazil

"If our nation ever needed to return to traditional values, it is now. We are committing suicide; but each of our problems has at its roots a moral solution found in the tenets of the Christian tradition that is at the foundation of our being. *Return to Order* does a great job of highlighting the source and solution to our impending demise."

— *Maj. Gen. Patrick H. Brady, USA (Ret.)*
Medal of Honor recipient

"Anyone who considers the ongoing public debate as superficial—indeed most reform proposals merely want to cure the symptoms, yet do not address the underlying causes—should study Mr. Horvat's *Return to Order*. It is to be hoped that this book reaches a large reading public and will have an impact on public policy, theoretical debates and personal decisions alike."

— *Gregor Hochreiter*
Director, Institute of Applied Economics and
Western Christian Philosophy (Vienna, Austria)

"[Horvat] would likely fall into the company of such traditional conservative scholars as Russell Kirk or Richard Weaver. This is a perceptive and exciting book explaining how these traditional understandings and principles can form the bedrock of our personal and corporate philosophy today."

— *G. Daniel Harden, Ph.D.*
Emeritus Professor of Education, Washburn University
Chairman, Kansas Governmental Ethics Commission

"This excellent work is an in-depth study of the history and cause of our present-day economic and spiritual crisis, and it gives us a well-reasoned solution to our plight as well. I am pleased to recommend it."

— *Most Rev. James C. Timlin*
Bishop Emeritus of Scranton

"Horvat calls for an order that combines the virtues of tested traditions with the creative potential of the free economy: a combination of a structured order based on traditional values and the spontaneous order of economic systems based on private property. He uses the term 'frenetic intemperance' to describe the type of life which does not leave room for family, creative leisure, and prayer. A call for more balance in our economies and our lives."

— Alejandro Chafuen, Ph.D.
President, Atlas Economic Research Foundation

"*Return to Order* is a refreshing breath of air in a time of economic and political distress.... [It] is a beacon on a hill enlightening the way for readers in a time of American uncertainty."

—Congressman Lou Barletta
U.S. House of Representatives, serving Pennsylvania's 11th District

"The restoration of economic and social peace in our disordered society is something for which all men of good will yearn. John Horvat has given us in his excellent book, *Return to Order*, a catechism of principles to guide all our efforts to restore economic and social peace to America."

— Most Rev. Rene H. Gracida
Bishop Emeritus of Corpus Christi

"It's rare that a book of this depth is also such a pleasure to read. Horvat's critique of contemporary America's 'frenetic intemperance' rings true, laying bare modern man's confusion and anomie amid plenty. An erudite cultural sculptor, Horvat chisels away materialism's false promises and points toward God as the source of the higher revelation that makes beauty, heroism, nobility, sacrifice and true vocation discoverable and meaningful."

— Robert Knight
Columnist and author

"*Return to Order* touches on matters that apply not only to America but everywhere. Modern economy is in trouble and this book zeroes in on the problem of frenetic intemperance in an original and convincing manner. Best of all, author John Horvat offers organic Catholic solutions that are both so needed and so refreshing. I hope this book gets wide circulation and recommend it to all those who want real answers to vital questions."

— H.H. Duke Paul of Oldenburg
Director, Brussels Office of Fédération Pro Europa Christiana

"*Return to Order* is a clear, engaging read that, by delineating some fundamentals of the natural order, will empower you to spot many of today's disorders— even some you may have unconsciously bought into. Such was my experience... I was enlightened.... The book is interesting, clear and enlightening."

— Patrick F. Fagan, Ph.D.
Director, Marriage & Religion Research Institute (MARRI)

"Horvat's thesis that frenetic intemperance has driven many, if not all, of today's economic problems bears close consideration....This book should be read and its recommendations followed by those who know a *Return to Order* in the twenty-first century is sorely needed."

— *Lt. Col. Joseph J. Thomas, USMC (Ret.), Ph.D.*
Distinguished Professor of Leadership Education,
United States Naval Academy

"Like the true cultural conservative he is, John Horvat takes on the idols of technological, economic, and political power. These powers exacerbate the human tendency toward frenetic intemperance."

— *Richard Stivers, Ph.D.*
Emeritus Professor of Sociology, Illinois State University

"In an intellectually compelling and practical way, *Return to Order* reminds us that economy and religion are deeply connected, and that, with the family at the center, we can hope to be freed from the frenzy in which our society finds itself. I highly recommend this book."

— *Rev. Frank Pavone*
National Director, Priests for Life

"This book proposes a revitalization of long standing Christian practices as an antidote to current economic discontinuities. Using practical minded recommendations to resolve massively complex societal issues, *Return to Order* is a proposal that should be welcomed by those looking for a path to economic recovery and a tempering of future disruptions."

— *John B. Powers*
President, Chicago Daily Observer

"A fabulous study!"

— *Malcolm S. Morris*
Chairman, Stewart Title Guaranty Company

"*Return to Order* offers a synthesis of Catholicism's invaluable contribution to the building of a humane and ordered society in which the human person can flourish. When culture, economy, polity, and religion form an ethical whole, children, families, businesses, religious communities and individuals find their fulfillment through making their contribution to the common good. *Return to Order* shows us a clear way out of the current cultural crisis which besets the great human project."

— *Most Reverend Donald J. Hying*
Auxiliary Bishop, Archdiocese of Milwaukee

"I highly recommend this book."

— *Rev. John Trigilio, Ph.D.*
Author and President, Confraternity of Catholic Clergy

* Titles and affiliation of the above individuals with businesses, institutions or organizations are for identification purposes only

RETURN TO ORDER

RETURN TO ORDER

From a Frenzied Economy to an Organic Christian Society

Where We've Been,
How We Got Here, and
Where We Need to Go

BY JOHN HORVAT II

York Press
York, Pennsylvania

Copyright © 2013 The American Society for the
Defense of Tradition, Family and Property*—TFP*
Second Printing, 2015

For information about special discounts for bulk sales, please contact:
Return to Order
P.O. Box 1337, Hanover, PA 17331
Tel.: (855) 861-8420
Email: Info@ReturnToOrder.org

Unless otherwise noted, all Scriptural references are from the
Douay-Rheims version of the Bible.

The American Society for the Defense of Tradition, Family and Property*,
TFP*, and York Press are assumed names of The Foundation for a Christian Civilization, Inc.,
a 501(c)(3) tax-exempt organization.

Book design: Jennifer Bohdal

ISBN: 978-0-9882148-0-4
ISBN: 978-0-9882148-2-8 (ebook)
Library of Congress Control Number: 2012953937

Printed in the United States of America
22 21 20 19 18 17 16 15   2 3 4 5

To Prof. Plinio Corrêa de Oliveira,
Catholic thinker, man of action, and champion
for the cause of Christian civilization.
His example and great virtue gave courage to many.
His Catholic vision inspired this work.

NINE AWARDS FOR *RETURN TO ORDER*

Return to Order was won nine awards since first published. It was named a finalist in the 2014 USA Best Book Awards in the philosophy category.

It has also earned honorable mentions at the following book events:

- Great Northwest Book Festival
- Great Southeast Book Festival
- Great Southwest Book Festival
- Indiefab Awards
- London Book Festival
- Los Angeles Book Festival
- New England Book Festival
- New York Book Festival

TABLE OF CONTENTS

PART II: The Road Ahead: A Return to Order

FOUNDATIONS OF AN ORGANIC ORDER

THE HEART AND SOUL OF AN ECONOMY

A PASSION FOR JUSTICE

A CORRESPONDING TEMPERANCE

THE SEARCH FOR MEANING

FOREWORD

BY HARRY C. VERYSER

The argument presented in this book is very unique in that it is at the same time very old and very new. It reaches back through the philosophers to the thoughts of Plato and Aristotle. In his book, *The Republic*, Plato presents an argument that the state of the Commonwealth is the state of the individual souls writ large. Plato saw in democratic societies a danger that the desires of the people for bodily satisfactions would outrun the resources of the State and result, eventually, in a tyranny.

Aristotle also was concerned about the problems of the democratic society in which people, being free, would allow their desires to become disorderly and inimical to the common good. To overcome this tendency, he recommended a mixed or constitutional regime.

This argument was taken up in the mid-twentieth century by the prominent writer Russell Kirk. In an important essay, "The Problem of Social Justice," Kirk argued that disorder in the soul reflects itself in disorder in the Republic.

Prof. Harry C. Veryser was the director of graduate studies in economics at the University of Detroit Mercy from 2007-2012. During his many years of teaching, he has served on the faculties of Northwood University, St. Mary's College-Orchard Lake, Hillsdale College, and Ave Maria College.

He is currently on the advisory boards of The Mackinac Center for Public Policy and the Acton Institute for the Study of Religion and Liberty.

He is the author of *Our Economic Crisis: Sources and Solutions* and *It Didn't Have to Be This Way: Why Boom and Bust Is Unnecessary and How the Austrian School of Economics Breaks the Cycle* (ISI Books, 2013).

In *Return to Order*, John Horvat II continues the argument by teasing out its application to the present twenty-first century. Applying it to the economic, financial, social, and finally moral crisis faced by Western civilization, he argues for a return to the cardinal virtues, particularly temperance. This is a new way of looking at the present economy and social order.

While Plato and Aristotle focused on the political factors—that of a democratic society and the inordinate desire of the population to use political measures to achieve their satisfactions—Horvat sees our enormous technological success, from the Industrial Revolution to our days as a major factor. With the increase in productivity, people were able to realize a standard of living hereto only dreamed of by past generations. As more desires were fulfilled, this led to frantic explosions of expectations. So great was the desire to fulfill these benefits that political society began to break down the necessary preconditions for a prosperous society. Intemperance reigned!

Since intemperance is a matter of habit, people became habituated to great expectations and fulfillment, until finally, in the words of one economist, they began to consume the seed corn of moral capital. In this way, self-interest exhausted itself in intemperance.

It was almost as if a young man, left with a great legacy by his grandparents, destroyed the trust fund. One could go back to Scripture to the story of the Prodigal Son where the young man, having received great wealth, wasted it on intemperate desires.

Horvat sees America as that type of society. He argues that the inability of many to control their desires led to "frenetic intemperance" setting the tone for society as a whole. And what was the consequence? The profligate wasting of a great inheritance.

Horvat calls us to return to our Father's House, not just individually, but collectively. If we do this, not only will we restore our individual souls to a more virtuous state, but America will be a great and prosperous nation once more.

Back on Course

I f there is an image that corresponds to the state of the nation, it would be that of a cruise ship on a never-ending cruise. On each of its multiple decks, we find every modern comfort and entertainment. The bands are playing, the theaters are full, the restaurants crowded, and the boutiques well stocked.

The atmosphere is outwardly marked by fun and laughter. Everywhere there is dazzling spectacle, amusing games, and gadgetry. There is always one more joke or one more dance to keep the party going. The cruise ship gives an almost surreal impression of fantasy, unrestraint, and delight.

Cruises are normally celebrations for special occasions, but this party cruise is different. Over the decades, many have come to see the cruise not as a holiday but as an entitlement; it is no longer an exceptional event but the norm. Rather than leave the ship, many seek instead to prolong the party on board without worrying about a final destination, or who will pay the bill.

Breakdown of a System

Even the best of cruises reaches a point of exhaustion. Even the best of parties can last only so long. Behind the festive veneer, things start to run down. Scuffles and disagreements break out among passengers. Crew members quarrel and cut corners. Financial problems curtail the festivities. Yet no one has the courage to suggest that the party should not go on.

This image is a fitting way to explain the present crisis. As a nation, we are in the same dilemma as those on a never-ending party cruise. Economically, we have reached a point of unsustainability with trillion-dollar deficits, economic crises, and financial crashes. Politically, we have reached a point of immobility as polarization and strife make it difficult to get anything done. Morally, we have stooped to such great depths with the breakdown of our moral codes that we wonder how

The state of the nation might be compared to a cruise ship on a never-ending cruise. The bands are playing and the decks are full of light and activity. No one wants to declare that the party is over.

society will survive. The course is plotted to send us to our ruin, but all the while the bands play on.

Instead of confronting these problems head on, many are looking for ways to prolong the party. No one dares to declare that the party is over.

Ill-equipped to Face the Storm

The problems inside our cruise ship are compounded by those outside it. We are facing an impending economic collapse that appears on the horizon like a gathering storm. Few want to admit the storm is approaching. When the full thrust of this storm will break—be it months or even a few years—is difficult to determine. We do not know exactly how it will strike or the precise means to avoid it.

What we do know is that a storm lies ahead. It is not just a passing tempest for we already feel its strong winds. By its sheer magnitude, we sense there is something about this particular crisis that touches the very core of our American order. It will have political, social, and even military consequences. What makes it so grave is that our ship seems so ill-equipped and its crew so divided as we approach the ever more menacing storm.

In the past, we had a unity and projection that helped us stay the right course in storms like these. We were a people solidly united around God, flag, and family, but now all seems fragmented and polarized. By our great wealth and power, we once held the respect and awe of nations, but now we are unexpectedly attacked by unforeseen enemies and forsaken by friends and allies. Now, our certainties are shaken; our unity is in doubt. There is anxiety and dark pessimism about our future.

Our Purpose

The American Society for the Defense of Tradition, Family and Property (TFP) is a group of Catholic countrymen concerned about the state of the nation. This concern prompted the formation of a study commission that would delve deeply into the causes of the present economic crisis. Motivated by love for God and country, we now enter into the debate with the findings of this commission. We will be indicating where we as a nation went wrong. Our desire is to join with all those practical-minded Americans who see the futility of prolonging the party. The time has come to declare the party over. Now is the time to batten down the hatches and plot a course in face of the raging tempest ahead.

Although the storm be treacherous, we need not sail on uncharted seas. That is why these considerations spring from our deep Catholic convictions and draw heavily from the Church's social and economic teachings, which gave rise to Christian civilization. We believe these teachings can serve as a lighthouse; they contain valuable and illuminating insights that will benefit all Americans since they are based not only on matters of the Faith but also upon reason and principles of the natural order.

Having this lighthouse is a matter of great urgency because we navigate in dangerous waters. We cannot follow the socialistic courses to anarchy and revolution that have shipwrecked so many nations in history. Unless we have the courage to draw upon our rich Christian tradition and place our trust in Providence, we will neither steer clear of disaster in the coming storm nor arrive to safe harbor.

Since the storm is principally economic in nature, that will be our main focus. However, this is not an economic treatise. Rather, we offer an analysis based on observations of economic developments in history from which we have constructed a number of theses, which we present succinctly without excessive proofs or examples.

To develop fully every thesis is a vast task beyond the scope of this work. Our purpose is to provide a platform for debate; to point in the general direction of a remedy. We invite those who enter into this debate to apply the broad principles found here to the concrete circumstances.

A Great Imbalance in Economy

Our main thesis centers on a great imbalance that has entered into our economy. We do not think it is caused by our vibrant system of private property and free enterprise as so many socialists are wont to claim. What is at fault is something much more profound yet difficult to define.

We believe that, from a perspective that will later become clear and not denying other factors, the main problem lies with a restless spirit of *intemperance* that is constantly throwing our economy out of balance. It is made worse by a *frenetic* drive generated by a strong undercurrent in modern economy that seeks to be rid of restraints and gratify disordered passions. We call the resulting spirit *"frenetic intemperance,"* which is now pushing the country headlong into the throes of an unprecedented crisis.

In the course of our considerations, we will first look at this frenetic intemperance and see how it manifests itself in our industrialized economy. We will look at the unbalanced drive to reach gigantic proportions in industry and the mass standardization of products and markets. We will analyze its urge to destroy institutions and break down restraining barriers that would normally serve to keep economies in balance.

We will then show how this frenetic intemperance has facilitated certain errors that extend beyond economy and shape the way we live. To illustrate this, we will discuss the frustrations caused by an exaggerated trust in our *technological society*, the terrifying isolation of our *individualism*, and the heavy burden of our *materialism*. We will highlight the bland *secularism* that admits few heroic, sublime, or sacred elements to fill our lives with meaning. Far from promoting a free market, frenetic intemperance undermines and throws it out of balance and even prepares the way for socialism. The tragic effect of all this is that we seem to have lost that human element so essential to economy. Modern economy has become cold and impersonal, fast and frantic, mechanical and inflexible.

The Missing Human Element

In their zeal for maximum efficiency and production, many have cut themselves off from the natural restraining influence of human institutions such as custom, morals, family, or community. They have severed their link with tradition where customs, habits, and ways of being are passed from generation to generation. They have lost the anchors of the cardinal virtues that should be the mooring for any true economy.

The result is a society where money rules. Men put aside social, cultural, and moral values, adopting a set of values that attaches undue importance to quantity over quality, utility over beauty, and matter over spirit. Free of traditional restraints, those under this rule favor the frantic dealings, speculation, and exaggerated risks by which they have sent our economy into crisis.

Finding Remedies

If frenetic intemperance is the main cause of this economic imbalance, the quelling of this restless spirit must figure in the solution. To this end, we need to reconnect with that human element that tempers the markets and keeps them free.

The model we will present is the organic socio-economic order that was developed in Christendom. Inside this organic framework, we find timeless principles of an economic order, wonderfully adapted to our human nature. This gives rise to markets full of exuberant vitality and refreshing spontaneity. There is the calming influence of those natural braking institutions—custom, family, the Christian State, and the Church—which are the very heart and soul of a balanced economy.

DEFINING THE PRESENT ECONOMIC CRISIS

When referring to the *present economic crisis*, we are not referring to any specific speculative bubble or financial crash. We are generally speaking of the cumulative effect of massive debt, unbridled government spending, economic instability, and other factors that are already threatening to coalesce into a single global crisis that is likely to cause a major economic collapse.

Economy becomes anchored in the virtues, especially the cardinal virtues. Inside this order, the rule of money is replaced by another rule that favors honor, beauty, and quality.

Yet we must stress that this is a Christian order suited to the reality of our fallen nature. It is well adapted to both the sufferings and joys that this vale of tears affords. Indeed, we are reminded that it was born under the constant shadow of the Cross with Christ as Divine model.

By studying the principles of this order, we can come to have a notion of what our ideal should be and how it might be obtained.

With the menacing storm on the horizon, the stage is set for a great debate over where we are now, and where we need to go. At this point, our principal concern will be to understand both the nature of the storm we face and that of the harbor we seek. Only then can we chart a course for the future.

PART I

THE LONG BREWING STORM

The present crisis is like a gathering storm that threatens to overwhelm the nation.

The dominant American model
is held together by a political consensus
where citizens agree to certain laws and
rules which allow them to get along. It also
includes a religious consensus loosely based
on a respect for the Ten Commandments.

CHAPTER 1

The Dominant American Model: A Cooperative Union

T hroughout our history, we have always relied upon a dominant socio-economic model that has helped us navigate through storms and shape our way of life. This American model has survived economic booms and busts, the Great Depression, world wars, recessions, and times of unrest. We find it portrayed in our literature and films. It influences how we live and interpret reality to such a degree that it is difficult to imagine life outside this model.

In the face of our present crisis, this model no longer works as it once did. It is breaking down, and hence our first task is to understand this dominant American model and where it went wrong.

A Description of This Model

We can identify two main elements in this dominant model. The first is a vibrant economic system with a great dynamo of production that churns out material comfort and well-being. With a healthy regard for private property and free enterprise inside the rule of law, this model has given us great abundance and prosperity.

The second element is a corresponding *American way of life* whereby we enjoy the fruits of this production. Above all, it supports a dream— the idea that everyone must have the maximum amount of freedom to pursue their personal happiness so long as it does not interfere with another's dream. The result is a practical way of life where all can pursue their dreams and celebrate life's small joys, domestic virtue, and financial success. This way of life supports an atmosphere of mutual cooperation where individuals and families within their communities all get along while pursuing their individual interests. This system promotes and rewards hard work, initiative, and an optimistic can-do mind-set.

Components of a Consensus

The key to the success of this model lies in a great universal consensus, a kind of spiritual glue that holds everything together, one where everyone agrees to get along. It is a flexible and deliberately vague consensus that tends to sweep aside any robust attachments to religious, ideological, or universal traditions that might prove divisive or stand in the way of each one's constant and ever-elusive search for perfect happiness.

This consensus is reflected in our normal political discourse, which does not question this dominant model but rather debates on how best to achieve our American dream. All parties in the political arena use the same concepts, imagery, and rhetoric to reach a consensus: God, freedom, the American flag, family, and apple pie. The dominance of this model is so great that it all but smothers the smattering of radical Communist, Socialist, or other fringe parties that dare to challenge it.

We can see this same consensus reflected in a similar attitude towards religion. Unlike the modern European model, which seeks to break any link between religion and public life, the American model welcomes religions with open arms—as long as they all get along. It is as if the American government has an unwritten agreement that establishes what many have called a "civil religion," one with a set of working rules in which certain things against God are prohibited. Although legally separate, the State maintains a reverence for a vague Judeo-Christian God in whom it trusts yet leaves undefined. "Our form of government has no sense," President Dwight Eisenhower once noted, "unless it is founded in a deeply felt religious faith, and I don't care what it is."[1]

Religion acts as a kind of guarantor of good order through a consensual Christian moral code loosely based on the Ten Commandments, which is adopted by the State, embedded in our laws, and engraved on our public buildings. Ideally, this model holds that everyone should have some kind of religion, preferably Biblical, so as to maintain an atmosphere conducive to prosperity and general well-being. This part of our consensus has had the good effect of deeply imprinting upon the national character a sense of morality, godliness, patriotism, and family devotion. Its moral code also has a healthy moderating influence on the economy.

---

1. Patrick Henry, "'And I Don't Care What It Is': The Tradition-History of a Civil Religion Proof-Text," *The Journal of the American Academy of Religion* 49 (Mar. 1981): 41.

A Co-op Nation

This American model presents a formula for running the country that we might liken to that used by a thriving farm co-op or public corporation of shareholders.[2]

This co-op mentality leads citizens to act as if their connection to our country works like a co-op membership full of legitimate benefits with distributed risks, voting privileges, few liabilities, and plenty of recreational opportunities. As long as an atmosphere of well-being and happiness exists, members renew their membership with great enthusiasm. Many have even taken their membership in the co-op as a kind of entitlement in which benefits are seen as rights. This enthusiasm is aided by a strong economic foundation that practically guarantees some degree of prosperity.

As a result, this cooperative union is remarkably resistant to crisis. Doomsayers have often predicted its ruin. Nevertheless, as long as this economic model maintains the outward appearance of prosperity and confers benefits, liberties, and entitlements upon its citizens, we will have the consensus necessary to maintain our union—even in times of great moral decadence like our own. In theory, it might be argued that our cooperative union can last indefinitely.

Despite its intensely self-interested nature, this American model has endeared itself to countless Americans since it has often delivered growth, prosperity and relative peace where everyone seemed to get along. Many even regarded this practical blueprint for success as a redemptive formula that should be adopted by all mankind, and they have preached this American way to the nations with almost missionary zeal.

America in Crisis

This model can only work as long as everyone agrees to get along and cooperate. When the economic dynamo stalls or sputters, discord arises. When the vague moral code of the consensus begins to crumble, trust and confidence disappear. In periods of prolonged crisis like the present one, this cooperative model breaks down.

---

2. We already find in the literature of the Founding Fathers references to the nation as a "commercial republic," a union of legitimate self-interest, providing prosperity and security. Matthew Spalding and Patrick J. Garrity, *A Sacred Union of Citizens: George Washington's Farewell Address and the American Character* (Lanham, Md.: Rowman and Littlefield, 1996), 65.

Then we see factions forming. Polarizing debates arise where each wants to blame the other for the failure of the co-op. Elections resemble shareholder brawls where officers are frequently changed. The opportunities for profit diminish. The co-op now appears to work contrary to the membership's interests. It is, so to speak, not paying out dividends but distributing uncertainties that cause anxiety, depression, and stress. This raises questions as to whether ours is really a redemptive formula for all mankind.

———————————— • ————————————

In presenting this American model, we do not wish to insinuate that all Americans equally adhere to it. We are not affirming that "co-op Americans" lack patriotic sentiments, or that other competing models do not exist. All we are saying is that, generally speaking, this cooperative model has dominated the American way of life and is now in crisis.

The unthinkable is now happening: Our cooperative union is unraveling; our consensus is crumbling; and the dynamo of our production is slowing down. We must now deal with this frightening prospect.

> ## DEFINING THE AMERICAN COOPERATIVE UNION
> Our American cooperative union can be defined as our dominant socio-economic model consisting of a vibrant economic system that produces a great abundance and a corresponding American way of life by which we enjoy it. Those adhering to this model see our country working like a farm co-op or shareholder company full of legitimate benefits, voting privileges, and entitlements.

CHAPTER 2

Why This Model Failed: A Frenetic Intemperance

T o understand the present crisis, we must now see why our cooperative union is failing. We believe the cause is found in an element of imbalance that has entered into the dynamic economic system that is the centerpiece of our American model. This, in turn, has had an effect upon our corresponding way of life.

Use of the Term "Capitalism"

When speaking of imbalance in our economy, many are quick to lay the blame upon capitalism as a system since we have long gloried in being the capitalist nation par excellence. We do not agree with such an evaluation. In its purely popular sense understood by most Americans, capitalism is a market system of production and consumption that protects the right of private property and free enterprise under the rule of law. In this sense, it is a useful system that has produced general prosperity for our nation. Hence, it cannot be the target of our criticism.

Yet capitalism also cannot be the battle line in our defense. The word has other meanings that we cannot endorse. The Left, for example, has long used this term to describe the system's shortcomings or excesses, while some libertarians have used it to promote a radical anarchical agenda.

That is why we must carefully avoid the trap of using the word indiscriminately. Because of the misuses of the word, it is wiser to follow the advice of Jesuit economist Fr. Bernard Dempsey, who claims that capitalism is a word incapable of scientific definition, and one that should only be used with great reluctance and care, commenting: "Only a very foolish general accepts battle on terrain of his adversary's choice."[1] We will henceforth use this vague term sparingly.

---

1. Bernard W. Dempsey, *The Functional Economy: The Bases of Economic Organization* (Englewood Cliffs, N.J.: Prentice-Hall, 1958), 162.

CAPITALISM: AN AMBIGUOUS WORD

The ambivalence of the term "capitalism" is very well expressed in the encyclical *Centesimus Annus* of Pope John Paul II when he answers the question of whether "capitalism" had triumphed over communism. He writes:

If by "capitalism" is meant an economic system which recognizes the fundamental and positive role of business, the market, private property and the resulting responsibility for the means of production, as well as free human creativity in the economic sector, then the answer is certainly in the affirmative, even though it would perhaps be more appropriate to speak of a "business economy," "market economy" or simply "free economy." But if by "capitalism" is meant a system in which freedom in the economic sector is not circumscribed within a strong juridical framework which places it at the service of human freedom in its totality, and which sees it as a particular aspect of that freedom, the core of which is ethical and religious, then the reply is certainly negative (*Centesimus Annus* [Washington, D.C.: United States Catholic Conference, 1991], no. 42).

Focus of Our Criticism

In our zeal to find the cause of the present crisis, we also believe that a broad attack upon our whole free market system would be a great mistake. Rather, we should distinguish between two currents in our economy. The first is a huge sector governed by the free market, which consists of the normal operation of millions of vibrant companies—small, large, and huge—that engage in healthy competition and amply supply goods and services to the nation.

This first bedrock sector, so much a part of our daily lives, cultivates those sturdy American virtues—diligence, moderation, thrift, and honesty—essential for the proper functioning of any free market. While undoubtedly important and avowedly "capitalist," the activities of this vast sector cannot be considered the cause of our crisis.

Frenetic Intemperance

We should instead focus on a second more unrestrained current, which is not, properly speaking, a formal sector but a volatile undercurrent that has a destabilizing effect on an economy.

This undercurrent is defined by what we will call *frenetic intemperance*—a restless and reckless spirit inside modern economy that foments a drive to throw off legitimate restraints and gratify disordered passions.

This frenetic intemperance is not specifically an economic problem but a moral and psychological one deep within the soul of modern man that manifests itself in economy. It tends to form an undercurrent that is manifested everywhere in varying degrees. It can be observed in individuals and groups of individuals. It operates in environments that neither include all big corporations nor exclude all small firms. Nor is wealth its defining characteristic since this restless spirit can exist in a simple shopkeeper or a multi-billionaire. We must insist, and will repeatedly insist, that unless frenetic intemperance be addressed, any solution, perfect though it may seem, will be found lacking.

Our first tasks will be very specific: tracing the origins of this undercurrent, and then defining and characterizing its spirit. This is also the key to understanding the present-day economic crisis—which is above all a spiritual one.

DEFINING FRENETIC INTEMPERANCE

We can define frenetic intemperance as a restless, explosive, and relentless drive inside man that manifests itself in modern economy by 1) seeking to throw off legitimate restraints; and 2) gratifying disordered passions. It tends to form an economic undercurrent whose action can be likened to that of a faulty accelerator or regulator that takes an otherwise well-functioning machine and throws it out of balance.

An Often Observed Phenomenon

We are not alone in our suspicions that this restless spirit of frenetic intemperance has long been at work gnawing at the bowels of Western economy.

So clearly does it appear that many have observed the effects of this mysterious drive and tried to identify it. Pius XI associates it with the force of "disordered passions."[2] Still others, like Max Weber, refer to activities of an "irrational and speculative character."[3] Sociologist Robert Nisbet complains of a "mental feverishness,"[4] while on the other end of the spectrum economist Robert Heilbroner speaks of a "restless and insatiable drive."[5] Hyman Minsky refers to an "inherent and inescapable" instability. [6] These are a few of many who have all sought to label this force without naming its cause.

We contend that the cause of this terrible force does have a name: it is called *Revolution.*[7]

The Origin of Our Economic Crisis

To put it simply, frenetic intemperance is much more than just a minor defect in economy but rather one manifestation of a greater Revolution.

History records dramatic changes in the general mentality of men. One such change was an outburst of pride and sensuality that shook medieval Christendom. It gave rise to a single historical process that Catholic thinker Plinio Corrêa de Oliveira calls *the Revolution.* This Revolution was a revolt against the very idea of restraint driven by an intemperate desire for pleasures and novelties, an explosion of disordered appetites and the gradual abandonment of the stabilizing forces of spiritual, religious, moral, and cultural values. We can trace the four phases of this process to: 1) the Renaissance which prepared a spirit of revolt found in the Protestant Revolution (1517); 2) the French Revolution (1789); 3) the Communist Revolution (1917); and 4) the Cultural Revolution of the Sixties (1968).[8]

Over the centuries, this Revolution has slowly entered all fields of life where it has had destabilizing effects. In this context, we affirm that frenetic intemperance is the manifestation of this Revolution in economy.

---

2. Pius XI, encyclical *Quadragesimo Anno* (1931) in *The Papal Encyclicals,* ed. Claudia Carlen (Raleigh, N.C.: McGrath, 1981), vol. 3, p. 436, no. 132.
3. Max Weber, *The Protestant Ethic and the Spirit of Capitalism,* trans. Talcott Parsons (New York: Charles Scribner's Sons, 1958), 20-21.
4. Robert A. Nisbet, *Twilight of Authority* (Indianapolis: Liberty Fund, 2000), 90.
5. Robert Heilbroner, *The Nature and Logic of Capitalism* (New York: W. W. Norton, 1985), 42.
6. Hyman P. Minsky, *Stabilizing an Unstable Economy* (New York: McGraw Hill Companies, 2008), 134.
7. See Plinio Corrêa de Oliveira, *Revolution and Counter-Revolution,* 3rd ed. (York, Pa.: The American Society for the Defense of Tradition, Family and Property, 1993).
8. A connection between the first three Revolutions can be found in Leo XIII's apostolic letter *Annum Ingressi* of Mar. 19, 1902. Other historians join Leo XIII in making similar connections between these first three revolutions without naming the whole historical process.

Charting Frenetic Intemperance

We can chart the ups and downs of this frenetic intemperance as it moved throughout the Western economies in history. It can be traced to its modest beginnings with the proto-capitalist Renaissance merchants to the Industrial Revolution to the globalism of our days. Although it may vary in intensity, with each new phase, its disorderly dynamism increases in scope.

In its more extreme and obvious forms, frenetic intemperance is to be found riding on the crest of speculative ventures whether it be the Dutch Tulip Craze (1633–37), major stock market crashes, or the 2008 sub-prime mortgage bubble.

More often than not, we see this restless spirit in lesser financial crises that frequently punctuate the history of modern economy. In fact, our business literature is strewn with dramatic expressions that include manias, blind passion, frenzies, feverish speculation, crazes, or rushes, all describing our precarious state of frequent financial crashes, crises, and cycles involving ever greater amounts of capital.[9]

In the vanguard of this undercurrent, we always find a relentless drive to throw off restraint and seek gratification which, like a bulldozer, runs over any neighborhood, custom, or cultural value that stands in the way. Those involved in this undercurrent might even be seen working against their own self-interest. Thus, we find them maximizing profits by collaborating with socialist or Communist governments that destroy free markets. They can be seen undermining market ethics and competition by engaging in crony capitalism or power lobbying.

In our daily lives as consumers, this undercurrent's influence can be felt in the prevailing tendency to live beyond our means and to borrow without regard for the future. It fosters a kind of consumption that goes beyond the mere acquisition of money and possessions. Rather, many have adopted fast-paced lifestyles facilitated by easy credit which project the idea of success. "The hard work and sacrifice that were part and parcel of the original [American] dream," writes marketing professor James A. Roberts, "have been replaced by wishful thinking of

---

9. This is but a partial listing of terms. For a longer list followed by a historical account of major panics and crashes, see Charles P. Kindleberger and Robert Z. Aliber, *Manias, Panics, and Crashes: A History of Financial Crises* (Hoboken, N.J.: John Wiley and Sons, 2005), 40.

material success, with no willingness to pay the dues necessary to create such wealth." [10]

On a more popular level, we know this undercurrent well since Hollywood—itself a part of this undercurrent—popularizes and even glamorizes its frantic wheeling-and-dealing archetypes throughout our culture. Moreover, while most firms do not fully engage in its practices, the influence of this undercurrent is such that it sets the tone for our whole business culture by creating a certain frenetic electricity in the air.

A Frenetic Nature

To understand this unrestrained undercurrent fully, we must highlight its *frenetic nature*. We are not speaking about mere intemperance that leads to the simple greed or ambition that has always plagued man throughout history. We also must not mistake frenetic intemperance for the legitimate and energetic practice of business and its risk-taking that leads to true prosperity.

Rather, frenetic intemperance is an explosive expansion of human desires beyond traditional and moral bounds. Its frenetic nature leads those of this undercurrent to resent the very idea of restraint and scorn the spiritual, religious, moral, and cultural values that normally serve to order and temper economic activity. Financial writer Edward Chancellor aptly observes an "anarchic, irreverent, and antihierarchic" spirit whose essence is not simply about greed but "a Utopian yearning for freedom and equality which counterbalances the drab rationalistic materialism of the modern economic system." [11]

To the degree that frenetic intemperance prevails, its self-destructive character will eventually destroy free markets and moral values. We might say of this unrestrained current what Marshall Berman harshly attributes to an innate dynamism in modern economy which, were it allowed to run completely free, would annihilate "everything that it creates—physical environments, social institutions, metaphysical ideas, artistic visions, moral values—in order to create more, to go on endlessly creating the world anew." [12]

---

10. James A. Roberts, *Shiny Objects: Why We Spend Money We Don't Have in Search of Happiness We Can't Buy* (New York: HarperOne, 2011), 66.
11. Edward Chancellor, *Devil Take the Hindmost: A History of Financial Speculation* (New York: Plume, 2000), 29.
12. Marshall Berman, *All That Is Solid Melts into Air: The Experience of Modernity* (New York: Simon and Schuster, 1982), 288. This freedom from restraint helps explain the paradox of why some

A Great Intemperance

The frenetic nature of this undercurrent's activity only makes worse the effects of its intemperance.

Temperance is the virtue whereby man governs and moderates his natural appetites and passions in accordance with the norms prescribed by reason. When this frenetic element enters into economy, the resulting intemperance can lead to periods of "irrational exuberance,"[13] resulting in frenzied activities, fabulous fortunes, and spectacular failures.

This intemperance in economy acts like a car that goes at remarkable speeds, yet lacks adequate brakes; it frequently crashes in order to slow down or stop. We might also liken it to a drug addiction that leads to ever more frequent alternating periods of frenzy and depression as the addiction grows. It may bring amazing energy and resources into markets. However, if modern economy has brought us great prosperity, it is not because of frenetic intemperance but in spite of it.

We can see the telltale footprint of this frenetic intemperance in today's economic crisis. It behooves us now to delve deeper into this ailment, so that we may better understand its workings. We will do this by first discussing how it undermines our economic system, and then how it affects our way of life.

Above all, we must realize that it cannot be stopped by imposing draconian laws upon the economy since this would only end up strangling all commerce. The only solution to this intemperance is a corresponding temperance.

As Edmund Burke notes: "Men of intemperate minds cannot be free. Their passions forge their fetters."[14]

---

extremely rich individuals support socialist, permissive, or liberal agendas even though they have everything to lose by opposing a moral order.

13. This was the expression used to describe one such period. See Alan Greenspan, "Remarks at the Annual Dinner and Francis Boyer Lecture of The American Enterprise Institute for Public Policy Research," Washington, D.C., Dec. 5, 1996, accessed Oct. 14, 2012, http://www.federalreserve.gov/boarddocs/speeches/1996/19961205.htm.

14. Edmund Burke, "A Letter From Mr. Burke to a Member of the National Assembly: In Answer to Some Objections to His Book on French Affairs. 1791," in *The Works of Edmund Burke, With a Memoir* (New York: Harper and Brothers, 1846), 1:583.

The nineteenth-century Industrial Revolution was a far-reaching revolution with cultural, social, and political consequences. It helped create our big cities and the modern masses.

CHAPTER 3

The Industrial Revolution:
A Defining Point for Frenetic Intemperance

W e can better understand frenetic intemperance in economy by going straight to that point in history when we can clearly observe this undercurrent beginning to exert great influence. We believe this defining point was the great transformations brought about by the first Industrial Revolution (1760-1840) and its subsequent cycles of technological change.

An Enormous Transformation

The Industrial Revolution was a defining point that historian Carlo Cipolla calls "an unprecedented and far-reaching revolution" with "economic, cultural, social and political implications."[1]

No one can deny that the Industrial Revolution resulted in great material progress and wealth of great benefit to society. However, much of this progress can be attributed to healthy factors already in place in the West prior to the Revolution, such as the expansion of commerce, the abundance of capital, the development of technology, and the existence of a vast infrastructure of social institutions.[2] What we criticize is the assertive role of the restless undercurrent of frenetic intemperance, which facilitated a frantic change of pace that set in motion economic trends and processes that caused great financial and social upheaval.

The Mark of the Industrial Revolution

It is not our intention here to criticize specific technological or eco-

---

1. Carlo M. Cipolla, *Before the Industrial Revolution: European Society and Economy, 1000-1700* (New York: W. W. Norton, 1976), 274.
2. Robert Nisbet claims family, church, and community ties had their role: "Freedom of contract, the fluidity of capital, the mobility of labor and the whole factory system were able to thrive and to give the appearance of internal stability only because of the continued existence of institutional and cultural allegiances which were, in every sense, precapitalist. Despite the rationalist faith in natural economic harmonies, the real roots of economic stability lay in groups and associations that were not essentially economic at all." Robert A. Nisbet, *The Quest for Community: A Study in the Ethics of Order and Freedom* (San Francisco: ICS Press, 1990), 212. About the abundance of capital prior to the Industrial Revolution, see Fernand Braudel, *The Wheels of Commerce*, vol. 2 of *Civilization and Capitalism 15th-18th Century* (Berkeley: University of California Press, 1992), 398-99.

nomic aspects of the Industrial Revolution. We limit ourselves to listing only those dramatic changes of attitude and mentality brought
about by frenetic intemperance that diminished the moderating influence of familial, cultural, and religious institutions. We can see
these changes:

- Economics is given precedence over social, political, cultural, or religious activity—or even adaptations of these
  activities to conform to economics.

- There is a change of attitude towards capital and credit,
  which led to their massive expansion and helped en-
  throne, as a *de facto* ruling elite, a reigning regime of
  bankers, businessmen, and technocrats—with powers,
  fortunes, and privileges far outshining those of the kings
  and princes of old.

- The Industrial Revolution set in motion a transformation
  of society by installing a colossal industrial infrastructure
  necessary for mass production, standardization, and
  economies of scale. It provoked the abandonment of the
  countryside and the establishment of big cities that centralized industry, trade, and finance.

- The Industrial Revolution fostered a secular, materialistic,
  and pragmatic attitude towards life. This materialistic
  view of scientific and technological progress advanced
  the dream of a material "paradise" that would redeem
  mankind and relegate religious and moral issues to a secondary plane.[3]

- There is the introduction of new technologies, work
  schedules, and rhythms of life that proved to be deper-
  sonalizing, brutalizing, and stressful.

---

3. Our technology and its emphasis on the physical, technical, and empirical led to what Sabino S.
    Acquaviva called a "desacralization process" affecting all formal and informal institutions of so-
    ciety where "the very organization of the modern day has become a hindrance to religiosity,
    squeezing out religious experience." Sabino S. Acquaviva, *The Decline of the Sacred in Industrial
    Society*, trans. Patricia Lipscomb (Oxford: Basil Blackwell, 1979), 137.

- The destabilizing changes of the Industrial Revolution prepared the ground for Karl Marx's theory of class struggle by establishing a conflictual relationship between owners and workers.[4]

Thus, our target is not the actual technologies that were involved but the manner in which the Industrial Revolution and each succeeding technological cycle—be it steam, electric, nuclear, or especially computer technologies—advanced the commanding role of the undercurrent of frenetic intemperance in modern economy.

Propelled by frenetic intemperance, this Revolution set in motion a dramatic throwing off of restraint inside economy that continues in our days. Our thesis is that our present economy would have been much more advanced and prosperous without frenetic intemperance.

---

4. Marx celebrated the triumph of industrialization over the old order. He credits the bourgeoisie as the principal agent of this destruction. "The bourgeoisie," he writes, "has played a most revolutionary role in history." Karl Marx and Friedrich Engels, "Manifesto of the Communist Party," in *Marx*, vol. 50 of *Great Books of the Western World*, ed. Robert Maynard Hutchins (Chicago: University of Chicago, 1952), 420.

Corbis/Sion Touhig

Gigantism often leads to the building of huge production facilities in nations with questionable, low-cost labor practices, limited rule of law, harmful environmental standards, and/or poor human rights records, especially as seen in still-Communist China.

Corbis/Wally McNamee

CHAPTER 4

The Drive to Gigantism

Perhaps there is no better example of frenetic intemperance furiously at work than its drive towards gigantic expansion. Of course, we do not criticize the idea of growth or large-scale production by those in that bedrock sector of our economy that often engages in big industry. We find no fault in those who desire to better themselves and their communities through the normal expansion of commerce.

We limit our criticism to those in the undercurrent of frenetic intemperance with their explosive and consuming drive towards ever more gigantic proportions in all fields of business and industry. Our focus is on those in this sector who have an inebriating desire to shake off all restraint and a willingness to use any means—legitimate or otherwise—to dominate markets and stifle competition. This destructive drive towards what we will call unbalanced gigantism is found at the core of the present crisis.

At the same time, any criticism of gigantism must be done with great caution. From the very beginning of the Industrial Revolution, a great controversy has raged around the issue, especially the dehumanizing aspect of its massive industrial processes. This discussion has often been exaggerated and exploited by the Left (including Marx himself). We must acknowledge that problems do exist and need to be addressed—without a leftist slant.[1] We believe this can best be done by addressing the central problem of frenetic intemperance.

The Industrial Revolution's Frantic Expansion

We can trace the drive to gigantism back to the Industrial Revolution of the nineteenth century when industrial development expanded on a scale and at a speed never before seen.

---

1. For discussion of the problem as it appears now, see George Ritzer, *The McDonaldization of Society 5* (Los Angeles: Pine Forge Press, 2008), or Nelson Lichtenstein, ed., *Wal-Mart: The Face of Twenty-First Century Capitalism* (New York: New Press, 2006).

Everything came together to put in place a vicious circle geared towards the gigantic. To compete in vast markets, companies had to build huge factories to mass produce standardized goods. To build these plants, colossal infusions of capital and loans were needed. To run the factories, companies expanded their labor force, which gave rise to huge sprawling cities that emptied out the countryside. To sell their products, firms had to target concentrated markets through mass marketing and advertising. To dominate the whole process, energetic captains of industry with fabulous fortunes, exceptional abilities, and often unscrupulous methods swept away obstacles and competition.

Inside this gigantic production, sectors driven by frenetic intemperance brought great imbalance into modern economy. In their frenzy to expand, these sectors unleashed speculative bubbles, financial crashes, and gigantic displacements that wreaked great havoc upon society and the economy in the turbulent transition to the industrial age.

The Formation of Massive Commercial Blocs

This drive to gigantism did not end with the first factories of the Industrial Revolution. It continued with the forming of blocs of firms, holding companies, and conglomerates that amassed even greater resources. There was also the proliferation of mergers, which culminated with the "merge manias" at the beginning and end of the twentieth century.[2] When these consolidations were driven by frenetic intemperance (and not all were), they exhibited the same disregard for restraint and employed similarly disruptive means of expansion as might be seen in stock market manipulations, hostile merge/takeover strategies, cutthroat competition, and the formation of powerful cartels and monopolies.

Today, globalization extends the scope of these blocs and the disruptive instruments whereby they might intemperately expand. When these global firms enter into crisis as a result of their intemperate actions, they can pull down whole economies, as was seen, for example, in the sub-prime mortgage crisis of 2008. In this way, we have reached

---

2. "Some 3,000 firms disappeared through mergers during the 1895-1904 decade. Three-quarters of these were absorbed in mergers combining five or more firms at once.... During the Clinton Administration alone, an estimated seventy thousand mergers and acquisitions were undertaken, with a cumulative combined value of $6 trillion" (Walter Adams and James W. Brock, *The Bigness Complex: Industry, Labor, and Government in the American Economy* [Stanford, Calif.: Stanford University Press, 2004], 24, 144).

situations where industries are supposedly too big and too interdependent to fail, and thus they can hold all society hostage to their needs.

Attack on Private Property and Free Enterprise?

Some might interpret this description of gigantism as an attack on private property and free enterprise. Quite the contrary. We favor the expansion of production and trade that is not driven by frenetic intemperance.

What we criticize is the disordered dynamism by which firms, cartels, and commercial blocs expand, concentrate, and manipulate industry and capital to the point of market disruption. We find fault with the pervasive mentality of perpetual wheeling and dealing that turns businesses into pawns in a ruthless war to control markets, circumvent regulation, and secure unfair advantages.

In fact, we contend that the drive to unbalanced gigantism upsets rather than stimulates markets. Had frenetic intemperance not entered into this process, modern economy would be more balanced, more proportional . . . and even more efficient.

Looking at the "Efficiency" of Gigantism

Many defend, almost as a dogma, the idea that the gigantism of huge companies is necessary and inevitable because it assures the most efficient use of available resources. They believe that only gigantic companies can maintain the production and research facilities necessary for progress and growth—and they must do so at the expense of lesser firms.

Economist F. A. Hayek takes issue with the flawed logic of those who claim that "large firms are everywhere underbidding and driving out the small ones; this process must go on until in each industry only one or at most a few giant firms are left." This argument that free markets inevitably lead to capital concentration, Hayek further contends, "receives little support from a serious study of the facts."[3]

His position is similar to that of economists Walter Adams and

---

3. F. A. Hayek, "The Road to Serfdom," in *The Road to Serfdom: Texts and Documents, The Definitive Edition,* vol. 2 of *The Collected Works of F. A. Hayek,* ed. Bruce Caldwell (Routledge, London: University of Chicago Press, 2007), 92. Moreover, F. A. Hayek complains of how these huge companies often achieve this superior position by sidestepping markets and forming monopolies and cartels in conjunction with deliberate State policies that favor the suppression of competition as an element of State planning. Hayek also stands out for his brilliant and courageous defense of the free market at a time when socialism had made it unpopular.

James Brock, who write that the evidence "repudiates the myth that society faces an agonizing choice between good economic perform-ance, on the one hand, and decentralized, competitively structured markets and industries on the other."[4]

Beyond Normal Limits

It is a fact that unbalanced gigantism is not always efficient. We might liken it to a man that frantically eats and becomes overly fat, or to a bodybuilder that exercises constantly and builds bulging muscles. In both cases, the person takes his body beyond its normal limits. Both suffer from lack of focus and efficiency as one loses the ability to move quickly while the other's brutal bulk prevents him from moving agilely.

To the extent that frenetic intemperance drives firms, conglomer-ates, and mergers to gigantism, they also tend to lose focus and effi-ciency. On one hand, they can grow fat in their monopolistic position in the market and become mired in bureaucracy. On the other, they can become unwieldy in their super-rationalized and machine-like structures. Precisely because of their gigantic size, both types of super-firms or commercial blocs suffer from a lack of agility and adaptability. Smaller, more agile companies will very frequently outperform these gigantic firms—if given a level playing field.[5]

Undermining the Free Market

In normal markets, we might expect such gigantic firms to be re-placed by other more efficient ones. However, just as an overly fat per-son might have recourse to expensive medicine to stay alive and grow yet fatter, and the bodybuilder might use steroids to appear more muscular, so also these firms driven by frenetic intemperance often survive and grow even bigger because they can make use of certain practices, facilitated by their immense resources, to stifle competi-tion, increase short-term profits, and secure advantages. Hence, we can cite as examples:

---

4. Adams and Brock, *Bigness Complex*, 61-62.
5. Adams and Brock continue by stating: "The validity of this assessment is reinforced, not only by dozens of individual case studies and scores of generalized statistical analyses, but perhaps just as persuasively by the resurgence of entrepreneurship, by the innovative vibrancy of small firms in an advanced 'high-tech' age, and not least by the inestimable powers of discovery that the computer revolution and the information age have placed at their disposal" (ibid., 62).

- The formation of monopolistic blocs of companies that agree among themselves to exercise such control over certain industries so as to severely restrict surviving owners of smaller businesses.

- The ability and willingness to build gigantic production facilities in nations with questionable low-cost labor practices, limited rule of law, harmful environmental standards, and/or poor human rights records, especially as seen in still-Communist China.

- The use of powerful lobbies to secure government contracts, subsidies, and benefits, and even using their influence to craft government regulations that favor their own monopoly-like status in their industry.

- A reliance upon competitive advantages gained through trade tariffs, special tax breaks, government bailouts, and crony capitalist dealings.

- The use of litigation and immense legal resources that render anti-trust prosecution woefully inadequate or ineffective.

These and other practices lead to unbalanced markets and help intensify the drive to gigantism. This does not favor a sound economy since, just as the overly fat or steroid-ridden body will eventually break down from self-abuse, so also are these firms susceptible to breakdown.

In analyzing the problem of unbalanced gigantism in general, Adams and Brock conclude: "Whether in its horizontal, vertical, or conglomerate guise, whether wielded by business, labor, or government—or by all three in coalition—it tends to undermine efficiency and obstruct technological progressiveness."[6]

Concentrate and Conquer

This drive becomes all the more critical because when gigantic blocs are in the hands of only a few, they become vulnerable targets to be confiscated or controlled by intrusive governments.

By suppressing all intermediary leaders who might come to his defense, the absolutist king prepares his own way to the guillotine. In a similar way,

---

6. Ibid., 317.

when huge commercial blocs devour smaller industry, they prepare their own way to socialist confiscation since it is much more difficult to confiscate a thousand medium-size companies than a single huge one.

When such blocs falter, they are deemed "too big to fail," and the government proves to be the only player large enough to bail out the ailing industry—and put it under its control. In this way, private property easily becomes collective property. Thus, as Pius XI warned, liberalism prepares the way for socialism.[7]

Diluted and Remote Ownership

Far from preserving the sense of private property, unbalanced gigantism tends to dilute it. This is especially true inside giant publicly-traded firms driven by frenetic intemperance, where the very sense of property ownership is watered down and remote since their huge assets juridically belong to shareholders with stakes so small as to render them powerless and anonymous.

Columbia professors Adolph A. Berle and Gardiner C. Means analyzed such diluted corporate ownership at the time of the Great Depression of 1929-1933 and concluded:

- The position of ownership has changed from that of an active to that of a passive agent. The owner now holds a piece of paper representing a set of rights and expectations with respect to an enterprise, but has little control. The owner is practically powerless to affect the underlying property through his own efforts.

- The spiritual values that formerly went with ownership have been separated from it.[8]

In these cases, the substance of a firm's ownership is transferred to highly salaried managers who put up no capital yet can take risks to increase their bonuses. We cannot sense in this manager that lively "will to fight, economically, physically, politically, for 'his' factory and his control over it, to die if necessary on its steps."[9] In a similar way,

---

7. See Pius XI, *Quadragesimo Anno*, especially no. 122. Marx also took note of the increasing concentration of capital to the detriment of smaller companies and uses this fact as a justification for a greater disorder—his Communist revolution.
8. Adolph A. Berle and Gardiner C. Means, *The Modern Corporation and Private Property* (New Brunswick, N.J.: Transaction, 2002), 64-65, quoted in John C. Bogle, *The Battle for the Soul of Capitalism* (New Haven: Yale University Press, 2005), 31.
9. Joseph A. Schumpeter, *Capitalism, Socialism and Democracy* (New York: Harper Perennial Modern Thought, 2008), 142.

the loyalty of the masses of anonymous workers, mere numbers in "their" huge company, evaporates. Even shareholders show little loyalty as many sell their shares to follow the latest stock fads. An apathetic attitude, devoid of real proprietary interest, easily prevails.

That is to say, such super-concentration of industry and capital prepares the mentality of executives to behave like functionaries, companies to become like governmental bureaucracies, and workers to become masses. It prepares the way for state capitalism, where the State, as lender of last resort, ends up owning or controlling most of the means of production and other capital.

Gigantism and a Global Culture

Finally, unbalanced gigantism favors a global culture that supplants our own way of life. Inside gigantism's climate of unrestraint, we find a manner of expansion that bulldozes over or absorbs local cultures and traditions. Its international markets offer a world of goods and luxuries that often have neither proportion to a given country's wealth nor connection to its culture.

Gigantism favors the emergence of pseudo-elite figures such as super-businessmen, jet-setters, entertainment stars, and others who are presented as glamorous role models for promoting this global culture.[10] It is the curious phenomenon of those who want all the benefits of elites yet refuse to behave as true elites by maintaining a connection to their communities. Historian Christopher Lasch writes of these pseudo-elites as those "turning their back on the heartland and cultivating ties with the international market in fast-moving money, glamour, fashion, and popular culture."[11]

Social commentator David Rothkopf explains how these "predominantly globally oriented, globally dependent, globally active" figures are shaping a whole society in their own global image.[12] In fact, Rothkopf claims the writing is already on the wall, and it is senseless

---

10. See Plinio Corrêa de Oliveira, *Nobility and Analogous Traditional Elites in the Allocutions of Pius XII: A Theme Illuminating American Social History* (York, Pa.: The American Society for the Defense of Tradition, Family and Property, 1993), 187-190. Professor Corrêa de Oliveira's detailed description of these inauthentic elites provides insight into their unbalanced nature and characteristics.
11. Christopher Lasch, *The Revolt of the Elites and the Betrayal of Democracy* (New York: W. W. Norton, 1996), 6.
12. David Rothkopf, *Superclass: The Global Power Elite and the World They Are Making* (New York: Farrar, Straus and Giroux, 2008), 320.

to oppose it. He warns that we would do well to "come to grips with the redefinition of core ideas like sovereignty, community, identity, local, and foreign."[13]

——————————— · ———————————

Thus we see how the disordered drive to gigantism is an expression of frenetic intemperance, which has grave consequences. Contrary to popular belief, it does not result in a greater efficiency of the free market but undermines markets, prepares a socialist mentality, and promotes a global culture.

The key to containing this unbalanced gigantism is not establishing ownership limits or enacting state regulations. The key lies in addressing those fundamental disorders within the souls of men that have taken us so far off course.

———————————

13. Ibid., 321.

CHAPTER 5

The Paradox of Mass Standardization

T he driving force of frenetic intemperance can be further seen in the mass standardization of products. Unbalanced gigantism is only possible if there is unbalanced consumption to absorb its massive production.

We will readily admit that standardization normally occurs in all economies to ensure adequate production. It is unreasonable to expect that all products must be handcrafted and different. Ordinary standardization provides stability to markets since it helps maintain regularity and unity in production. Standardized grades of gasoline, for example, guarantee a uniform and efficient manner of providing fuel.

Inside the unity of this standardization, there also exists in man a great desire for diversity whereby he might express his individuality. For this reason, he searches for ways to customize, individualize, and tailor products to satisfy the unique needs essential for his personal development and limit the leveling effect of standardization. The bland and standardized fashions of Communist countries were rightly criticized for their blatant disregard for man—and his dignity.

A healthy economy balances standardization with individuality and unity with diversity. This balance is lost when frenetic intemperance enters, and what we will call *mass standardization* becomes the norm.

A Tradeoff of Priorities

Traditional markets tend to unite producer and consumer as a means to bring about this balance. In a real consumer-driven market, the producer's primary concern is to make and adapt the product to satisfy the consumer. The producer may even use standardized processes to achieve this satisfaction, but the end result is that the consumer and producer cooperate in distilling a product. A traditional tailor, for example, would see his principal task as making and fitting the suit according to the tastes and figure of the customer and at a reasonable price. The suit is "custom-made" for the customer. Such subtle coop-eration connects markets to culture since it makes of the production of goods a true expression of a people.

Frenetic intemperance throws off the restraints of this distilling process. By making the feverish search for expanding production and profits primary concerns, cooperation between consumer and pro-ducer is suppressed; mass standardization necessarily takes place. It is true that such standardization offers convenience and low prices. Nonetheless, the consumer is expected to sacrifice quality, comfort, and specific tastes for a rough equivalent. When mass standardization dominates a certain industry, custom-made products may still exist, but they become costly exceptions and not the rule.

In reality, mass standardization reduces the creative process to a statistical exercise where the consumer decides, with millions of fellow consumers, which of the many standardized products to buy. In this way, the consumer becomes "standardized." That important human touch that develops culture and tempers markets is thus lost.

A Process of Separation

This mass standardization was largely achieved through the separation of production and consumption. We note that the role of merchants has always been to unite producer and consumer by bringing to mar-ket products that they perceive will fill the needs of customers. The provision of such goods, even large quantities over great distances, performs a real service to society in satisfying individual needs.

This traditional role of uniting consumer and producer was sup-planted by a class of pre-industrial merchants in the sixteenth century that started to separate them by sidestepping the self-regulating cus-toms of the local markets that protected the independence of the pro-ducer. In their stead, they developed private supply chains by directly and cheaply cornering the market of large quantities of local goods or raw materials, especially in the wool and clothing industries, and sell-ing them in distant markets.

Such a separation put the local producer at the mercy of interna-tional market fluctuations and the terms of the new class of mer-chants. The decision of what, how much, or how it should be produced shifted from the producer to the trader. Likewise, the trader could dictate the terms of consumption. Freed from the level playing field of local competitive markets, such merchants could then form trade monopolies and cartels.

"This intervention of commerce between production and consumption was more than just a division of functions," write Peter Kriedte et al. "It gave rise to an economic dependence which gradually undermined the formal independence of the petty commodity producer and in the end destroyed it." They later continue: "In times of crisis and personal difficulty he [the merchant] was in a position to extend credit to the producer against the unfinished product and thereby obligated him to sell to nobody else."[1]

By keeping producer and consumer separate and distant, this new class of merchants could free themselves from the transparency of local, regional, or even national markets and dictate the terms of trade at both ends of the market, which allowed them to make huge profits. From that point on, the great merchants with their immense cash reserves tended to *control*, not unite, both producer and consumer. Such business practices later made frenetic intemperance practically inevitable.[2]

The Mass Economy

Although such commerce represented only a small portion of the pre-industrial market, the Industrial Revolution generalized this separation. On one side, its huge factories churned out massive amounts of goods developed by the producers to appeal to a mass market. On the other, an army of marketers, advertisers, brokers, retailers, and middlemen converged to create and shape those same markets.

Globalism only brings this separation to a frenetic climax with far-flung networks of outsourced producers and its masses of anonymous consumers that span the globe. As with the aforementioned pre-industrial traders, opportunities for control and profit are enormous.

---

1. Peter Kriedte, Hans Medick, and Jurgen Schlumbohm, *Industrialization before Industrialization: Rural Industry in the Genesis of Capitalism*, trans. Beate Schempp (Cambridge: Cambridge University Press, 1981), 99.
2. A recent example of such separation might be seen in the 2008 subprime mortgage crisis. As long as lender and borrower were united in the mortgage process, these loans were generally stable. When mortgage traders separated the two by bundling up bad mortgages on one hand and selling them to avid investors on the other, they freed themselves from all restraint, harvesting great profits by engaging in the selling frenzy of toxic assets that led to the subprime crisis.

Occasions for producer-consumer cooperation are minimized because global markets are detached from the unique needs of the individual or a local culture.

Standardizing Both Products and Consumers

The simple fact is that mass standardization can only be profitable to the point that it can aggregate consumers into large blocs.

Hence, global markets must impose universal standardization upon products, for if this brand of economics is to survive as an exact deductive science to interpret markets, everything must be quantified. There is no room for nuance outside the bar code. Likewise, mass markets impose standardization upon consumers, who must also be quantified since marketing must identify the largest possible general and niche markets. Consumers are in this way reduced to sets of cold statistical categories, where "the individual is stripped of his qualities and then reconstituted in terms of quantities."[3]

Consumption without Restraint

Mass standardization not only allows us to produce without restraint but creates the illusion that we might consume without restraint. Hence, the unrestrained consumer also participates in frenetic intemperance by gratifying disordered passions, buying impulsively, and seeking to throw off the legitimate restraints of keeping demand within limits and living within one's own means.

Modern economy encourages this unrestrained consumption by constantly creating, stimulating, and expanding markets to consume the flood of its products. By the massive scale of its production, it can offer cheaply made goods at low prices. With mass marketing techniques, modern media can mold consumer preferences to these markets. Moreover, modern economy gives rise to fads and fashion, encouraging consumers to buy based not on their real needs but on what they perceive others are buying. Finally, super-consumption aided by advertising, hype, and easy credit can induce demand for products that consumers neither need nor really want, bought with money they do not have.

---

3. Richard Stivers, *Technology as Magic: The Triumph of the Irrational* (New York: Continuum Publishing, 2001), 104.

The Proliferation of Choices

Mass standardization can unify markets, but it cannot address the problem of individuality whereby we desire products to be tailored to express our personalities. Marketers try in vain to compensate for this deficiency by offering a vast proliferation of choices of their standardized products.

In this sense, the mass market is a utopian market seemingly without limits where any standardized product may be marketed in any standardized store (and bought by any "standardized shopper"). It is a single market driven by frenetic intemperance since it creates a psychological climate where it is held that all desires can be satisfied by a plethora of goods within our reach. This impression is further extended as marketers adjust the color, size, packaging, or flavor of their standardized products to create the dazzling spectacle of ever more superficial choices.

The reality is different. The mass market is a huge but limited universe since it can only offer those goods produced in marketable quantities. In this sense, it limits, since it excludes the much greater universe of goods that cannot be produced in mass quantities.

Mass markets may proliferate choices, but they end up proliferating the same assortment of choices everywhere. Thus, shopping centers appear the same wherever they are found. Where once there was a wide variety of unique and affordable products suited to the tastes of a given market, there are now thousands of outlets offering strikingly similar arrays of global products detached from any locality. Each product category is usually dominated by a few giant industries that control the market everywhere.

It is not only the arrays of products that are similar but the products themselves. In malls and supermarkets worldwide, a spirit of dreary sameness has descended upon the market as all these products must conform to uniform global regulation, shipping standards, and demands of a massive economy of scale. This sameness becomes yet bleaker when the State enters into the markets, issuing myriad regulations and specifications that control the minutest details of the production, processing, and sale of products. While mass standardization offers its choices, conveniences, and low prices, everything takes on the air of bland uniformity. It is one thing to buy a package of thick-skinned, chemically treated tomatoes, and quite another to buy a peck of tangy fresh ones.

The Paradox of Choice

Despite such shortcomings, there are those who claim that the inebriating idea of unlimited choice is itself an expression of a marvelous consumer culture. They celebrate the endless possibilities open to them despite the evident impossibility of exercising even a fraction of these options.

Such "unlimited" choice does not maximize satisfaction. Without reasonable limits, the proliferation of choices becomes a tyranny by overloading the individual with too many superficial decisions. The overwhelmed consumer is more susceptible to purchasing based on fads and crazes that everyone else appears to be following. "Unlimited" choice can and does easily lead to unrealistic expectations and frustration.

"As a culture, we are enamored of freedom, self-determination, and variety, and we are reluctant to give up any of our options," writes Barry Schwartz. "But clinging tenaciously to all the choices available to us contributes to bad decisions, to anxiety, stress, and dissatisfaction—even to clinical depression."[4]

Complexity of Current Markets

We have described mass standardization as a driving force of today's economy. In so doing, we did not wish to imply that all modern consumption is equally dominated by this mass standardization. Such a regime would be unbearable.

The desire of men to express their individuality is such that markets are always receiving bursts of creativity and innovations that run contrary to mass standardization. Even those that do engage in mass standardization feel compelled to respect individuality as they make constant attempts to imitate the custom-made aspect of traditional production or encourage a more personal or customized approach to doing business. There has also been a considerable backlash against

---

4. Barry Schwartz, *The Paradox of Choice: Why More Is Less* (New York: Harper Perennial, 2004), 3.

standardized products and a concerted effort to diversify some production. The recent growth of certain niche markets of quality goods such as local wines or micro-breweries shows how attractive and competitive contrary models can be. Nonetheless, we must note that these positive trends survive in constant tension with mass markets. Successful companies are all too often bought out and absorbed by larger firms. The general tone of modern economy remains set by mass standardization.

As global markets continue to expand, mass standardization will only intensify the frenetic intemperance now undermining our economy and culture. It will only increase the bland sameness of the markets and the frustration of consumers. Our challenge is to detach ourselves from the illusions of the mass markets that promise happiness and unrestrained consumption. We need to explore ways to reunite once again producer and consumer to the measure possible, thus returning the primary focus of production to *satisfying* the individual needs rather than *shaping* them to suit mass markets. This can only be done by dealing with the problem of frenetic intemperance. Only then will economy return to its proper course.

Under the influence of frenetic intemperance, modern men exulted in tearing down the monuments, traditions and institutions of their past. Such destruction helped bring about massive changes, but it did so at the expense of that essential human element that serves to temper and order economy.

CHAPTER 6

Breaking Down Barriers

U p to this point, we have discussed those driving forces that construct and produce at a furious pace. Now, we will look at frenetic intemperance's fundamental urge to destroy by breaking down barriers.

This urge to destroy is more a temperamental state than an economic or philosophical doctrine. It is an impatient restlessness that drives modern man constantly to tear down and build anew. It creates an electric excitement in the air, reinforcing the cherished myth that economies are like unstoppable machines spontaneously breaking down all barriers in their way so that a liberating progress might prevail.

To oppose this restless impulse is seen as opposing modernity and progress. Hence, most modern men, even today, exult in the inebriating excitement of this forward movement and trust in its promises of always "new and improved" technologies—even as they themselves rush to tear down the monuments, traditions, and institutions of their past that stand in the way.

An Imposed Revolution

We must emphasize that this has always been an imposed revolution. As much as some economists like to present modern market economies as the spontaneous interplay of unfettered economic forces, the State has always played an important role in this transformation. The action of Adam Smith's benevolent "invisible hand" was only made possible by the force of the State's quite visible iron fist.

Sociologist Robert Nisbet notes that laissez-faire capitalism "was brought into existence by the planned destruction of old customs, associations, villages, and other securities; by the force of the State throwing the weight of its fast-developing administrative system in favor of new economic elements of the population."[1]

This destruction of restraining institutions was deemed necessary

---

1. Nisbet, *Quest for Community*, 247.

since modern economy needed what Adam Smith called "a system of natural liberty" where markets would be freed from all such constraints.[2]

Selective Laissez-Faire

It is revealing to note that one of these institutions that Smith considered the most constraining was the Church.[3] Indeed, theology professor D. Stephen Long explains that "the free market first sought freedom not from the state but from the Catholic church."

"When Adam Smith published *The Wealth of Nations*," Long continues, "he stated that the church of Rome posed the greatest threat to the civil order, liberty and happiness of humankind that the free market could guarantee. To secure a free market, the church's charity must first be contained so that it would not 'disturb the state.'"[4]

The reason for this hostility was that economic liberals viewed the Church's insistence upon an economic order based on justice and charity as an obstacle to its "system of natural liberty." They held that "perfect liberty required a curtailment of interference in the market: whether that interference be political, based on justice, or ecclesial, based on charity. The central virtue necessary for the logic of Smith's system was the prudence to seek one's own advantage."[5]

In the name of "natural liberty," the Church's liberty was attacked. Her "oppressive" charity supposedly discouraged the poor from work or entering into markets. The liberal idea was that unfettered markets would discipline and regulate the needs of the poor and even prevent them from bearing too many children.

Thus, throughout the nineteenth century, the State increased its powers and curbed the Church's charity by confiscating Her assets. Much of the charitable and educational infrastructure that the Church had so painstakingly built up over the centuries to help the poor was torn down, and the poor were left to fend for themselves or have re-

---

2. Adam Smith, "An Inquiry into the Nature and Causes of the Wealth of Nations," in *Adam Smith*, vol. 39 of *Great Books of the Western World*, 300. Smith held that this system of perfect liberty, working under the natural constraints and competitive drive of human nature, will give rise to an orderly self-regulating society directed as if by an "invisible hand."
3. "The constitution of the Church of Rome may be considered as the most formidable combination that ever was formed against . . . the liberty, reason, and happiness of mankind" (ibid., 350-51).
4. D. Stephen Long, *Divine Economy: Theology and the Market* (New York: Routledge, 2000), 74. Professor Long further declares that "this is clear in Adam Smith's writings and it is a narrative economic historians share" (ibid).
5. Ibid., 189.

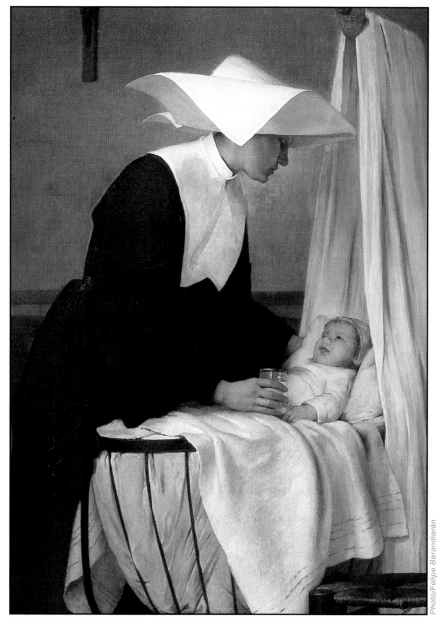

Charity by Uranie Colin-Libour (1833-1916). Some economists held that the Church's charity was "oppressive" and needed to be suppressed. They claimed it discouraged the poor from working and participating in the market.

course to the State's reluctant and compassionless welfare relief.[6]

A Tearing Down

We can see this same kind of action in the sudden emancipation from centuries-old customs and internal regulations—admittedly in need of reform—that had long governed pre-industrial society. The modern State, for example, suppressed guilds, common law, primogeniture, entail, and local customs, all of which had long stabilized pre-industrial society. It is important to note that these institutions were not the creations of faceless bureaucrats but the practical solutions of the population adapted over time to the local circumstances.

This "liberation" from custom was done in the name of removing any fetters that hampered trade. Yet it also took away those structures and associations that protected and sheltered producer and worker alike. The local customs, internal regulations, and craftsman traditions, all of which could well have served to temper economy, were discarded to make way for frenetic intemperance's rapid advance.

Indeed, economist Joseph Schumpeter notes: "In breaking down the pre-capitalist framework of society, capitalism thus broke not only barriers that impeded its progress but also flying buttresses that prevented its collapse."[7]

In fact, the pre-industrial order did collapse, and the result was the "loss of moral certainties, a confusion of cultural meanings, and a disruption of established social contexts"[8] that so characterized the early Industrial Revolution.

"Creative Destruction"

The dawn of the industrial age did not only bring down the flying buttresses of local traditions past; it also put up in their place the steel girders of our twentieth-century cooperative union.

The industrial age set in motion a dynamo of production that con-

---

6. It is well known that the anti-clerical movements of the nineteenth century, especially in France, plundered religious orders and congregations of their properties often to the enrichment of opportunists. We might also mention the massive despoliation of Church properties wrought by Napoleon and his troops. *The Catholic Encyclopedia* reports that "The history of the nineteenth century reveals a constant opposition to the Church. Her influence has been straitened by adverse legislation, the monastic orders have been expelled and their property confiscated, and, what is perhaps most characteristic of modern persecution, religion has been excluded from the schools and universities." *The Catholic Encyclopedia* (1911), s.v. "persecution."
7. Schumpeter, *Capitalism, Socialism and Democracy*, 139.
8. Nisbet, *Quest for Community*, 70.

stantly churned out new consumer goods, manufacturing methods, markets, and technologies. At the same time, we see the restless urge of frenetic intemperance already seeking to be free of these structures and creating new ones in their stead. It is what Schumpeter so expressively calls a "process of Creative Destruction" that "incessantly revolutionizes the economic structure *from within*, incessantly destroying the old one, incessantly creating a new one."[9]

As mentioned before, our American cooperative union fashioned some of its own braking mechanisms and moral restraints to ensure that everyone got along, and our cooperative ran efficiently. Part of our present crisis lies in the fact that, according to the logic of the process, the most cherished "fetters" of our American cooperative union—our religious and political consensus around God and country—are now being swept aside.

The Cables that Bind

In today's feverish globalism, the rusty steel girders of the industrial age have now become barriers themselves and are being hurled down and scrapped. From the ruins of our rust belts, fiber-optic cables are spinning the web of a new networked global society radically different from our own.

Like the transformation before, this one also advances by breaking down not local but national trade, political, and economic barriers while creating ever bigger global networks and structures. At the same time, the cables that connect also bind since all are tethered to these giant networks and are subject to their rules.

Thus we see the framework of a global economy being built where huge markets are opened, but the regulations of new supranational structures impose themselves upon the nations, as can be seen in global trade rules, monetary unions, or United Nations' protocols and treaties. Likewise, the same technologies that supposedly empower the individual to pursue his own happiness also give rise to the massive databases of intrusive government that pry into the private lives of individuals, record their every movement, and monitor the operation of markets.

---

9. Schumpeter, *Capitalism, Socialism and Democracy*, 83. While we believe that the term "creative destruction" can apply to the normal renovation of products, it can also be interpreted so as to describe the restless spirit of frenetic intemperance.

A Human Element

But the most destructive part of this new transformation is the force by which it sweeps aside those remaining national institutions that could serve to temper frenetic intemperance. Even the most optimistic promoters of flattening all barriers are forced to admit the disruptive challenges that threaten the "particular cultures, values, national identities, democratic traditions, and bonds of restraint that have historically provided some protection and cushioning for workers and communities."[10]

To the extent that these barriers are torn down, they erode that human element, which does not fit into the fast-paced sterile environments of vast networks. It is what Russell Kirk referred to as the "permanent things," those norms of courage, duty, courtesy, justice, and charity that owe their existence and authority to a power higher than the markets—indeed to a transcendent God.[11]

In making these observations, we are not criticizing technology, the free market, or innovative change. Rather, we are targeting the frenetic force by which modern technology aided by the State has effected massive changes at the expense of that essential human element that protects the individual. If we do not react, by the same dynamism and logic with which unrestrained industrialism destroyed the pre-industrial order, the present order will destroy its own substratum—and what little is left of Christian civilization.

---

10. Thomas L. Friedman, *The World Is Flat: A Brief History of the Twenty-first Century* (New York: Picador, 2005), 237.
11. Russell Kirk's reference to the "permanent things" can be found in many of his works such as *Enemies of the Permanent Things: Observations of Abnormity in Literature and Politics* (New Rochelle, N.Y.: Arlington House, 1969).

CHAPTER 7

Interdependence and Complexity

We will briefly consider yet another driving force that facilitates the advance of frenetic intemperance and the throwing off of restraint. It is a great impetus towards interdependence and complexity, which permits the rise of institutions, networks, and State regulatory agencies that tend to exercise control over everything.

This can be seen in today's huge interdependent global networks—in communications, Internet, transportation, shipping, finance, and so many other fields. We will admit that these interdependent networks facilitate the delivery of prodigious quantities of goods that flood our markets. Many consider them to be the basis of our richness, the cause of our progress, the pillar of our stability, and the guarantee of our security.

Nevertheless, these global networks also constitute a source of enormous fragility.

Exposed Neuralgic Chokepoints

These immense networks are fragile because we have made them so necessary and complex. Everyone is totally dependent upon them. Things have become so intertwined, operate so tightly coupled, and move so quickly that there is little margin for error. The slightest maladjustment, natural disaster, human error, or socialist regulation can have dire effects upon the whole. In this way, we have set up a world of vulnerable neuralgic chokepoints that range from geographic straits to oil supply chains to Internet servers to electric grids.

Moreover, the more complex the systems put in place, the more unpredictable life becomes. The number of unintended consequences is multiplied, and the very technology employed to deal with them becomes inadequate. "No mathematical model is sufficient to get all the variables," notes Richard Stivers. "Many of the most important can't be quantified. Furthermore, the use of systems analysis (as with information systems) actually militates against the flexibility required to deal with that which is unexpected."[1]

This is especially true of our worldwide financial markets, which analyst Richard Bookstaber claims "are now so complex, and the speed of transactions so fast, that apparently isolated actions and even minor events can have catastrophic consequences."[2]

NEURALGIC CHOKEPOINTS

Neuralgic chokepoints can be found everywhere in our interconnected world. They can be physical places like the Straits of Hormuz, the Panama Canal, or international airports. Our communications, Internet, and electric grid networks are all neuralgic chokepoints. The control of markets or commodities such as oil, gas, minerals, or credit are all fragile points of risk. Even certain practices such as just-in-time inventory production or high-frequency stock trading can easily throw systems out of balance and put all society at risk.

A Disappearing Moral Responsibility

In ordinary epochs, this vulnerability would already be alarming. However, in our times of disappearing moral responsibility, all it takes to bring these great networks to a grinding halt is a concerted attack by a terrorist group, an irresponsible act of a politician, or an uncalculated risk by a rogue broker. What seems so strong can suddenly be at the mercy of a few.

In fact, the probability of such irresponsible actions is no longer remote. With relatively unsophisticated means, today's terrorists, as evidenced by the 9/11 attacks, inflicted huge damage upon our networked infrastructure using simple box cutters as their weapon of choice. Likewise, we see how the unethical actions of a relative few in the financial markets can result in enormous monetary losses that extend far beyond a single financial institution.

All these damages can be multiplied by the psychological effects caused by sensational reporting in the media—yet another network

---

1. Richard Stivers, *Shades of Loneliness: Pathologies of a Technological Society* (Lanham, Md.: Rowman and Littlefield, 2004), 115.
2. Richard Bookstaber, *A Demon of Our Own Design: Markets, Hedge Funds, and the Perils of Financial Innovation* (Hoboken, N.J.: John Wiley and Sons, 2007), 1.

that can be exploited and manipulated by the unscrupulous few to cause great damage.

———————————— · ————————————

The unpredictable acts of unprincipled men, coupled with the ever-increasing complexity and interdependency of our integrated systems, make it extremely difficult to employ all possible safeguards to avoid disasters and system crashes.

Thus, as the present crisis deepens, we face the prospect of our own systems turning against us. By yielding to frenetic intemperance, we unleash what Bookstaber calls in the title of his book a "demon of our own design." As we will see, ours is the task to confine this demon by returning to moral restraint and then take back our future.

A Threatened Way of Life

Suburban scene. Our cooperative union has produced a way of life that is threatened by the present crisis.

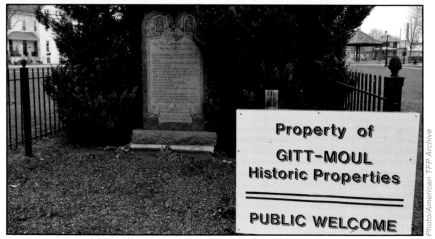

There is a growing frustration as our way of life appears to be unraveling. In the practical order, things seem congested. An airport scene of cancelled flights (top). Our political discourse (middle) has become polarized, embittered, and uncivil. The religious consensus around the Ten Commandments is breaking down as debate over public monuments leads to fencing them off as if a source of possible harm (bottom).

CHAPTER 8

Unraveling a Way of Life

Our American cooperative union consists of an economic dynamo of production and a corresponding way of life. We have described how frenetic intemperance has thrown this economic dynamo out of balance. It now remains for us to see the effects of this flight from temperance in our American way of life.

By broadening our outlook beyond the field of economic processes, we avoid the error of believing that prosperity can be restored simply by making some major, and even painful, adjustments to the economy. Other issues must also be addressed.

A Single Revolution with Many Facets

Frenetic intemperance helped generate profound transformations that contributed to the present crisis. This in turn threatens the stability of our American way of life.

Working in parallel in the political, intellectual, and religious fields, the statesman, philosopher, and theologian joined the businessman in bringing about profound changes in society as a whole. Just as an undercurrent dominated by frenetic intemperance produced unrestrained processes in economy, similar undercurrents in academia, the arts, religion, and political life unleashed their own destructive processes. Together, all these undercurrents brought about huge transformations. They constitute, as we have seen, a single Revolution that targets for destruction what little remains of our Christian civilization.

Thus, like our economy, our way of life has also become unbalanced and unsustainable. As a result, the glue of the consensus that binds our cooperative union together can no longer hold.

We will now look at those profound changes that are inextricably intertwined with our present economic model. In this way, we will understand the full extent of the crisis that is affecting the way of life we once believed unshakable, the progress we judged inevitable, and the consensus we thought indestructible.

The Frustration of Technology

N one of the processes by which our modern economy throws off restraint would be possible without our transformation into a technological society.

In truth, we are immersed in technology. Especially today with computer technology, it has become an unquestioned part of our lives since all our practical necessities depend upon it. Our purpose is not to condemn technology since it exists precisely to serve man. It is proper that scientific knowledge be applied to the practical aims of bettering human life.

What we criticize is the intemperate manner in which modern technology is applied to society and the exaggerated climate of great expectations that promises an always brighter and better future.

Promises and Great Expectations

These expectations were embraced with great enthusiasm at the time of the Industrial Revolution of the nineteenth century. The prospect of a kind of technological utopia electrified the air. There was a subconscious yet unbounded confidence in technology, vaguely analogous to the absolute confidence medieval man placed in Divine Providence.

"Along with technology's material domination, however, came its spiritual domination," writes Richard Stivers. "It assumed the form of an absolute value, a sacred; western societies looked upon it as the engine of progress, the solution to all problems."[1] In a similar vein, Lewis Mumford refers to the demands of technological progress as having "the effect of a divine ordinance, sacrilegious to challenge, impossible to disobey."[2]

---

1. Richard Stivers, *The Culture of Cynicism: American Morality in Decline* (Cambridge, Mass.: Blackwell, 1994), 162.
2. Lewis Mumford, *The Pentagon of Power,* vol. 2 of *The Myth of the Machine* (New York: Harcourt Brace Jovanovich, 1970), 158.

So great was the hope of expelling misfortune from our path that even the banishing of death was considered possible through the marvels of technology.[3]

Needless to say, while our technology is credited with providing enormous material abundance, it has failed to deliver upon its promise of permanent happiness. While it may still hold its fascination, the wildly optimistic enthusiasm of earlier times no longer reigns. Instead, technology has produced many undesirable and unintended consequences.

The Birth of the Masses

One such consequence was massification—the reduction of modern men into insignificant equals performing mechanical tasks. Our technological society facilitated the rise of the "masses," the shapeless multitudes that first worked in the factories and crowded the industrial cities of the nineteenth century. Some rightly affirm that mass society was born when most economic functions were taken away from the family at this point of industrialization.[4]

The effects of this change were devastating. This can clearly be seen in the statements of Pius XII who denounced the formation of egalitarian "masses" where men are "reduced to the minimum status of a mere machine." Such masses, he affirms, can become, upon an "impulse from outside, an easy plaything in the hands of anyone who exploits their instincts and impressions; ready to follow in turn, today this way, tomorrow another." Industrialization did much to produce what the Pontiff describes as "a mechanical level, a colorless uniformity." He speaks of how a sense of true honor and a "respect for tradition, of dignity—in a word all that gives life its worth—gradually fades away and disappears."[5]

Today's Masses

Massification still continues in our day. Everyone is in some way put

---

3. One example of such hopes was the development of the science of cryonics in which bodies and brains are frozen and preserved at extremely low temperatures in the expectation that future technological advances will be able to revive them.
4. This is the position of Peter Laslett who writes of the devastating effects of the economy outside the context of the family and household. See Peter Laslett, *The World We Have Lost—Further Explored*, 3rd ed. (London: Routledge, 1983), 18.
5. Pius XII, "1944 Christmas Message," in *Christmas Messages*, vol. 2 of *The Major Addresses of Pope Pius XII*, ed. Vincent A. Yzermans (St. Paul: North Central, 1961), 81-82.

into standardized categories, identified with bar-coded tags, or simply reduced to statistical numbers. Technological advances have only served to facilitate and increase enormously the extent of our massification. Society even defines itself in terms of mass transit, mass media, and mass production—which now extend to global markets.

Cheap mass-produced goods on a global scale, for example, play a role in creating global masses. "You would not refer to peasants in a medieval village as a mass, nor even the peasants in all of, say, Germany or France," comments Lawrence Friedman. "Mass *is* a way of describing people who live in a world where one can of soup is exactly like a billion other cans."[6]

Thus, the technology that enables standardization, globalization, and interdependency has done much to broaden the leveling, uniformity, and lack of respect for tradition and dignity mentioned by Pius XII. As much as we might try to defend our personal individuality, technology's dehumanizing and massifying effects tend to dominate and contribute to this assault upon the soul.

People Functioning Like Machines

We can cite the mechanization of society as a corollary of this massification. Perhaps one of the most brutal manifestations of our technological society is its system that transforms man from *organism* to *mechanism*. Against our organic nature, we are impelled to function like machines because we have become so enmeshed in the production process as to be reduced to human resources.

The victory of the machine is that it has become our model. Machines do their monotonous work with apparent perfection and obedience and tend to be automatically imitated. But the machine should not be our model. It cannot create but only copy. The computer does not think but processes. Mass technology cannot define itself in human terms; it admits no exceptions or nuances since the machine treats everyone with strict equality and speed.

Technology Everywhere

We note that technology does not refer only to the machines and computers that make up our industry. It also refers to those identical methods,

---

6. Lawrence M. Friedman, *The Horizontal Society* (New Haven: Yale University Press, 1999), 70.

procedures, and practices that men employ equally upon others and in this way imitates the action of efficient machines. This can be seen in the development of bureaucracy, teaching methods, advertising, and public relations practices. All these techniques tend to imitate the processes of a machine or computer.

We, in our turn, tend to organize our own lives into machine-like techniques and processes. "It would be a major error to limit technology to mere machinery and to material culture as such," warns sociologist Robert Nisbet. "Technology is no less present in rationalized, efficiency-oriented structures of organization in education, entertainment, and government than it is in the churches of our day, and even in family life."[7]

The family, for example, often delegates its functions to experts outside the family and home who provide uniform child-care, education, entertainment, and counseling to its members.

Today there is no field of human action that in some aspects is not modified in such a way as to impel men to act like a machine or computer. Inside these systems, all must be simplified, planned, and engineered to adapt to the machine and subsequently minimize individuality and maximize efficiency. In our turn-key franchises, for example, every procedure is planned out in detail to ensure "discipline, order, systematization, formalization, routine, consistency, and methodical operation."[8] In such a regime, the individual is reduced to a depersonalized "unit" to be inserted, replaced, and deleted at will in the industrial processes.

The Unintelligible Universe

Our transformation into a technological society has given us a rationalized mechanistic outlook on the world. The whole universe is perceived as one huge machine, and God is, at best, seen as a mere clockmaker who winds up the clock He built and leaves the world to its whims.

About this outlook, we may agree with Gilbert Simondon when he writes, "By reducing the object to nothing but its dimensions, technol-

---

7. Robert A. Nisbet, *The Social Bond: An Introduction to the Study of Society* (New York: Alfred A. Knopf, 1970), 245.
8. Ritzer, *McDonaldization of Society*, 97.

ogy does not recognize in it any internal or symbolic meaning, or any significance beyond its purely functional utility." He later concludes: "For this reason, one might say that 'technology desacralizes the world' to the extent that it progressively imprisons man in nothing but objects, without allowing him to catch a glimpse of a higher reality."[9]

In fact, modernity unofficially adopts "scientific" materialism as its explanation of the world. Philosopher William Barrett describes this worldview as the belief that "the ultimate facts of nature are bits of matter in space, and that all the varied phenomena of experience are to be explained by the movement and configuration of that matter." This matter-in-motion concept is the *de facto* dominant mentality of the West still reigning today, not necessarily as a formal philosophy but as "an unspoken attitude, habit and prejudice of mind."[10]

By reducing everything to the mechanical properties of mass and movement in space, this perception strips the universe of all metaphysical meaning and purpose. According to this random vision of nature and man himself, everything becomes unintelligible since all appears as a "flux of blind and aimless causation."[11]

The result of this view is that, since we cannot assign meaning to nature, we are limited to understanding only that which we make ourselves. Hence, the only way to deal with nature is not to understand it but to conquer and control it by our technology. We impose ourselves upon the universe, even to the point of abusing the nature with which we were created to live in harmony.

Inside an unintelligible universe, we doubt all past certainties, narratives, and even our own technology. We fall prey to a cynical skepticism, which is, in the words of Leo Strauss, "the inevitable outcome of the unintelligible character of the universe or of the unfounded belief in its intelligibility."[12]

---

9. Gilbert Simondon, *Du mode d'existence des objets techniques* (Paris: Aubier, 1958), quoted in Acquaviva, *Decline of the Sacred in Industrial Society*, 140.
10. William Barrett, *Death of the Soul: From Descartes to the Computer* (New York: Doubleday Anchor Press, 1986), 7.
11. Leo Strauss, *Natural Right and History* (Chicago: University of Chicago Press, 1953), 173. We are also reminded of John Locke's definition of the identity of man: "The identity of the same *man* consists; viz., in nothing but a participation of the same continued life, by constantly fleeting particles of matter, in succession vitally united to the same organized body." John Locke, "An Essay Concerning Human Understanding," in *Locke, Berkeley, Hume*, vol. 35 of *Great Books of the Western World*, 220.
12. Strauss, *Natural Right and History*, 174.

Technology, which seemed to hold so much promise at the time of the Industrial Revolution, has not delivered on those promises. Instead, the unintended consequences of massification and the mechanization of life have taken hold. Had frenetic intemperance not entered into the advance of technology, man could well have enjoyed the advantages offered by technology within the context of an intelligible universe.

BERTRAND RUSSELL'S DESPAIRING WORLDVIEW

Bertrand Russell gave bleak expression to this unintelligible vision of the universe in 1903:

> That man is the product of causes which had no prevision of the end they were achieving; that his origin, his growth, his hopes and fears, his loves and his beliefs, are but the outcome of accidental collocations of atoms; that no fire, no heroism, no intensity of thought and feeling, can preserve an individual life beyond the grave; that all the labors of the ages, all the devotion, all the inspiration, all the noonday brightness of human genius, are destined to extinction in the vast death of the solar system, and that the whole temple of Man's achievement must inevitably be buried beneath the debris of a universe in ruins—all these things, if not quite beyond dispute, are yet so nearly certain, that no philosophy which rejects them can hope to stand. Only within the scaffolding of these truths, only on the firm foundation of unyielding despair, can the soul's habitation henceforth be safely built ("A Free Man's Worship," in *Mysticism and Logic and Other Essays* [London: George Allen and Unwin, 1959], 47-48).

CHAPTER 10

The Consequences of the Abuse of Technology

When we function like our machines and computers, we adopt habits outside the normal rhythms of our nature. When we believe in modern technology's mechanistic worldview, it leads to what Plinio Corrêa de Oliveira calls an "adoration of novelties, speed, and machines" and a "deplorable tendency to organize human society mechanistically."[1]

This technological view of society cannot fail to have practical consequences in the way we experience life. To the grave economic crisis brought about by frenetic intemperance, we can add a corresponding culture that hinders our ability to react and negatively affects the psychological well-being of the nation.

A Brutal Pace of Life

One harsh consequence of our technological society is a mania for speed and novelty. Most early inventions of the Industrial Revolution, whether train, steamship, or telegraph, celebrated speed more than any other aspect.

These new technological advances helped unleash pent-up disordered passions deep inside man that exploded like fireworks and found their expression in an unbridled appetite for ever greater speeds, sensations, and pleasures.

This adoration of movement and change manifests itself by a desire for all that is instantaneous without the natural progression of intermediary phases of speed or reaction. It creates impatience with time and space based on the idea that nothing should stand between ourselves and the objects of our gratification. It stimulates inside man a restless desire to leave himself and his normal environment in search of new sensations. It can be seen, for example, among those who misuse an array of gadgets and electronic devices to multiply an instant

---

1. Corrêa de Oliveira, *Revolution and Counter-Revolution*, 80.

Boys on cell phones. When we are bombarded with constant stimuli, it taxes our ability to know things profoundly.

yet superficial connectivity with others or the intense addiction of those who find fast-paced gratification in video games.

Thus we are victims of a brutal and exhausting pace of life. This cult of speed is facilitated by a technology that allows us to make our machines, computing devices, and therefore our lives go ever faster.

A Nausea for Reflection

Are we really victims of speed? Yes, but we note that many modern men do not reject this harsh pace of life but rather embrace it.

Inebriated by the frenetic intemperance of our economic progress, many have come to relish the nanosecond networks that supply us with immediate sensation and novelty—be it in entertainment, communication, advertising, or sports. Speed becomes a "form of ecstasy the technical revolution has bestowed on man."[2] It becomes a means whereby modern men "escape subjective reason and lose themselves in the sensation of the moment."[3]

Amid noisy distractions, there is little time for that true leisure so necessary for the human soul to function. Leisure is not "freedom from work," but, as Lewis Mumford writes, it is "freedom within work; and along with that, time to converse, to ruminate, to contemplate the meaning of life."[4] The failure to seek or even desire that psychological repose leads to much anxiety and stress.

As a result, many have come to disregard tranquility, recollection, and true leisure in favor of the exhaustion of constant activity. The mania for speed leads to a nausea for reflection. Those proportional spiritual pleasures—joys like conversation, art, and silence—have ever less attraction. "Instead of contemplation," writes Daniel Bell, "we find substituted *sensation, simultaneity, immediacy,* and *impact.*"[5]

A Shallowness of Thought

As part of this quickening of the pace of life, we might especially mention how information technology, social networking, and the Internet

---

2. Milan Kundera, *Slowness* (New York: HarperCollins, 1996), 2, quoted in Stivers, *Shades of Loneliness*, 38.
3. Stivers, *Culture of Cynicism*, 146.
4. Mumford, *Pentagon of Power*, 2:138. See also Josef Pieper, *Leisure: The Basis of Culture*, trans. Gerald Malsbary (South Bend, Ind.: St. Augustine's Press, 1998).
5. Daniel Bell, *The Cultural Contradictions of Capitalism* (New York: Basic Books, 1976), 111.

are affecting our thought processes with a mania for all that is superficial and shallow. We are bombarded with the external stimuli of gadgetry whereby we remain instantly connected with the virtual world by means of ever shorter bursts of information. Scholars point out that such distractions tax our ability to concentrate and come to know things profoundly. The mind cannot relax and ponder meaning or nuance, thereby reducing us to a shallowness of thought that inhibits our ability to communicate face-to-face with others.

"The more distracted we become, the less able we are to experience the subtlest, most distinctively human forms of empathy, compassion, and other emotions," warns journalist Nicholas Carr. This assault on our mind's processes leads to an erosion of our humanness that "diminishes our capacity for contemplation" and is "altering the depth of our emotions as well as our thoughts."[6]

The Sterilization of Time

Within this hurried pace of life, time itself loses meaning. Inside our rushed schedules, we experience the double sensation of having no time to do anything and doing nothing with our time.

Without using time to reflect upon and interpret experiences, even the most organized life can become a jumble of insignificant events, passive entertainment, and mechanical routines. It is something Richard Stivers calls the "sterilization of time": "When time loses its meaning—the memory of significant events and transformations within a narrative framework—it becomes the space within which we produce and consume as much as possible."[7]

Within this paradox where we have no time yet waste so much time, we experience the boredom, exhaustion, and psychological stress that leads so many to conclude that there is nothing beyond the aimless flux of immediate experience.

Destruction of Place

The mania for movement and change contributes to an unsettled state of mind that manifests itself in a generalized loss of the sense of place.

---

6. Nicholas Carr, *The Shallows: What the Internet Is Doing to Our Brains* (New York: W. W. Norton, 2010), 221.
7. Stivers, *Culture of Cynicism*, 172.

Facilitated by technology, Americans have become a restless people constantly on the move inside this rushed pace of life. We have become a nation of strangers without anchorage in any place and disconnected from community. In the expressive words of Plinio Corrêa de Oliveira, we have built a vast network of nameless or numbered viaducts and bridges that become "anonymous passages for anonymous people to go to unknown places."[8]

As a result, this mobility tends to make all places appear the same. As Richard Weaver notes, our ability to travel anywhere at any time on these "anonymous passages" diminishes "the separateness of places" that were once protected and appeared different because of their "isolation, privacy and . . . identity."[9]

In fact, our electronic networks have now contributed to this destruction of place to such a point that it no longer matters where we are inserted into what has been so aptly called the lonely—and now so virtual—crowd.[10] In our networked society, one can work, live, and communicate anywhere. A public place like an airport or city park is "no longer a communal space but a place of social collection: people come together but do not speak to each other. Each is tethered to a mobile device and to the people and places to which that device serves as a portal."[11]

Granted, our technologies do facilitate contact with others at great convenience and over great distances. Nevertheless, they can also encourage making our messages more superficial by increasing their volume, brevity, and speed. While instant connectivity can supplement personal relationships, it can also make them more distant when mediated and hidden behind a screen or in short text messages. The very real danger is allowing these technologies to replace

---

8. See Plinio Corrêa de Oliveira, MNF meeting, Aug. 21, 1986, Plinio Corrêa de Oliveira Documents, American TFP Research Library, Spring Grove, Pa. (This collection consists of transcribed audio recordings and is hereafter cited as Corrêa de Oliveira Documents. All references are American TFP translations.) Twentieth-century urban planners like Le Corbusier conceived of a new street which would become a "machine for traffic" where the pedestrian could not obstruct traffic flow. By making it easy to get out of the city, the planners built the highways which inadvertently helped turn the cities into empty shells of themselves and sent people into the suburbs.

9. Richard Weaver, *Visions of Order: The Cultural Crisis of Our Time* (Wilmington, Del.: Intercollegiate Studies Institute, 1995), 37.

10. Cf. David Riesman, Nathan Glazer and Reuel Denney, *The Lonely Crowd: A Study of the Changing American Character* (New Haven: Yale University Press, 1989).

11. Sherry Turkle, *Alone Together: Why We Expect More from Technology and Less from Each Other* (New York: Basic Books, 2011), 155.

the face-to-face contacts and sense of community that make place so important in our lives.

When we allow our instant communications to uproot the anchors of place in us, we lose more than just physical location. We lose the stage for our relationships within our communities, the locus of legend and myth, and the place where our lives gain context and meaning. The result is a world that, to use the harsh words of Charles Reich, "has obliterated place, locality and neighborhood, and given us the anonymous separateness of our existence."[12]

A Crushing Disproportion

We cannot fail to mention in passing how we are also affected by a crushing disproportion whereby our technological society constantly affirms its overbearing triumph. Where once only steeples rose heavenward, massive skyscrapers stand, as if consigning past tradition to insignificance and reducing men to mere ants seemingly unable to affirm their individuality.

We might also mention the contrary disproportion where technological miniaturization makes its own brutal statement since, in its nanosecond and terahertz processing, it introduces a disproportion between tiny size and massive function incomprehensible to the human mind.

The Cult of Ugliness

The proliferation of massive, unadorned, and cold structures that tower over our cities represents not only the triumph of technological progress but a quantitative exaltation of matter that has been powerfully called a "cult of ugliness." Such structures, states Fr. Anthony Brankin, are "stunning and awesome in their utter inhumanity, their complete lack of scale, their thorough and total sterility, and their horrifying proportions."[13]

To this can be added the widespread promotion of modern art, which flaunts an esoteric ugliness and disproportion yet all the while suffers from a lack of understanding from a public that largely rejects it. All this sends postmodernity's relentless message of nihilism, empti-

---

12. Charles A. Reich, *The Greening of America* (New York: Crown Trade Paperbacks, 1970), 7.
13. Anthony J. Brankin, "The Cult of Ugliness in America," *Crusade Magazine*, May-June 2001, 12.

ness, and nothingness that Father Brankin describes as the belief that there is "neither nature, nor beauty, nor God."

A Universal Culture

Mass technology establishes a single universal culture in the face of globalized production and markets. On one hand, it assimilates local cultures, taking from them what little that might be globalized or commercialized, while turning the rest into folklore. For example, a giant chain of Italian restaurants can reduce Italian culture to a collection of recipes and "a handful of quaint old customs, maintained like bones in a museum."[14]

On the other hand, this society that technology created imposes its own common universal culture without reference to place, where music, food, cinema, fashions, and entertainment are increasingly the same.

Wearing Away of All That Is Most Human

These are some of the unintended consequences of our transformation into a technological society. We are given machines that we misuse to carry out the designs of our intemperance, and these very machines have served to alienate us from ourselves.

Suffice it to say that the crisis of a failed utopia is brewing because our mechanical and virtual relationships are wearing away the human element that makes us crave the warmth and security of those personal and intelligible things so proper to our rational nature.

Far be it from us to condemn technology. We only want to free technology from that which makes it inhuman. We want to return technology to its role of serving mankind—amply and freely. Alfred North Whitehead writes, "The greatest invention of the nineteenth century was the invention of the method of invention."[15] He rightly credits this frenzied method with the breaking up of the foundation of the premodern world. Because of an explosive intemperance, this whirlwind

---

14. Friedman, *Horizontal Society*, 62.
15. Alfred North Whitehead, *Science and the Modern World* (New York: The Free Press, 1967), 96.

of inventions dazzled man and whetted his appetites for ever greater speed, sensations, and pleasures.

To use the metaphor of Plinio Corrêa de Oliveira, pre-modern technology used to serve man as a horse serves its rider. But today's modern technology is like a galloping horse that drags its fallen rider from the stirrup. The rider falls because he does not have sufficient zeal for his own individual development, and has not rejected the standardization and dehumanizing elements of technology.[16]

---

16. See Plinio Corrêa de Oliveira, American Studies Commission meeting, Dec. 21, 1987, Corrêa de Oliveira Documents.

CHAPTER 11

The Implosion of Individualism

Perhaps no other conception of life played such an important role in the construction of modern society as the rise of individualism. In fact, many economists work on the premise that modern economy assumes an extreme individualism.

First expressed in the writings of Thomas Hobbes (1588-1679), the concepts that later gave rise to individualism radically changed our idea of society. No longer considered a community of individuals ordered to the perfection of man's nature, Hobbes saw society as a "sand heap" of individuals, each guided by his own self-interest and kept in order by a strong rule of law.

Individualism is a fundamental part of our own American culture and identity. It is the foundation of the cooperative union that serves as our dominant model. Individualism is popularized as a belief in the dignity and sacredness of the individual whereby one thinks and does as one wishes. Like technology, it also is enshrined as sacred in our secular pantheon since any violation of this right to do as one pleases is viewed as "not only morally wrong, [but] sacrilegious."[1]

This individualism now has its own points of tension and contradiction that put it in a state of crisis.

The Autonomous Man

First, let us analyze the substance of individualism so as to disentangle it from its myths and simplifications.

Individualism is much more than just doing as one pleases. Rather, it is a philosophy of life that declares self-preservation and its corollary self-interest to be the most common and inalienable of all rights and the root of all morality and justice. "There are, then, no absolute or unconditional duties," writes Leo Strauss of this system. "Duties are binding

1. Robert N. Bellah et al., *Habits of the Heart: Individualism and Commitment in American Life* (Berkeley: University of California Press, 1985), 142.

INDIVIDUALITY VERSUS INDIVIDUALISM

We make a distinction between individuality and individualism. Man manifests his individuality when he fully develops his personality and talents by which he is different from others. At the same time, individuality encourages man to develop his intensely social character by participating in life together in community, acknowledging a moral law, and promoting the common good. The more specific, richer, and stronger this personal life, the more intense the social life. Thus, individuality results in stronger community.

Individualism is a deformation of individuality by which man closes himself up in and makes himself the center of an enclosed world of personal self-interest that tends to disregard the social character of man and his role in community.

---

only to the extent to which their performance does not endanger our self-preservation. Only the right of self-preservation is unconditional or absolute."[2]

Hence, according to this vision, we are all involved in our own inebriating pursuit of self-interest. Each is a totally autonomous self-made man, who is the sole architect of his own freedom and destiny. Each is a being of infinite possibility completely free to construct an eternally new self.[3]

In this grandiose conception of self, this self-made man sees himself as the product of his own personal ingenuity and strength. He is the ultimate judge of what is right and wrong. This opinion can be found in the U.S. Supreme Court decision, *Planned Parenthood of Southeastern Pennsylvania v. Casey*: "At the heart of liberty is the right to define one's own concept of existence, of meaning, of the universe, and of the mystery of human life."[4] In this search, writes Daniel Bell, "there is a denial of any limits or boundaries to experience. It is a reaching out for all experience; nothing is forbidden, all is to be explored."[5]

This concept holds that an individual becomes a perfect and com-

---

2. Strauss, *Natural Right and History*, 181.
3. Individualists are divided on the true meaning of individualism. The English school tends to take a more natural, less reasoned, and spontaneous attitude towards human action. The French school is rationalist and Rousseauan. Both contain this idea of self-interest and self-determination.
4. *Planned Parenthood of Southeastern Pa. v. Casey*, 505 U. S. 833 (1992). Justice Anthony Kennedy later cited this passage, which he had written, as support for his central thesis for striking down all sodomy laws in *Lawrence v. Texas*, 539 U.S. 558 (2003).
5. Bell, *Cultural Contradictions of Capitalism*, 14.

plete being when "unencumbered" by strong ties to tradition, family, custom, or moral law. Such a vision sees everyone as being equally and entirely free of special obligations to one another. When working with or even under others, we engage in a "social contract" or partnership where each seeks one's own advantage or pleasure. Even the State is seen as a mere mechanism to facilitate these contracts in the pursuit of self-interest.

We note that, like technology, the giddy freedom promised by individualism also has unintended practical consequences that have led to disillusionment and crisis.

Alas, man is too much of a social being to endure individualism in its pure form. His human nature craves the richness of the very social bonding from which he is "liberated" by individualism. He perceives the limits of his lonely search for his own destiny; he finds that the unencumbered self easily becomes an impoverished and empty self. He senses the difficulty in engaging in what Hobbes calls a "war of every man against every man,"[6] which leads to the tension of looking upon others with suspicion and as competitors.

Society Is "Atomized"

Thus, individualism brings about two contrary movements: isolation and conformity.

"In the absence of any objectifiable criteria of right and wrong, good or evil," write sociologist Robert Bellah et al., "the self and its feelings become our only moral guide."[7] Far from unencumbering this self-made man, individualism actually isolates him like an atom. His lone search for self-fulfillment ends up encapsulating him inside his own self-enclosed micro-world, where he is entirely free within its limited domains "in glorious, but terrifying, isolation."[8]

Living as an isolated atom actually gives a sensation of emptiness, anonymity, and loneliness that is profoundly anti-natural. Man's social nature is such that the frustrated individual, asphyxiated by his enclosure, cannot live up to his imagined self-aggrandizement; he must look for solace outside.

---

6. Thomas Hobbes, "Leviathan," ed. Nelle Fuller, in *Machiavelli, Hobbes*, vol. 23 of *Great Books of the Western World*, 86.
7. Bellah et al., *Habits of the Heart*, 76.
8. Ibid., 6.

Thus, we reach a great paradox. No longer having tradition, community, or social mores to sanction his judgments or measure his achievements, the self-made man turns to conformity with those similar "atoms" around him for validation. "Thrown into society as isolated human beings, literally *individua* and human atoms, people hunger for 'integration,' and they allay this hunger by means of the intoxicating thrills and crowds of mass society," writes economist Wilhelm Röpke.[9]

That is to say, the great individualist who takes great pride in being free to do everything, usually ends up doing what others are doing. This is how the masses are formed. The individualist becomes what is called the "other-directed man," constantly gauging himself by what he perceives are the reactions of the other anonymous atoms that make up the masses.[10] Since these perceptions are not always clear, the individualist feels the insecurity of never knowing exactly where he stands.

The implicit messages contained in media advertising and television programs essentially play on this insecurity of individualists. All are led to believe that security is found in mass-produced products and their corresponding lifestyles whereby they can become like smiling celebrities. Worse yet, they believe they are crafting for themselves unique lives of success and happiness by their own choices. In reality, they are merely integrating themselves into our mass society by conforming to what every other "atom" thinks.

In such an atmosphere, life, work, and even politics come to be molded by the spectacular and theatrical since it is the only way to call people out of their isolation and convey the sense of universal happiness to be found in being part of the masses.

With few mediating social structures, the individualist, like a grain of sand, suffers himself to join the anonymous masses by allowing himself to be directed by mass media, mass culture, mass markets—or even big government. In promising individualism, modernity paradoxically delivers its own stifling brand of collectivism.

Practical Consequences: The Demise of Community
One major consequence of our mass culture is that we no longer see

---

9. Wilhelm Röpke, *A Humane Economy: The Social Framework of the Free Market* (Chicago: Henry Regnery, 1960), 57.
10. See Riesman, Glazer and Denney, *The Lonely Crowd.*

FREEDOM IS NOT CHOICE

There are those who confuse freedom with choice. They do not realize that freedom is the ability to choose the means to a determined end perceived as good and in accordance with our nature. It is not the choice itself. When a person makes a bad choice or chooses a bad end, the result is not freedom but a type of slavery to the passions. Thus, a person who overeats when satisfying natural hunger or another who chooses an excellent wine with the intent of getting drunk, does not exercise true freedom but rather its abuse. The more we master our nature, the more freedom we have. Supernatural virtue gives us yet more freedom since we not only master our nature but surpass it.

Saint Thomas teaches: "But man is by nature rational. When, therefore, he acts according to reason, he acts of himself and according to his free will; and this is liberty. Whereas, when he sins, he acts in opposition to reason, is moved by another, and is the victim of foreign misapprehensions. Therefore, 'Whosoever committeth sin is the slave of sin'" (quoted in Leo XIII, encyclical *Libertas* [1888] in *The Papal Encyclicals*, vol. 2, p. 171, no. 6).

ourselves as social beings, but rather as the center of a separate little world with no essential need of betterment through society. In such a vision, notes philosopher Alasdair MacIntyre, we "see in the social world nothing but a meeting place for individual wills, each with its own set of attitudes and preferences and who understand that world solely as an arena for the achievement of their own satisfaction, who interpret reality as a series of opportunities for their enjoyment."[11]

That is why extreme individualism leads to the demise of community. This can be seen, for example, in the aftermath of the sixties when powerful currents swept away the remaining traditional bonds that once held the social fabric together so tightly. The result is now evident. Silently and imperceptibly, the life of communities is dissolving with shocking rapidity as most Americans withdraw from civic and community involvement and become less engaged with family, friends, and neighbors.

---

11. Alasdair MacIntyre, *After Virtue: A Study in Moral Theory*, 3rd ed. (Notre Dame, Ind.: University of Notre Dame Press, 2007), 25.

This process is facilitated by the modern megalopolises which, by their anonymity, make social relation more difficult and impede the natural formation of local leaderships. Nevertheless, notes Robert Putnam: "No part of America, from the smallest hamlet on up the scale has been immune from this epidemic." He observes that this "anti-civic contagion" is found in every social class, ethnic group, racial category, and marital status group.[12]

Types of Social Groups

We are not saying that the individualist is necessarily a lonely person without social relationships. Association with others, a circle of family and friends suited to taste, is admitted or even encouraged by individualist thinkers. In fact, our modern world is full of organizations of all types providing numerous opportunities to interact socially.

However, what we are saying is that these associations tend to be shallow. These relationships are often deliberately superficial and casual and, as a result, well suited to the individualist who links and unlinks with others according to personal whims and immediate interests. There are a vast number of legitimate and useful organizations that loosely engage the individual around specific interests. These might be organizations centered, for example, on self-help, sports, education, or stamp collecting. While these free and voluntary associations serve a purpose, they are set up without major commitments or allegiances, and do not seek to define or form the person.

Richard Stivers claims that mass society makes these superficial and voluntary organizations especially necessary. He notes that, "With the disappearance of extended family and community, the individual requires some identity and security in relation to the centralized power of the state and corporation."[13]

These organizations differ from the family and those traditional groups of community or parish, which help define the person and are deliberately formative. Membership in these cohesive social groups plays an important role in the perfection of a person's social nature, conferring status, identity, meaning, and structure upon one without

---

12. Robert D. Putnam, *Bowling Alone: The Collapse and Revival of American Community* (New York: Simon and Schuster, 2000), 208, 247.
13. Richard Stivers, *The Illusion of Freedom and Equality* (Albany, N.Y.: State University of New York Press, 2008), 53.

destroying individuality. This can also be seen, for example, in universities, military services, or church organizations that enhance, not absorb, the individual.

While individualists might admit the usefulness of the family and intermediary groups, they do so in the pursuit of their self-interest and tend to deny this intense social context.

War on Cohesive Communities

It is no surprise that modern individualist thinkers and politicians have waged a veritable war on these cohesive mediating groups. Such ideologues celebrate their demise as "liberating" and insist that the individual must reign supreme. In reality, none save the State ultimately ends up reigning since it is the only entity capable of absorbing (and badly carrying out) the functions of the smaller groups.

THE REVOLUTION'S HATRED OF INTERMEDIARY ASSOCIATIONS

Distrust of intermediary social bodies can already be seen in Hobbes' support of the strong State in his book *Leviathan*. Rousseau did not hide his own dislike for "partial associations" (See Jean Jacques Rousseau, "The Social Contract," in *Montesquieu, Rousseau*, vol. 38 of *Great Books of the Western World*, 387). In 1791, the French Revolution abolished guilds and trade corporations. It later imposed the infamous *Le Chapelier* law, which, under the pretext that no corporation should stand between the individual and the State, forbade the establishment of intermediary associations. Napoleon broadened and systematized such laws when, in 1810, he extended the prohibition to include any association of over twenty persons. An uproar led to progressive relaxing of these restrictions. The controversy continued until the laws were repealed at the end of the nineteenth century.

Even where these cohesive societies manage to survive, the alienating forces of modernity have done much to deprive them of their functions and reduce the old communal institutions of clan, village, or church to almost folklore status. More conservative individualists might even tragically turn these same cohesive societies into voluntary societies aimed at self-interest.

Thus, for example, the family, stripped of its functions, comes to be considered as a mere voluntary social unit, no more or no less than any other association, to be used to advance the individual's pursuit of happiness. This can be seen in the proliferation of divorce or the demand for same-sex "marriage." As mentioned before, many see the nation, which should be the supreme cohesive body, as a cooperative union from which one can take great advantage.

Hostility Towards the State

Individualism eventually leads to hostility towards the State. It is seen as a mere keeper of order that becomes necessary as property is accumulated.[14] For John Locke, "Government has no other end but the preservation of property."[15] Its purpose is diminished to the safeguarding of those individual rights associated with self-interest. In the words of Adam Smith, "Civil government, *so far as it is instituted for the security of property*, is in reality instituted for the defense of the rich against the poor, or of those who have some property against those who have none at all."[16]

Thus, the individualist sees the State as a regulator of the social contracts that keep society running. "The state is a mechanical apparatus or a mutual insurance corporation," writes Heinrich Rommen in criticism of this model. "The taxes are insurance premiums, the state and its government a kind of property-owners' protective association."[17]

Any set of objective moral values outside this framework has no validity. The more radical libertarians refuse to see the State as a source of social union and even long to see the State abolished entirely and have all its regulating functions put in private hands. The socialist, on the other hand, sees the State as the supreme regulator that must plan all things.

The modern State is only too eager to fill its role as regulator by establishing its intrusive presence everywhere. The State arrogates to itself the great number of tasks that once belonged to the family and

---

14. "The acquisition of valuable and extensive property, therefore, necessarily requires the establishment of civil government. Where there is no property, or at least none that exceeds the value of two or three days' labor, civil government is not so necessary." Smith, *Wealth of Nations*, 309.
15. John Locke, "Concerning Civil Government, Second Essay," in *Locke, Berkeley, Hume*, vol. 35 of *Great Books of the Western World*, 46.
16. Smith, *Wealth of Nations*, 311. (Emphasis added.)
17. Heinrich A. Rommen, *The State in Catholic Thought: A Treatise in Political Philosophy* (St. Louis: B. Herder, 1947), 128.

other intermediary associations. The State establishes a growing presence in the economic activities of the nation, thus fostering a socialist mentality. It must have frequent recourse to an army of faceless bureaucrats that have the onerous task of regulating the action of its citizens. To this effect, it must also tax and spend, even to the point of incurring great debt.

Hence, the State is no longer seen as the highest social union, the holder of legal authority, or the promoter of the common good. Rather, it plays the role of the intrusive regulator of individual interests to be looked upon with utmost suspicion.

The Destruction of Higher Law

We also note that the individualist concept of law tends to deny the obligations to follow a higher or eternal law. This concept greatly simplifies moral law, which is based on human nature, by limiting it to merely the natural right of self-preservation.[18] Such law is severely limited in both scope and content since it does not consider the role of law and justice in the perfection of our nature.

"If the only unconditional moral fact is the natural right of each to his self-preservation, and therefore all obligations to others arise from contract, justice becomes identical with the habit of fulfilling one's contracts," explains philosopher Leo Strauss. "Justice no longer consists in complying with standards that are independent of human will."[19]

Thus, law is reduced to mere regulation aiding individual self-interest, safeguarding property or contracts, and keeping public order. Without references to any universal principles, civil law easily embraces positivism, a philosophy that holds that the foundation of law is no longer found in natural law but the State itself.

The individualist order extends beyond simply doing what one wants. It tends to develop shallow and loose associations favorable to self-

---

18. Hobbes and others tried to deduce a law of nature (*lex naturalis*) based not on human nature but self-preservation, "a precept, or general rule, found out by reason, by which a man is forbidden to do that which is destructive of his life." Hobbes, *Leviathan*, 86.
19. Strauss, *Natural Right and History*, 187.

interest but which break all those strong ties that lead to the social cohesion so necessary for our troubled times. The immense freedoms that we as Americans enjoy would gain much if we could once again acknowledge those natural social institutions that temper yet give meaning and context to this freedom. Without this recognition, far from enhancing true freedom, individualism has only served to destroy it.

CHAPTER 12

Postmodern Individualism: Splitting the Atom

There is yet one more aspect of individualism to be considered. For decades we have lived in a society where this classical individualism has had great influence. This has created an internal tension inside countless Americans who yearn for community yet search for individual self-fulfillment. Individualism satisfies neither desire.

On one hand, there is the crushing pressure to conform to the false "community" found in the media, markets, and culture that rule over our mass society. On the other hand, there is the sobering experience of our "atomized" isolation that continually haunts us in our search for meaning.

Breaking an Uneasy Peace: Postmodern Individualism

Our American way of life found a way to make an uneasy peace between these two impulses. In theory, our culture extols the desirability of pure individualism, although this ideal is often adulterated in practice to adjust to a more human reality.

Many Americans find meaning and identity in private life by clinging to what little remains of family, church, and other social structures. At the same time, they alternatively put up with and embrace those mass structures (like mass media and mass marketing) that seem so beyond their control and comprehension.

This uneasy peace was broken in the sixties. There was a revolt against this accommodation with classical individualism, and a new more radical postmodern individualism exploded onto the scene.[1]

The classic individualist enshrined self-preservation as the sole standard of order. By the same logic, the postmodern individualist makes the "right" of self-gratification the only absolute right even when such

---

1. Charles Reich wrote about this revolution in 1970 in his counter-culture classic book *The Greening of America*. He said it was a revolution unlike any of the past. "It will originate with the individual and with culture, and it will change the political structure only as its final act. . . . This is the revolution of the new generation." Reich, *The Greening of America*, 2.

behavior is self-destructive. If individualism turned individuals into isolated atoms, its postmodern mutant splits the atom.

This new individualism is an extension and radicalization of what came before. The difference is that the modern individualist destroyed external structures—tradition, custom, or community—that encumbered self-interest. The postmodern individualist seeks to destroy those internal structures—logic, identity, or unity—that impede instant gratification.

Unlike violent revolutions of times past, this silent yet relentless movement strikes at the core of our culture and its morality. It is an instance of what Edmund Burke calls "the most important of all revolutions . . . a revolution in sentiments, manners, and moral opinions."[2] When this revolution heads towards decadence as it is now doing, it spreads slowly, imperceptibly, and contagiously by decay, inertia, and torpor. To use a metaphor of Plinio Corrêa de Oliveira, it "conquers and overthrows everything with all the nonchalance of a smiling Buddha."[3]

Manifestations of Postmodern Individualism

This postmodern individualism manifests itself everywhere as can be seen in the following ways:

- The "liberation" from the constraints of logic by fragmenting unity of thought and the blurring and blending of all distinctions. There is a concerted effort to avoid definitions and accept the most blatant contradictions. Just about anything can be blended and blurred together: religions, nations, economies, "genders," or computer networks.

- The deconstruction of identity by questioning nationality, sexuality, personal name, or any aspect of what is considered an "imposed identity." Some even go to the point of fragmenting into several identities, "genders," or online avatars based on the whim and imagination of the moment.

- An aversion to that which is reasoned, structured, or systematized, and as a result a "need to escape into fantasy,

---

2. Edmund Burke, "Reflections on the Revolution in France," in *The Works of Edmund Burke, With a Memoir*, 1:490.
3. Plinio Corrêa de Oliveira, Medical Commission meeting, May 12, 1991, Corrêa de Oliveira Documents.

dreams and ecstasy."[4] Hence comes our culture's obsession for the spontaneity found in the experience of drugs, sexual promiscuity, and online fantasies.

An Illusion of Greater Freedom

All this is done in the name of greater freedom. Yet today's postmodern man is no freer from the mass structures that so enslaved the individualist before him. He actually isolates himself yet more by throwing off the restraints of logic and identity that bind him to his culture. He seeks to integrate himself even more by throwing himself into the now globalized masses of the vast virtual world networks, which are removed from any concrete social order. And all this is done at a pace and volume that is overwhelming.

Russell Kirk observes: "Whenever people cease to be aware of membership in an order—an order that joins the dead, the living, and the unborn, as well as an order that connects individual to family, family to community, community to nation—those people will form a 'lonely crowd,' alienated from the world in which they wander. And to the person and the republic, the consequences of such alienation will be baneful."[5]

"So long as a strong cultural heritage existed, and with it a sense of membership, the modern ethic of individualism was tolerable," writes Robert Nisbet of this extreme individualism. And he continues, quoting Paul Tillich, "But when the remnants of a common world broke down, the individual was thrown into complete loneliness and the despair connected with it."[6]

Thus we reach a point of terrible irony, full of pathos and tragedy.

Today, the freedom or autonomy promised by classical individualism or its postmodern version has not materialized. In these times when all talk of diversity, never has there been less diversity and more

---

4. Stivers, *Technology as Magic*, 203.
5. Russell Kirk, *The Roots of American Order*, 3rd ed. (Washington, D.C.: Regnery Gateway, 1991), 473.
6. Nisbet, *Quest for Community*, 11.

conformity. Never have so many worn the same clothes, eaten the same fast foods, or listened to the same popular music as today's globalized masses. While all believe themselves to be free and autonomous, never have so many been compelled to think and act in the same politically correct way.

In our crowded cities, many are lonely. In our interconnected world, there are those who feel entirely isolated, tormented by apathy, boredom, and restlessness. Is it any wonder that we cannot unite to find solutions? Is it any wonder that so many feel abandoned and full of anxiety?

CHAPTER 13

The Exhaustion of Materialism

W e are a practical and restless people blessed with a land of great bounty. Throughout our history, we have pursued unlimited progress with great optimism and relentless drive. The resulting material prosperity seems to support the idea that we are a people set apart, impervious to the misfortunes others have suffered in history.

In truth, we have built this robust material order with hard work, a practical spirit, generosity, and good will towards others. With almost missionary zeal, we have spread this spirit of great enterprise to other parts of the world in the sincere hope that it might bear similar fruits— and yet we often see such efforts rejected.

We do not criticize this extraordinary drive or the desire to better our lives materially. However, we do criticize the materialistic spirit— so often linked to the so-called consumer society that motivates many of the actions in this process—and its failure to address the spiritual nature and needs of man.

Farewell to Perfection

A materialistic society cultivates an excessive fixation on addressing the pleasures and bodily comforts of everyday life. Even mental or intellectual improvement and development is made to serve material advancement. As a result, it does not sufficiently deal with those specifically spiritual desires that are so much a part of our human nature. It does not deal with anything metaphysical since it does not address the good, the true, or the beautiful but only the useful. There is little room in this materialism to respond adequately to any great yearnings for perfection, heroism, or sanctity.

In fact, this materialist order, born of the Industrial Revolution, explicitly rejected the high ideals that motivated the Christian era. Christian virtues were replaced by the civic virtues that favor a commercial culture. The ideals of Christian perfection that had so inspired the marvels of Christendom were deemed impracticable, prideful, and even impoverishing.[1]

Describing the spirit of the time, Michael Novak writes of the call to reject those "human ideals too high for the ordinary mundane business of life." The French philosopher Montesquieu denounces "glorifying ideals too perfectionist for ordinary life." By subjecting all to common sense, Novak explains this new ethic of commerce as being "proportioned to man as he is, not as dreams would have him." Hence, the founders of this new order embraced "the common, the useful, the mundane" as the best expression of what they considered a natural system of justice and liberty.[2]

The more accessible (and less demanding) moral qualities of business and commerce were suddenly thrust into the limelight as the virtues to govern all society. In fact, virtues were only considered virtues to the extent they favored self-interest. "Useless" virtues like humility, modesty, and chastity were replaced by honesty, fairness, moderation, thrift, or utility. It is a purely naturalist vision of society that excludes a notion of heroic virtue—sanctity—and rejects the supernatural.

Dangers of the New System

Yet even the optimistic advocates and commentators of this new civilization saw the great dangers that could befall humanity if the pursuit of perfection were abandoned. Montesquieu, Tocqueville, and Adam Smith all realized the perils that this change of values could entail.

Hence, Tocqueville foresaw situations that could degenerate into servitude, barbarism, and wretchedness.[3] Adam Smith himself believed that "the new order would narrow and demean the human spirit, such that the 'heroic spirit' would be 'almost entirely extinguished.'"[4]

The result is a moral-cultural order that avoids all that smacks of

---

1. Michael Novak notes how the founders of the new economic industrial order dismissed the marvelous monuments, masterpieces, palaces, and buildings of the Christian era as products of "aristocratic pride" that produced no real wealth, corrupted practical wisdom, and impoverished society. See Michael Novak, *The Spirit of Democratic Capitalism* (New York: Touchstone, 1983), 117.
2. Ibid., 117-18.
3. See Alexis de Tocqueville, *Democracy in America*, trans. Henry Reeve (Cambridge: Sever and Francis, 1863), 2:412.
4. Novak, *Spirit of Democratic Capitalism*, 120. Smith further believed "the division of labor would force some into tasks that would mutilate their minds, encourage gross ignorance and stupidity, and corrupt 'the nobler parts of human character'" (ibid).

ideals, and instead prides itself on its ordinary "middling" virtue, mundane pleasures, and practical wisdom.

Such a materialistic society imposes wrong standards. It creates unhappiness by replacing a metaphysical vision of order that corresponds to our nature with another that frustrates it. Indeed, we were created to pursue a spiritual heaven, and, failing this, we try to construct an earthly paradise.

As a result, materialism fails to satisfy, even though we maximize our every material comfort and minimize every physical suffering. It is a bland secular society officially stripped of its spiritual elements, from which we can expect "no high nobility of purpose, no selfless devotion to transcendental ends, no awe-inspiring heroism."[5]

Moreover, we impose our unlimited expectations for the spiritual order on our earthly consumer paradise. When material goods fail to live up to these spiritual expectations, this leads to increasingly unreasonable and insatiable demands upon society for yet more goods or entitlements. Hence we naturally experience frustrated expectations and make grueling efforts to find happiness in consumption by which, Richard Stivers notes, we all become "free and equal in our pursuit of banal pleasure."[6]

Practical Consequences: "Institutionalization of Envy"

This frustration manifests itself in many ways. One practical consequence is the frustration of status buying. This happens when, for example, certain specialized product lines and brands, whether shoes, foods, or cars, are marketed and perceived as the finest and most avant-garde in their field. When the powerful engines of mass media are employed to support this universal perception, consumers are induced to think that they will obtain an imagined status and happiness when they buy such products.

When consumption is based solely on this assumed status, it pressures a person to buy an item not because it corresponds to a need or want, but rather to a desire for something that belongs to another. Such covetousness is a moral deformation since each is convinced to acquire that which is not proper to the person. Each desires to appear

---

5. Irving Kristol, *Two Cheers for Capitalism* (New York: Basic Books, 1978), 178.
6. Stivers, *Illusion of Freedom*, 94.

inauthentically like others, rather than as one truly is. The heightened expectations promised by such demand might well be called what Daniel Bell terms "the institutionalization of envy."[7]

Advertising: Marketing Dissatisfaction

In a similar way, we cannot fail to mention modern advertising as a major mechanism of our materialistic culture. By its imagery and message, advertising employs advanced techniques that heighten expectation and promise happiness through consumption. It tends to rely more on impulse than intellect. New products are presented under an artificial light whereby the consumer feels great pressure to follow the fashion and even go into debt to avoid the stigma of being left behind.

Ironically, advertising does not maximize satisfaction but only dissatisfaction. The function of advertising, notes sociologist Robert Lane, "is to increase people's dissatisfaction with any current state of affairs, to create wants, and to exploit the dissatisfactions of the present. Advertising must use dissatisfaction to achieve its purpose."[8]

In fact, modern advertising is a veritable machine of psychological pressure to make us leave the real world and seek happiness in a wonder world of consumption. "This promised land is likewise a world of total consumption, where people possess perfect health, beauty, and eternal youth," writes Richard Stivers of this almost religious observance. "They are free to do whatever is pleasurable and thus experience complete happiness. The myth of technological utopianism is promulgated through the liturgy of advertising." [9]

In fact, advertising creates a world of unreality, a "mythological world" that exists outside time and space and where it appears that "our unlimited desires are perfectly fulfilled."[10] In the words of Daniel Bell, "It is a world of make-believe in which one lives for expectations, for what will come rather than what is. And it must come without effort."[11]

But such expectations are often disappointed. Consumer culture exults in the fact that it offers a proliferation of choices. While it is true that we have the freedom to choose thousands of items, the fact that

7. Bell, *Cultural Contradictions of Capitalism*, 22.
8. Robert E. Lane, *The Loss of Happiness in Market Democracies* (New Haven: Yale University Press, 2000), 179.
9. Stivers, *Shades of Loneliness*, 108.
10. Stivers, *Culture of Cynicism*, 67.
11. Bell, *Cultural Contradictions of Capitalism*, 70.

we may choose between fifty different brands of corn flakes or soda does not confer happiness or meaning to life. Advertising becomes necessary to create the illusion that, through variety, we might reach complete happiness. To do this, it has recourse to spectacle to make competing products more distinguishable and thus avert the boredom of the consumer.

Avoiding Suffering

We find a similar effort to banish suffering from life. There seems to be an unwritten rule that suffering must be avoided at all cost. Implicit is the idea that any suffering is an anomaly, mistake, or injustice. According to this materialist view, we must make every effort to organize our lives to eliminate all appearances of suffering and tragedy.

One application of this unwritten rule is to label the demand for any exertion or effort as a cause of suffering. According to this view, parents who discipline their children cause them to suffer. Likewise, teachers who correct their students cause suffering. Instead of effort, we are encouraged to postpone suffering by throwing ourselves into the pleasures of the here and now. Such an attitude leads youth to embrace immaturity for as long as possible with a refusal to grow up. Tragically, this outlook does not rid life of its suffering but often only increases it by exposing us to the consequences of our postponements.

A second application is an optimistic outlook on life strongly promoted by our Hollywood culture and consumer society. It is what Richard Stivers calls, "the media assumption of universal happiness"[12] where all must put on the appearance of great happiness, even when torn by loneliness and great personal tragedy. Such an appearance becomes necessary because our culture promises everyone great success yet cannot possibly meet such expectations. To avoid thinking of ourselves as failures, we are expected to mask any suffering by covering it up with smiles and laughter since "for us to admit we are not happy is tantamount to saying there is something wrong with us."[13]

The Denial of Tragedy

A terrible consequence of materialism is that it introduces into the

---

12. Stivers, *Shades of Loneliness*, 1.
13. Stivers, *Culture of Cynicism*, 171.

culture the denial of a great spiritual reality: the existence of tragedy.

Since the materialist man cannot account for the spiritual reality of tragedy, he resolves the problem by claiming an almost voluntary ignorance of our limited and fallen nature. He adopts the erroneous Enlightenment idea of an unlimited and perfectible world that is devoid of Original Sin, a world where we will all one day be united in a universal brotherhood of man.

Thus, the materialist man tries to exclude anything that might threaten what he sees as an earthly paradise. He holds, for example, the belief that deep down no one is really bad and everyone is basically good. This vision exudes a natural optimism with a happy end to every story, and a theme of wishful thinking that is repeated in classic Hollywood movies, advertising, and literature.

Of course, we cannot always live up to these optimistic expectations. Not every story has a happy ending. Because of Original Sin, everyone is capable of malice, wrongdoing, and vice. All must face the tragedy of death. In fact, tragedy is the normal matter that makes up the grand pageant of history where the destiny of souls is decided.

But instead of facing up to the reality of tragedy and evil, the materialist man remains steadfast in his belief in the natural goodness of man, attributing the existence of evil to simple ignorance, misunderstanding, or psychological maladjustment. Instead of confronting disaster when it strikes, he seeks to disguise it, dismiss its real causes, and start over again hoping it will turn out better next time around.

LEAVING PROBLEMS BEHIND

"The philosopher George Santayana once observed that Americans don't solve problems, they leave them behind. If there's an idea they don't like, they don't bother refuting it, they simply talk about something else, and the original idea dies from inattention. If a situation bothers them, they leave it in the past" (David Brooks, *On Paradise Drive: How We Live Now (And Always Have) in the Future Tense* [New York: Simon and Schuster, 2004], 47).

Hollywood—Vicarious Fantasy

Hollywood has long had a special role in encouraging the avoidance of suffering and the denial of tragedy. The film industry actually takes this vision to an extreme.

Hollywood stars radiate health, youth, and vitality. The standard Hollywood film has settings that are idealizations of our material paradise that do not exist in real life. Film plots include incredible escapades and happy endings that an adoring public is invited to imagine themselves reenacting.

It is a world so unreal that the scandal-ridden film stars themselves cannot even imitate the happy lives of the characters they play. Yet, Hollywood proposes a kind of vicarious fantasy in which one imagines leading a life not one's own. Such a tragic situation is like living with the discomfort of an organ from another person that the body has only partially accepted while pretending that all is well.

We thus conclude that our materialistic society provides only a superficial happiness that hides the frustrations of a sad and melancholic people.

There are many who propose as solutions the rejection of material goods or the adoption of idyllic and simpler lifestyles. But such "solutions" only compound the problem by adding a material impoverishment to a spiritual one.

They fail to address the premise at the foundations of materialism: its denial of metaphysical, spiritual, and supernatural reality. To resolve this problem, we must address our great metaphysical yearnings for transcendental meaning. We must unmask the frustrating promises of a material happiness that can never satisfy the spiritual side of our nature. Finally, we must embrace the reality of tragedy and suffering that is becoming ever harder to deny.

Alas, even material abundance is now failing us as a real economic crisis is upon us. Our materialism, no longer able to live up to its own promises, is worn out. What we feel is the kind of exhaustion that comes from a never-ending party.

The Beinecke Rare Book and Manuscript Library at Yale University. In a
secular society, references to any reality beyond that of a naturalistic and
materialistic world are purged out to the point that a library no longer
need be a stately building but a mere warehouse of knowledge.

CHAPTER 14

The Absence of the Sublime

Secular society is the logical consequence of a predominantly materialistic society. By "secular society," we do not wish to affirm that God is denied. Quite to the contrary, *personal* belief in God is allowed and even encouraged as long as it is confined to the personal unofficial realm. A secular society in general is one which is officially purged of all references to a reality beyond that of our naturalistic and materialistic world. There is an indifference to or confusion about what constitutes the meaning of life.

Secularism, asserts Plinio Corrêa de Oliveira, is a curious form of atheism affirming that "it is impossible to be certain of the existence of God and, consequently, that man should act in the temporal realm as if God did not exist; in other words, he should act like a person who has dethroned God."[1]

"Secularization is the liberation of man from religious and metaphysical tutelage, the turning of his attention away from other worlds and toward this one,"[2] exults Harvey Cox, one of many modern "theologians" who celebrate this dethronement as a liberating experience.

Weariness for Spiritual Things

This "liberating" secular society inevitably leaves a profound void inside the soul of modern man creating a frustration and desolation that many have termed a spiritual wasteland.

Such an attitude calls to mind the condition that Saint Thomas Aquinas calls *acedia*, which he defines as the weariness for holy and spiritual things and a subsequent sadness of living.[3] As a spiritual being, the man afflicted with *acedia* denies his spiritual appetites. "He

---

1. Corrêa de Oliveira, *Revolution and Counter-Revolution*, 47-48.
2. Harvey Cox, *The Secular City: Secularization and Urbanization in Theological Perspective* (New York: Macmillan, 1966), 15. Cox goes so far as to recommend a secular religion without the mention of God.
3. See Aquinas, *Summa Theologica*, II-II, q. 35, a. 1.

does not want to be what God wants him to be," notes Josef Pieper, "and that means that he does not want to be what he really, and in the ultimate sense, *is*."[4] This refusal cannot help but bring sadness and even despair.

The modern version of *acedia* includes both a weariness *and* a wariness for all things spiritual. There is the conscious turning away from holy and spiritual things as well as a cultural regime where sublime goals or religious ideals are looked upon with suspicion and simply not considered to be an important part of our lives. The intensive feverish activity of modern life often is an attempt to hide *acedia's* effects of listlessness, low spirits, and lack of joy.

The Flight of Happiness

Indeed, a great sadness has descended upon the land.

"Amidst the satisfaction people feel with their material progress," writes sociologist Robert E. Lane, "there is a spirit of unhappiness and depression haunting advanced market democracies throughout the world, a spirit that mocks the idea that markets maximize well-being and the eighteenth-century promise of a right to the pursuit of happiness under benign governments of people's own choosing."[5]

Despite huge opportunities for entertainment, pleasure, and excitement, happiness eludes us. This is all the more incomprehensible since the unhappiness persists even among those surrounded by riches, consumer goods, technological progress, or good health.

Moreover, Lane notes, "The richer the society and its individuals become, the less purchasable are the goals that bring them happiness."[6] This unhappiness, in turn, breeds frustration and can be a major cause of the pervasive sadness and depression that afflict us.

There is a generalized dissatisfaction with life that is different from times past. Before the sixties, surveys found the exuberance and optimism of youths made them generally happier than old people. By the end of the century, such findings were reversed. Younger people are now generally unhappier than the older generations, a fact that can be verified by its impact "in terms of headaches, indigestion, sleepless-

---

4. Pieper, *Leisure*, 28.
5. Lane, *Loss of Happiness*, 3.
6. Ibid., 63.

A GREAT SADNESS OVER THE NATION

The number of professionals treating those afflicted with mental unhappiness and depression reflects a growing sadness over the nation.

"As Ronald Dworkin pointed out in a 2010 paper for the Hoover Institution, in the late '40s, the United States was home to 2,500 clinical psychologists, 30,000 social workers, and fewer than 500 marriage and family therapists. As of 2010, the country had 77,000 clinical psychologists, 192,000 clinical social workers, 400,000 nonclinical social workers, 50,000 marriage and family therapists, 105,000 mental-health counselors, 220,000 substance-abuse counselors, 17,000 nurse psychotherapists, and 30,000 life coaches" (Stephen Marche, "Is Facebook Making Us Lonely?" *The Atlantic,* May 2012).

A study by Prof. Myrna Weismann and associates finds that "about a quarter of the population experiences some of the clinical symptoms of depression during some portion of their lifetime; another study reports that almost half of the population (48 percent) has suffered from depression severe enough to inhibit functioning for two weeks or more, and nearly 20 percent qualify for a lifetime diagnosis of major depression or dysthymia" (Lane, *Loss of Happiness,* 22).

---

ness, as well as general [dis]satisfaction with life and even likelihood of taking your own life."[7]

It is evident that the happiness people seek goes beyond mere gratification, material goods, and consumption. Studies show that people express their desires in spiritual terms of peace of mind, equilibrium, or tranquility.[8] This suggests that our modern brand of *acedia* has much to do with the discontent that so mocks and haunts our modern civilization.

Rejecting the Sublime

This aspect of our crisis has been ascribed to many causes. We would attribute it to the absence of the sublime.

The sublime consists of those things of transcendent excellence that

---

7. Putnam, *Bowling Alone,* 263.
8. "Self-satisfaction and equilibrium," "being satisfied," "feeling content with myself," "feeling fulfilled and worthwhile" are some of the other expressions cited by Robert Lane in his overview of studies in the field. Lane, *Loss of Happiness,* 15.

cause men to be overawed by their magnificence. It invites men and nations to turn beyond self-interest and gratification and look towards higher principles, the common good, or ultimately towards God, thus giving meaning and purpose to their lives. Whether manifested in works of art, fabulous cultural achievements, great feats of men, or religious piety, the sublime has the capacity of inciting in us sentiments of loyalty, dedication, and devotion that can fill the emptiness of our modern wasteland.

Alas, our secular society strongly rejects the sublime option. It generally presents only the physical or economic good whereby individuals and nations lose the notion of the sublime. The sublime becomes an abstract or poetic matter while the concrete thing is portrayed as the only reality.

DEFINING THE SUBLIME

Something can be called sublime if it is of such excellence that it provokes a great emotion that causes men to be overawed by its magnificence or grandeur. The sublime might be found in extraordinary panoramas, works of art, ideas, virtuous acts, or the heroic feats of men.

Two Options Open

This great conflict between the poles of the practical and the sublime often sets in motion a great internal crisis in the souls of men—and analogously in civilizations. That is to say, we are frequently called to make a choice between self-interest and sublime principles, as might be seen in a person's dilemma between simply enjoying life and pursuing a soldier's selfless devotion to country or a priestly vocation.

Sometimes the same situation can lead to a solicitation from both poles, as in the case of a politician that feels both the noble desire to serve the common good and the temptation to enrich himself at the public's expense. An image of this bipolar solicitation might be seen in the case of wine. There are those who are able to derive great spiritual satisfaction from wine, and yet others who can only become physically intoxicated from the same wine.

Tocqueville warns us of the danger of the absence of the sublime when he comments on "a taste for physical gratification: this taste, if it become excessive, soon disposes men to believe that all is matter only; and materialism, in turn, hurries them back with mad impatience to these same delights."[9]

Reign of Normality

The post-World War II period of economic expansion introduced one such period of gratification. It was not only a period of unparalleled prosperity but also one of excessive materialism—which persists to our day.

Ours is officially a secular world simplified and purged of any transcendence beyond the ordinary experience of daily life. This world is dominated by money, science, and technology with its overwhelming emphasis on all that is pragmatic, organized, and "reasonable."

This rejection of the sublime is especially notable in our present culture, which favors the superficial and pleasurable. Hollywood and the media invite us to celebrate that which is comic, sentimental, and sensual. Ours is a culture that glorifies comfort and health and exudes carefree optimism, giving us the mistaken impression that we have somehow obtained the aforementioned perfect *material happiness* in this vale of tears.

Thus, such a shallow regime of excessive materialism has long been considered "normal," while the option of the sublime and spiritual has been consigned to the risky bygone adventures of saints, heroes, and poets that are to be avoided by all sensible people.

Revenge of the Sublime

Many were surprised when the post-war normality of the fifties did not generate yet more normality. They were shocked to see that it brought frustration and rebellion instead.

The explosion of the sixties was an expression of the absence of the sublime. "They [baby boomers] then discover[ed] that a life that is without a sense of purpose creates an acute experience of anxiety," writes Irving Kristol, "which in turn transforms the universe into a hostile, repressive place."[10]

And yet our pursuit of the sublime cannot be suppressed. Man cannot remain long without the goods of the spirit. Our natural tendency for the

---

9. Tocqueville, *Democracy in America*, 2:175.
10. Kristol, *Two Cheers for Capitalism*, 179.

sublime must find some way to express itself even if in a distorted way.

Our materialist culture asphyxiated the spiritual desires of the younger generations. As the "normal" baby boomers grew up, they found increasingly "abnormal" outlets for their spiritual hunger in the drugs, religious sects, and bizarre lifestyles that so destroyed their lives.

Ever since the sixties, we have been living amid the ruins of this normality that still maintains its materialist facade. Yet behind the facade, the frustration has only deepened. In our postmodernity, we see "normality" fragmented into a thousand subcultures, deviations, and alternative lifestyles. But we also see a hunger for marvelous, sublime, and heroic things by those who never knew the splendors of Christian civilization.

Thus, an uneasiness hangs over our normality. Disillusioned by materialism's promises, discontented segments of society now appear, searching the mists of our past tradition and asking about the sublime that was so brutally rejected.

CHAPTER 15

The Rule of Money

We have focused upon the driving forces of frenetic intemperance and its effects upon our way of life. If we were to synthesize all these considerations in a few words, we would say *a rule of money* has been established and is now in crisis.

By rule of money, we mean, of course, the *misuse* of money. The rule of money turns money from a common means of exchange into the principal measure of all relationships and values. Everything is reduced to terms of a commercial trade. It is a state of things where the human element, so essential to the proper functioning of society and economy, is diminished. Modern economic activity becomes cold and impersonal, mechanical and inflexible. In this context, money becomes the most important consideration; it rules.

In truth, money is a jealous master that tolerates little opposition and, when misused, easily rules over any competing values with ruthless efficiency. "Money is not content with being just another final purpose of life alongside wisdom and art, personal significance and strength, beauty and love," writes German sociologist Georg Simmel. "But in so far as money does adopt this position it gains the power to reduce the other purposes to the level of means."[1]

A Set of Values

Tragically, under this rule of money, men adopt a corresponding set of values that takes root in society. We see an entirely different way of looking at life where social, cultural, and moral values are put aside. In their place is a set of values that attaches more importance to quantity over quality, utility over beauty, matter over spirit.

With this set of values, the rule of money undermines society, as Lewis Mumford notes: "Money, as the nexus in all human relations and

---

1. Georg Simmel, *The Philosophy of Money*, trans. Tom Bottomore and David Frisby, 2nd ed. (London: Routledge, 1990), 241.

as the main motivation in all social effort, replaced the reciprocal obligations and duties of families, neighbors, citizens, friends."[2]

Separate from Social Life

We can cite as an example of this separation from social life the modern outlook towards labor. In pre-industrial times, productive activities
were embedded in the social, cultural, and religious organization of
society. Employers assumed family-like links with those whom they
employed, as might be seen in the family-like ties in the guild system.
There often existed cases where reciprocal social obligations and affection between employer and employee would span generations.

The tendency of modern economy is to turn labor into a mere commercial and abstract relationship where labor represents a unit of effort to be put on the market. As economic historian Karl Polanyi
observes, "To separate labor from other activities of life and to subject
it to the laws of the market was to annihilate all organic forms of existence and to replace them by a different type of organization, an atom-
istic and individualistic one."[3]

Likewise, property loses its social significance in the rule of money.
It too becomes a commodity bought and sold indifferently on the market without regard for any connection it might have had with family,
history, or society. Inside the rule of money's set of values, such human
sentiments have little commercial value.

When these values take hold in a society, everything can be commercialized. This can be seen, for example, in the sad commercializa-
tion of Christmas in which the great mystery of the Incarnation is
overshadowed by festive yet soulless holiday spending.

Markets and the Rule of Money

The rule of money also has its economic consequences. We cannot ac-
cuse it of directly disrespecting the right of private property and free
enterprise. Quite to the contrary, under the rule of money, men actively
and frantically engage in commerce that often leads to high levels of
prosperity.

---

2. Lewis Mumford, *Technics and Human Development*, vol. 1 of *The Myth of the Machine* (New York: Harcourt Brace Jovanovich, 1967), 281.
3. Karl Polanyi, *The Great Transformation: The Political and Economic Origins of Our Times*, 2nd ed. (Boston: Beacon Press, 2001), 171.

Photo/Felipe Barandiarán

The Accountant's Bank Note Office, **Bank of England (1870). The rule of money reorganized society by making money the principal measure of relationships, prestige, and values.**

However, this rule can also change mentalities and indirectly undermine markets. When the rule of money dominates, we see the disappearance of the transparent marketplace where goods change hands between known buyers and sellers who transact business using the same moral norms on a more or less level playing field. Such transparent markets favor stability, security, and equity inside the context of social relationships. They are truly free since they are regulated by justice.

In their stead, there are increasingly abstract markets where goods and services change hands many times between unknown buyers and sellers in the absence of moral norms where the playing field is far from level (as might be seen with China). We also see the increasing participation of the State in determining large segments of trade. While these factors may facilitate trade volume and free up capital, they also create, by their opaqueness, conditions that favor speculation, exaggerated risk, and frenetic intemperance. They can eventually lead to unfair conditions that undermine free markets.

Fraught with Risk

That is why the rule of money is fraught with vulnerability and risk. When money becomes the primary concern, it creates a dynamism of its own by empowering banks and other financial institutions to expand the money supply.[4] This rule encourages many financial institutions to develop complex new financial products, credit innovations, and speculative instruments that enable them to profit from a tense climate of boom or bust. A central bank, as lender of last resort, can reinforce such risk-taking since it is often left to pick up the pieces by bailing out overextended institutions popularly deemed "too big (or important) to fail."

The creation of easy money leads to a situation where the money supply no longer corresponds to that which is needed for the normal exchange of goods and services that should characterize a sound economy. Instead, it leads to enormous amounts of money being used for speculation, leveraging risks, and investment bubbles that make frenetic intemperance possible, if not inevitable.

Such a system invites crises. As Mervyn King, governor of the Bank of England, noted in 2010: "Banking crises are endemic to the market economy that has evolved since the Industrial Revolution. The words 'banking' and 'crises' are natural bedfellows."[5]

"Although many now-advanced economies have graduated from a history of serial default on sovereign debt or very high inflation," write Carmen Reinhart and Kenneth Rogoff, "so far graduation from banking crises has proven elusive. In effect, for the advanced economies during 1800-2008, the picture that emerges is one of serial banking crises."[6]

A Credit Culture

When the rule of money holds sway, it is no surprise that we find a culture strongly conditioned by finance and credit.

In the face of the rapid expansion of industrial processes and consumption, society gives utmost importance and prestige to the financial establishment that must raise and lend massive funds. It creates a business culture where what really matters are credit instruments that exploit all possible opportunities for profit. Every dollar is leveraged many times beyond its value, every debt exploited and marketed, and every speculation promoted and wagered. Edward Chancellor ob-

---

4. One way this is done is through fractional reserve banking, where banks give loans with only a fraction of cash reserves to back them up.
5. Mervyn King, "Banking—from Bagehot to Basel, and back again," *BIS Review* 140 (2010): 1.
6. Carmen M. Reinhart and Kenneth S. Rogoff, *This Time Is Different: Eight Centuries of Financial Folly* (Princeton: Princeton University Press, 2009), 141.

serves that "Credit was the Siamese twin of speculation; they were born at the same time and exhibited the same nature; inextricably linked, they could never be totally separated."[7]

This rule, where banks easily become mini-mints, makes the supply of fast and easy credit a fixture in modern society. Every effort is made to make this credit instantly available and used. Advertising often induces the urge to buy right away the latest automobile or electronic device. Credit cards and financing are easily provided. As a result, consumers frequently buy beyond their means.

In short, the problem lies not in the actual credit itself but in the climate that brings much pressure to bear upon business and society to think in terms of instantly available money and credit. Nouriel Roubini and Stephen Mihm note that most financial crises are associated with "an excessive accumulation of debt, as investors borrow money to buy into the boom," and "an excessive growth in the supply of credit." They are further made possible by "the creation of newfangled instruments and institutions for investing in whatever is the focus of a speculative fever."[8]

Although this world of finance seems to have led to unprecedented material prosperity, no one can deny that it has also created a debt-ridden society, credit-driven economy, and deficit-laden big government inside of which people live regularly beyond their means. No one can deny that, by force of its own internal dynamism, the rule of money is now in crisis.

This crisis is a matter of great concern to us since the vacuum left by the breakdown of this rule could have catastrophic consequences. The rule of money at least served to unify our cooperative union. Without these factors of material self-interest, our mass culture could well fragment the nation. Now appearing on the horizon are dangerous and false alternatives that should be avoided at all costs.

---

7. Chancellor, *Devil Take the Hindmost*, 32.
8. Nouriel Roubini and Stephen Mihm, *Crisis Economics: A Crash Course in the Future of Finance* (New York: Penguin Books, 2010), 17.

At a Crossroads

The present crisis
brings us to
a crossroads
between the path to
order and another to
disorder.

Anarchical protesters from the Occupy Wall Street movement in New York City. Radical false alternatives must be rejected as they will fragment the nation.

CHAPTER 16

Rejecting False Alternatives at the Crossroads

With the rule of money in crisis, there are those who propose false alternatives that will greatly imperil our nation since they include bankrupt socialist systems, ecological models, or populist demagoguery.

As long as a consensus formed around our cooperative union, there was little danger that these alternatives could have any chance of success. On the contrary, they usually formed fringe positions far from the mainstream.

A Temperamental Distrust

This situation could change if there is a general frustration with the present system. It might give rise to a temperamental distrust of modern institutions, governing structures, or economic systems. This, in turn, could contribute to the further fragmentation of society since this distrust easily erodes social unity.

We might cite as an example today's marked hostility towards the modern State and elites. In times of crisis, this hostility can lead to a distrust of all authority and the idea that there is no solution, save each becoming his own authority. It could also lead to confused notions of freedom that bring individuals to disregard the remnants of the moral or natural law existing today and declare every man to be a law unto himself.

Thus, as we stand at a crossroads, some of those positions once considered so extreme are presented as real options. If only for want of a better solution, these proposals may be mistakenly embraced in desperation.

A Real Danger

We believe these are false and dangerous alternatives since they are not based on natural law and objective reality. Rather, they represent subjective positions that cling to no principles and have few links with our history. At a time when the situation calls for firm principles, decisive action, and unity, we could find ourselves scattered in a confusing jumble. A psychological climate could reign where there is a doubting of all certainties, a supremacy of the emotions, and a rule of relativism. What characterizes these false solutions is a general loss of faith in political solutions and a corresponding tendency not to believe in anything at all. We run the risk of a reaction driven, not by convictions, but only by frustration, whim, and rage.

Volatile new masses, called forth from viral computer networks, can easily erupt against an established order and take on a disproportional importance. This was seen, for example, in the theatrics of the anarchical Occupy Wall Street movement that brought together a menagerie of discontents in the autumn of 2011. If a more serious spirit of discontent takes hold, it could result in another outbreak of protest and instability that could jeopardize our ability to deal with the present crisis.

Radical Alternatives

Today's fragmented discontents coalesce around certain false alternatives and subcultures. While it is not possible to describe all these alternatives, we can categorize some of them as follows:

- Ecological alternatives that advocate a return to more primitive lifestyles coupled with an almost mystical attachment to the earth. The more benign elements introduce magical, tribal, and indigenous paradigms into our culture while its radicals decry man's existence and civilization as destructive and seek massive reductions in population and draconian limits on our impact on the environment.

- A revolt against consumer society resulting in subconsumerist models that often include distorted views of Christian poverty. Such simplified lifestyles devoid of adornment strive to leave little or no impact on the environment.

- The throwing off of all remaining moral structures of society, advocating the most radical expressions of sexual freedom and aberrational lifestyles. These find their expression in myriad subcultures as might be seen in cyberpunk and Goth groupings or socio-political movements.

- Various reincarnations of socialism, including those elements who, in face of the failure of socialistic models, call for even more extensive regulations and global structures as a solution, or those who engage in the ever-elusive search for a "third way" between capitalism and socialism.

- A professed hostility towards the State and an unfocused populism driven by frustration that introduces elements of libertarian anarchy. Its more extreme elements tend to renounce the need for any government and promote a radical individualism and isolationism.

Constructing a Brave New World

These and other currents are already manifesting themselves. While they may appear as isolated fragments, we can discern common threads that unite them. We can envision the brave new world they could engender.

What unites those who propose these false alternatives is their discontent with the present system. They display a generalized skepticism about America's past and present. There is a rejection of the heritage and morality that has been entrusted to us and came to us from Christian civilization.

These discontents are not without influence. While they are disconnected from our present culture, they remain connected to our computer networks to spread their message. They can count on powerful governmental, academic, and other allies that already call for "global structures" to implement ecological and financial reforms. Despite their scanty numbers, most discontents can always rely upon a liberal media ever ready to magnify their actual projection.

Inside these alternatives we still find the restless spirit of frenetic intemperance seeking to break down barriers and throw off moral restraint. Far from resolving the present crisis, these new alternatives would fan the explosive expansion of human passions to greater intensity.

The results of this new disordered world could be similar to the modern individualists who look to the masses to form their opinions. In this case, today's postmodern discontents would practice extreme individualism by looking beyond the mass structures of the past and throw themselves into new global masses coordinated and controlled by the great computer networks, other global structures, or by mystical means yet unknown.[1]

One thing is clear. The proposed alternatives would not resolve our present crisis but only make it worse. Our response to the present crisis must be different from all these false alternative currents. We need to search for solutions that unify rather than disperse. We need a future that builds upon our rich Christian past. Our love of country calls upon us to be true to our nation and explore with urgency solutions that will preserve our identity, unity, and history.

---

1. Such a possibility is by no means unforeseen. Marxist theorists have long spoken of a time when the State would wither away and be replaced by a structureless, utopic, egalitarian society.

CHAPTER 17

Returning to an Economy without Frenetic Intemperance

W e believe the solution to the present economic crisis is to return purely and simply to an economy without frenetic intemperance.

That is why we have gone to such lengths to point out all the problems that stem from frenetic intemperance. Our aim is to show, almost to excess, how this great imbalance is now destroying our economy, the great powerhouse of our prosperity. We seek to leave no doubt that this flight from temperance is now throwing our way of life out of balance and breaking down our society. Frenetic intemperance has now spread like a cancer, causing distress and forcing us to take a position against it.

There are four things we must do to begin our return to order.

We Must Have No Illusions

The first thing we must do is to be convinced that frenetic intemperance is leading us to our ruin. We can have no illusions. There are those who think that it is enough to regenerate the present system, and America will prosper. Return to the strong economic foundations of our past, they argue, and we will see new benefits and freedoms bestowed upon the citizenry of the land. If we could but practice once again the common and practical virtues, we would again follow our self-interest and rebuild our lost consensus and forge once again our cooperative union.

But such measures are not enough. Our cooperative union is in crisis today because it has long carried within itself the unbalanced undercurrent of frenetic intemperance that now dominates. As long as frenetic intemperance is free to act, we cannot rely upon any kind of regeneration to restore this model to health. Any attempt to jump start the system will be merely postponing a remedy with stopgap measures, false stimuli, or quick fixes to give the outward appearances of a healthy body where inside a cancer festers. The solution lies in ridding ourselves of this frenetic intemperance; otherwise nothing will be accomplished.

We Must Resist the Temptation to Isolation

The second thing that we must do is resist the temptation of simply writing off the present system with all its problems. We must avoid the defeatist attitude of those who advocate isolating themselves from society and awaiting better days. In individualist fashion, they would take care of their own little worlds and disregard the cause of the common good.

Nothing could be more contrary to our way of thinking. We cannot abandon our nation in her time of need. It is in times like these that all Americans must show their true mettle and resist the selfish option of isolation. A policy of fragmentation always ends in defeat. Our goal should be that of uniting as many as possible and not shattering the nation into a thousand pieces.

We Must Defend What Is Good in America

While we must kill the cancer, we must also defend the body. For this reason, the third thing we must do is vigorously defend the many excellent values that still exist in America. In the order of economics, we must defend sound principles such as private property and free enterprise, which form the foundation of our prosperity and are according to natural law. They are *not the causes* of our great crisis. That is why we must vigorously oppose those who, like the socialists, unjustly attack these sound and legitimate economic principles as causes of our crisis.

Moreover, these sound economic principles—even when tainted by frenetic intemperance—buttress what remains of natural order in society. Despite many shortcomings, our industrial civilization is still built upon rational foundations that require discipline, logic, hierarchy, and the rule of law—much of which was inherited from Christian civilization.

We must defend this rational order since our enemies attack us because they see this order as hateful and restrictive to their agendas. The world's terrorist organizations see this order as an oppressive instrument of Western hegemony. As the world's only superpower, we do not hesitate to affirm that America still represents a bulwark of order that must be defended, even militarily, in a chaotic world. In this sense, the 9/11 attacks were assaults not just on the nation, but on the unified, rational, and universal order that undergirds Western prosperity. A misdirected isolationism is simply not an option.

In addition to these sound economic remnants of a Christian order, we are also attacked for yet another reason—our adherence to the moral remnants of this order. As was mentioned, our American consensus had the good effect of imprinting on vast sectors of the public a great respect for a consensual moral code loosely based on the Ten Commandments. The result is what we might call a "Ten Commandments America," which still preserves a healthy attachment to moral values. Such an attachment is hardly a conversion since, like our economic principles, it is often flawed in its application. Nevertheless, this imperfect adherence to family, traditional marriage, property, religion, morality, and country is enough to pose an obstacle to the Left's revolutionary agenda, which seeks to bring down these remnants.

That is why America's Cultural War over moral values takes center stage. The attachment of so many Americans to "backward" conservative and moral values serves as a rallying point to all who defend Christian morality worldwide. It also makes America the target of those who virulently oppose any kind of Christian order. Today, the United States is perceived by many to be a conservative power that must be destroyed since it is an obstacle to the kind of amoral egalitarian society longed for by the Left.

America is hated by her anti-Christian enemies not for her defects (and there are many) but for what she represents of good. And that is what we must now defend.

We Must Look Beyond the Status Quo

Finally, we must look beyond those good elements of the status quo that we must vigorously defend. While these poor remnants of Christian civilization are the object of the attack upon us, they cannot be the sole basis of our defense. Partially or badly applied principles are the stuff of which rearguard actions and retreats are made; they do not deliver victories.

What we must do is broaden our outlook and articulate a grand vision of an economic order without frenetic intemperance. This would require returning to our distant roots and changing our frenzied premises. Key elements of this vision are to be found in the timeless principles and institutions that served as the foundation for the organic socio-economic order that existed in medieval Christendom.

If we have the courage to look without prejudice beyond the status quo, this will allow us to explore a universe of refreshing and original applications of those principles that could address our problems. By expanding our horizons in this way, we open the floodgates of Christian wisdom to slake the thirst of our parched and narrow-minded secular age.

The present crisis clearly shows how frenetic intemperance is bringing the nation to ruin. There are many concerned Americans who want to vigorously defend America and her good values. What is missing is a vision of a socio-economic order without frenetic intemperance that we will now present.

If this vision is applied to our times with wisdom and courage, we believe the resulting economic order would restore balance and calm while remaining open to progress and technology. It would produce in great abundance yet also with great quality. Such a vision would provide the basis of a true regeneration of both society and economy in accordance with the nature of man and the law of God. If all this is done, we will have the elements for victory. We will witness a grand return to order.

PART II

THE ROAD AHEAD: A RETURN TO ORDER

Like a lighthouse, order is that set of illuminating principles by which we orient ourselves.

Iwo Jima Memorial at Arlington National Cemetery. There are many who do not see America as a cooperative union but rather as a nation formed around God, family, and country, for which they are willing to sacrifice, especially in times of crisis.

CHAPTER 18

A Salvific Debate:
Becoming a Nation, Becoming a People

Our search for solutions is made all the more urgent by the increasing polarization of our country in the face of our failing cooperative union. As a result, we sense a paralysis in the governing of our nation. There is a lack of direction and purpose.

A new consensus must be formed. The stage is set for a great internal debate, which we might even call a salvific debate, since the fundamental issues to be discussed will determine our future. It is no longer a question of whether we must change course, but how and when this change will take place.

A Great Divide: Two Americas

This debate has been long in the making since not all are enamored by our cooperative union. It would be a mistake to generalize and conclude that everyone has adopted the individualistic mentality driven by frenetic intemperance that we have criticized. We will admit that there are undoubtedly many who are enthusiastic about the materialistic progress of our cooperative union. They are inebriated by its speed and sensations and revel in its frenzied excitement.

On the other hand, there has always been a significant number of Americans who have resisted the harsh mechanistic aspects of this super-industrialized civilization. They do not feel comfortable in this stressful and inorganic world. They yearn for calmer times with a more reflective pace of life. They admire, with distant longings, the remnants of a Christian civilization they never knew.

Hence, although not immediately perceptible, America has long been divided to such a point that we can question whether we form a cohesive nation. In fact, many political analysts have identified a divide in America that they characterize in many ways.[1] The growing

---

1. Everyone is familiar with the division of red state vs. blue state, retro vs. metro, conservative vs. liberal, and other formulations. We feel such classifications are too general, and that the real cause of this division is much more profound, as will be shown.

polarization makes this divide increasingly hard to hide.

We believe that this divide is defined by a growing discontent with our modernity and its frenetic intemperance. It is a divide where both sides find surprising adherents belonging to all classical categories of party, class, ethnicity, and religion. In truth, we can say our country has long been involved in a struggle between two spiritual nations that live physically intermingled.

Another America: A Self-Sacrificing Nation

We already defined the first America as a model centered on an economic powerhouse, united by a consensus and generating a way of life. This model, organized as a cooperative union, has dominated our culture for most of our history. It has adherents on both liberal and conservative sides of the political spectrum.

There is a second America that is quite different, one that has never dominated our culture. On the surface, those in this America often feel the pressure to conform to the rules of the cooperative union. They may even enjoy and value the benefits of our way of life just like those in the cooperative union. Yet these Americans do not see America as a co-op but rather as a nation formed around vague Christian notions of God, family, and country for which they are willing to sacrifice. They acknowledge God's blessings and nurture a love for America that impels them to go beyond self-interest and sacrifice themselves for the common good, especially in times of crisis.

Such an America could be seen, for example, in the anti-Communist reaction that began in the fifties when numerous Americans embraced the "better dead than red" slogan of the Cold-War era and put sacrifice for their country above the economic interest of the co-op. This second America is a generous America, given to sacrifice, risk, and derring-do. Indeed, many went so far as to give their lives for our country. In so doing, these Americans took steps towards forging what we will call, not a co-op, but a unified nation.

Another example can be seen in the reactions to the Sexual Revolution of the sixties when large numbers of Americans first started putting their concern for moral matters above their own self-interests and pleasures. They confronted media and public opinion and now engage in a true Cultural War. This segment of the American public embraces a broader selection of issues. It includes those who question the cheapness, materialism, and vulgarity of our industrial civilization and sacrifice themselves to make a preferential option for quality and beauty.[2]

A Shifting Debate

While these two Americas have long been engaged in a struggle, the focus of this internal debate has now shifted with the present crisis. On one hand, the cooperative model that represents the first America is failing. On the other hand, the vague formulations of the second America do not have sufficient definition to bring about the needed transformation in society.

The focus of the debate now revolves around how these two Americas will answer the following questions: In the face of the current crisis, what will replace our cooperative union? Will our union shatter and its members gravitate to the dangerous socialist, ecological, or other alternatives which threaten to fragment the country? Or will we put country before self-interest and unify around our own tradition of self-sacrifice to forge a new consensus?

Evidently we favor and work towards this latter option.

Forging a New Consensus

We thus propose that we articulate a clear set of guiding principles around which we might rally. From these principles, we can define an organic socio-economic order *taken from our distant past and adapted to the future.* We propose calling upon that self-sacrificing spirit that has served us so well before to call forth the heroes that the hour demands.

Contrary to the co-op mentality that abandons the country in times of crisis, out of love for our country, we must adopt a path that embraces those sacrifices and sufferings that lie ahead. In this way, we can help forge the consensus that will make of us not a co-operative of stockholders but a courageous people, a nation of true heroes.

---

2. A list of the numerous concerns involved in this Cultural War includes such sensitive issues as the defense of the traditional family, the fight for the unborn, those who fight for chastity and abstinence, families who promote homeschooling or private schools, and so many other causes where Americans have confronted the terrible pressure of public opinion. We might also mention certain movements that strive towards a more healthy and organic lifestyle in accordance with these moral principles. We should also record the spiritual odyssey of many Americans that results, for example, in more than 100,000 conversions to the Catholic Church each year.

A New Element to Be Considered

There is one surprising element in this scenario that should be mentioned.

Mugged by the terrible reality of this crisis, we can observe that Americans of both currents sense the social and psychological emptiness of the present course and are searching for other options. Surprisingly, many are expressing a desire, yearning, and admiration for once-rejected traditions. From Gregorian chant to specialty beers to Gothic architecture, they manifest an astonishing openness for the marvelous fruits of Christian civilization.

That is to say, this crisis has served to remove much of the prejudice against Christian civilization so long imposed upon us by modernity. It serves to bring to light yearnings that can help us choose options that have long been suppressed from open discussion.

⁂

Our proposal is simple and straightforward. We seek a return to the principles that brought forth a Christian order. We use the term "order" not to mean an imposed set of principles upon a society. Rather, this term refers to a resulting *organic society* that corresponds to the natural development of man and society, and which will, in turn, lead to an economy without frenetic intemperance.

This Christian order has the advantage of being an alternative with a proven record. It has worked before when civilizations were in decline and chaos reigned. Ours is the same call to Christian principles that echoed amid the ruins of the Roman Empire. It is this same call that brought forth order in primitive lands and peoples.

We do not seek to revive a historical epoch or turn back the clock but rather to return to those timeless principles—valid for all peoples and all times—that spontaneously gave rise to organic solutions.

This is, of course, a return that will be much maligned by those attached to our frenetic modernity. Many principles to which we want to return are so blotted out of memory that we only recognize them in glimpses of the past actions of saints and heroes, or in the grandeur of historic monuments.

Hence, such a return resembles a homecoming to an ancestral dwelling that we know only through faded pictures that cause vague longings to well up in our hearts. It is also like a return of descendants of a prodigal son that is also an act of confidence made in expectation of a great pardon for a regrettable past. This "return home" is the basis of the organic model that we will soon describe. It is the basis for a truly salvific internal debate where we can enter into those paramount problems that lie at the root of the present crisis and which are now shaping our future.

ORDER: THE FIRST NEED OF THE SOUL

Order is that state of things where everything functions according to its nature and end. When everything is doing what it is supposed to be doing, there is order "because nature is a cause of order" and "whatever does not possess order is not according to nature" (Saint Thomas Aquinas, *In Physic.*, lib. 8, lect. 3, n. 3).

Order stems from the principles of natural law by which we orient ourselves. Everyone needs some semblance of order to function properly. It is a primary need from which we get our bearings, as with a compass.

As Russell Kirk states, "Order is the first need of the soul" (Kirk, *Roots of American Order*, 6). This same necessity of order can be affirmed about society: it is also the first need of the nation lest society decay into chaos. Freedom, justice, law, or virtue are all very important, but order is the first and most basic need. A return to order is thus a return to the principles of natural law.

The Beer Brewers. Fifteenth century stained glass, Tournai Cathedral, France. Our proposal does not seek a return to the historical medieval economy but to those basic and timeless Christian principles that can be applied to any economy.

CHAPTER 19

Preliminary Objections:
Can Medieval Economy Be a Solution?

Photo/Felipe Barandiarán

Some might object that we seem to be proposing a medieval economic order as a solution to the present economic crisis. They would protest that the differences between medieval and modern economies are so great as to render any return to a past order impossible.

Obviously, we do not seek a return to the historical medieval economy. However, it is not too much to suppose that we might return to the basic framework and timeless Christian principles that undergirded that medieval economic order. We could benefit from the order, calm, and balance that existed in those times. In fact, any observer of history must recognize the fact that such principles are already a part of the present order since so many modern economic and legal concepts and institutions have medieval roots.[1] There is no reason why basic premises of medieval economic thought cannot be adapted to our modern times as a means of suppressing the frenetic intemperance that plagues us.

The Proper Role of Economics

The first premise involves the very role of economics itself. We can begin by rejecting the modern obsession to see everything through the single prism of economics to the exclusion of all others.

We readily admit that economics is a necessary practice and science that deals with that human activity by which, through production, administration, and exchange of goods and services, we create the material means for society to exist. It has its own set of principles

---

1. So strong is this influence upon modernity that we tend to agree with the generalization of Lord Acton, who claimed: "Modern history tells how the last four hundred years have modified the medieval conditions of life and thought." Quoted in Nisbet, *Quest for Community*, 73.

(such as private property and free enterprise) and its laws (like that of supply and demand). We will not deny that it is an important human field without which other activities would be impossible or extremely arduous.

Nevertheless, we hold that *economics is not the most important human field.* Man does not live by bread alone (Lk 4:4). Man has another side that is spiritual and superior. This superior side is recognized by our own Western tradition which, even to our days, rightly affirms that every man is a unique and "spiritual creature with spiritual needs and spiritual desires."[2]

This superior side of man's nature is what makes him unique and establishes his dignity. This gives rise to political, social, cultural, and religious activities and sciences that tower above mere material economic sustenance and deal more directly with our spiritual needs and ultimately our eternal salvation.

When economics dominates, man himself is demeaned. "The great pageant of history thus became reducible to the economic endeavors of individuals and classes," writes Richard Weaver of this obsession, continuing: "Man created in the divine image, the protagonist of a great drama in which his soul was at stake, was replaced by man the wealth-seeking and -consuming animal."[3]

Economics Is Limited

A second premise of the medieval economic order takes this idea yet further by affirming that *economics alone is limited*; it must have recourse to other sciences.

The focus of economics is limited to a very specific part of human activity. It describes the process of wealth creation, acquisition, production, and consumption. But these economic processes often involve moral actions. It is outside the competence of economists to judge, order, and interpret these moral actions as such. Rather, economics must be subject to those higher normative sciences like ethics that deal with all human actions.

The medieval economic order seamlessly makes this link. Normative

---

2. Barry Goldwater, *The Conscience of a Conservative* (N.p.: Bottom of the Hill Publishing, 2010), 11. This affirmation has come to define the conservative tradition, as it is a central thesis of Goldwater's *Conscience of a Conservative.*
3. Richard M. Weaver, *Ideas Have Consequences* (Chicago: University of Chicago Press, 1984), 6.

sciences such as ethics, logic, and aesthetics have as their focus the full length and breadth of all human activity, and they define norms that serve as general orientation for all the empirical and social sciences. Ethics, for example, deals with the right or wrong of all human acts, be they economic, cultural, or social. In fact, pre-modern scientists found no problem in appealing to the normative sciences. It was part of their training. It is no coincidence that Adam Smith taught moral philosophy.[4]

For example, a purchase might be a real bargain, but if it is found to be unjust (as in today's case of trading with Marxist or totalitarian regimes that systemically violate human rights), then it must be rejected since it violates a moral code that binds all men to the practice of justice. On the contrary, medieval common sense would hold that if a purchase is found to be just but does not make sense economically, a person would be foolish to proceed with it. To the medieval mind, economics without ethics was ultimately self-destructive as it undermined society in general.

Respecting the Human Aspect

Perhaps the most important premise of the medieval economic order is its insistence that economic activity be considered in the context of a social order bound by *general rules of sociability, charity, or justice that must govern human relations*.

To use an analogy, a doctor, for example, must know medical science well, even though it be a science that is cold and objective. Yet when treating patients, he must go beyond the level of a technician and treat them with warmth, charity, and compassion due to their dignity as human beings. That is why doctors have long taken the Hippocratic Oath—a code of medical ethics valid for all times and places.

On an organizational level, this comprehensive approach could be seen in the medieval guilds. Georg Simmel explains that "A guild of

---

4. Religious and moral perspectives helped broaden the horizons of scientists to think beyond their narrow disciplines while making prodigious advances in science. Writing about a period of great technological progress, Lynn White, Jr., notes: "Every major scientist from about 1250 to about 1650, four hundred years during which our present scientific movement was taking form, considered himself also a theologian: Leibniz and Newton are notable examples. The importance to science of the religious devotion which these men gave their work cannot be exaggerated." Lynn White, Jr., *Machina Ex Deo: Essays in the Dynamism of Western Culture* (Cambridge: MIT Press, 1968), 101.

cloth-makers was not an association of people who merely represented the interests of cloth-making, but a living community in technical, social, religious, political and many other respects. Even though such an association was centered around objective interests, it rested directly on its members and they were absorbed in it."[5]

Inside this framework, many modern economic problems are even superseded. Such was the social cohesion of the members of medieval society that Joseph Schumpeter affirms that "its structural design excluded unemployment and destitution." Because everyone had a place in society, unemployment was normally "quantitatively unimportant," and "the charity enjoined and organized by the Catholic Church was perfectly able to cope" with those facing hardships outside the established social structures. Schumpeter concludes: "Let us remember in particular that mass unemployment, definitely unconnected with any personal shortcomings of the unemployed, was unknown to the Middle Ages except as a consequence of social catastrophes such as devastation by wars, feuds, and plagues."[6]

The Error of Modern Economy

Our great error is that we have turned economic activity into an end in itself. We have separated economics from the influence of those human sciences and norms that should orient all human actions. Economics, which should be a faithful servant to help man reach his end in life, thus becomes a domineering master.

———————————— • ————————————

By insisting that economics work in harmony with the other sciences and be subject to those that are higher, we do not flee from the economic debate but embrace it.

We ground ourselves on an understanding of reality long abandoned. We do this noting that ever since economic thought broke free from its moorings in moral philosophy and ethics, there have been those who have sought to keep such considerations out of this debate.

5. Simmel, *Philosophy of Money,* 343.
6. Joseph A. Schumpeter, *History of Economic Analysis,* ed. Elizabeth Boody Schumpeter (New York: Oxford University Press, 1986), 270.

The time has come for such reflections to return.

The need for this great return is made evident by the fact that we are suddenly faced with the terrifying specter that material progress and money alone will not resolve our crisis, calling to mind the words of Scriptures: "What doth it avail a fool to have riches, seeing he cannot buy wisdom?" (Prv 17:16).

What we must now seek is a return to this wisdom.

Medieval clock on the exterior of Wells Cathedral in England. The Middle Ages was a pre-industrial period of great dynamism and technological advances. Among the many inventions of that time was the mechanical clock.

CHAPTER 20

What Might Have Been, What Could Still Be

S ome might further object that our suggestion of a framework of timeless Christian principles found in the medieval economic order is at best a quaint and nostalgic proposal that has little connection to reality or economic theory. This second preliminary objection holds that we seem to ignore the advances of the Industrial Revolution, which resulted in unprecedented technical progress and production. We thus face the accusation that we are necessarily advocating backward ideas that would hurl us into a primitive Dark Age.

We categorically deny such a charge. The testimony of history comes to our defense. The timeless principles to which we refer were and can be the foundation of incredible material progress and production. Our objectors fail to acknowledge that the Middle Ages was a pre-industrial period of incredible dynamism and enormous technological advances. As historian Samuel Lilley reports, "The technological changes of the Middle Ages were greater in scale—by a very large factor—and more radical in kind than any since the start of civilization."[1] Never in history had man advanced so much—materially as well as spiritually.

Medieval Industrial Revolution

This society was not an enemy of technology. Men in medieval times "introduced machinery into Europe on a scale no civilization had previously known."[2] Even the Industrial Revolution, which so transformed the world, cannot be regarded as a radical departure from medieval technology. In fact, many historians affirm that the technological aspects of the Industrial Revolution were better considered as an *"enor-*

1. Samuel Lilley, "Technological Progress and the Industrial Revolution 1700-1914," in *The Industrial Revolution 1700-1914*, ed. Carlo M. Cipolla (New York: Harvester Press, Barnes and Noble, 1976), 214.
2. Jean Gimpel, *The Medieval Machine: The Industrial Revolution of the Middle Ages* (New York: Penguin Books, 1977), 1.

mous acceleration" of processes that were conceived and begun early in the Middle Ages.[3]

Historian Joel Mokyr affirms that, already in the eighth and ninth centuries, medieval society began to show signs of what he calls "a torrent of technological creativity."[4] Historian Lynn White remarks that medieval Europe developed into a technological society that, for the first time in history, built "a complex civilization which was upheld not on the sinews of sweating slaves and coolies but primarily by nonhuman power. The century which achieved the highest expression of the cult of the Virgin Mary likewise first envisaged the concept of a labor-saving power technology which has played so large a part in the formation of the modern world."[5]

Nor could it have been otherwise, for as M. Stanton Evans states, "*A harmonious objective order intelligible to man* is an obvious prerequisite of modern science." Contrary to pagan ideas that inhibited progress, the Christian worldview favored progress by offering "biblical teachings concerning man's dominion over nature, rejection of pantheistic magic, the idea of progress over linear time, a contingent rather than eternal cosmos."[6]

Lacking this objective worldview, the initial impulses of civilizations in China, Japan, and the Arab nations all eventually ran out of steam, lost their creative momentum for technological advance, and even regressed. Christian civilization suffered no such limitations. In fact, not only did Christian civilization develop its own technology, but it also took the ideas of others, "applying them in new combinations, adapting them to novel usages, and eventually surpassing the original ideas to the point where the original inventing society had to borrow its own ideas back, often unrecognizably altered and improved."[7]

Technology Did Not Dominate the Culture

Finally, we should point out that in the midst of great technological development, medieval man did not lose his ability to produce person-

---

3. Lilley, "Technological Progress," 187.
4. Joel Mokyr, *The Lever of Riches: Technological Creativity and Economic Progress* (New York: Oxford University Press, 1992), 31.
5. White, *Machina Ex Deo*, 71.
6. M. Stanton Evans, *The Theme Is Freedom: Religion, Politics, and the American Tradition* (Washington, D.C.: Regnery Publishing, 1994), 305.
7. Mokyr, *Lever of Riches*, 44.

alized and highly regionalized products. Rather, medieval man knew how to develop his tools so that "they [were] integrated into the culture in ways that [did] not pose significant contradictions to its worldview."[8]

"The techniques of the past were concerned as much with aesthetic expression as with efficacy," writes Richard Stivers. "Moreover, they were integrated into the larger culture and thus symbolically related to other activities. Because these techniques were imbued with moral and religious significance, they did not dominate the culture."[9]

RESPECTING THE DIGNITY OF MAN

It was not by chance that the Middle Ages was the first civilization in history to abolish slavery. Nor was it by chance that the Church ennobled and facilitated manual labor to the point that the Benedictine Order claimed prayer and work were complementary. There was a reason why this happened.

As Lynn White explains: "The labor-saving power machines of the later Middle Ages were harmonious with the religious assumption of the infinite worth of even the most seemingly degraded human personality, and with an instinctive repugnance toward subjecting any man to a monotonous drudgery which seems less than human in that it requires the exercise neither of intelligence nor of choice" (White, *Machina Ex Deo*, 73).

We might contrast this consideration for human nature with the quote attributed to industrialist Henry Ford: "Why is it every time I ask for a pair of hands, they come with a brain attached?" (Matthew Stewart, *The Management Myth: Why the Experts Keep Getting it Wrong* [New York: W. W. Norton, 2009], 57).

In other words, had technology been allowed to develop normally—without frenetic intemperance—a much more splendorous and advanced Christian civilization *could well have arisen* without the abrupt social and economic upheaval wrought by the Industrial Revolution. Progress, which should have been smoothly carried upward by the wings of the virtues of the Faith, was hurled forward by the explosion of intemperance.

---

8. Neil Postman, *Technopoly: The Surrender of Culture to Technology* (New York: Vintage Books, 1993), 25.
9. Stivers, *Culture of Cynicism*, 72.

An Economic Framework That Might Have Developed

Even in the field of economics, there were consistent advances in theory. Contrary to the popular myth, the science of economics was not invented by Adam Smith. We can find the early foundations of economics in the writings of medieval figures like Saint Bernardine, Saint Antoninus, Saint Thomas Aquinas, and other early Scholastics. They prepared the way for Spain's School of Salamanca (1500-1650), which began to shape such "conceptual milestones as the subjective theory of utility, the quantity theory of money, opportunity cost, and liquidity preference" in terms often clearer than those of the modern economists who followed them.[10]

That is to say, many elementary economic principles claimed as modern can be traced back to medieval or Scholastic times. As economic historian Raymond de Roover points out, Adam Smith's "'thunderous broadside' against monopolies can be traced back to Aristotle and Roman law, and especially to the Middle Ages when a theory of monopoly was truly formulated. The Schoolmen's aversion to monopoly hinges on their doctrine of just price."[11]

Governed by Principles

Again we find here a position that did not contradict the medieval worldview but rather worked inside its framework. Economic matters were judged not only by the efficient functioning of markets but above all by whether they were just and, ultimately, if they benefited the *cura animarum*, the care of souls.

A most significant feature of the Scholastic school of economics was the universal uniformity of its principles. The Scholastics agreed on general methods and principles while disagreeing on certain points of concrete application. Their general style and logic were consistent and focused on virtue. They dealt with economic principles of commutative justice, which are, like all general principles of morality, the same in all times and places.

However, the mercantilist and other schools that came after the

---

10. Julius Kirshner, ed., *Business, Banking and Economic Thought in Late Medieval and Early Modern Europe: Selected Studies of Raymond de Roover* (Chicago: University of Chicago Press, 1976), 20.
11. Ibid., 21. It should be noted that Adam Smith acknowledges no such sources although the ancient condemnation of monopolies was the common heritage of Western civilization and widely taught in his time.

Scholastics had neither uniformity nor method. Not unlike the Protestant ethos of free interpretation, everyone became his own economist unbound by precedents and guided by his own inspiration and self-interest.

In other words, had Scholastic economics developed freely, it could have adapted to the increasing complexity of economic systems and resolved with a body of consistent principles the difficult problems of usury, mass production, or labor conditions. Even so, medieval economic thought laid the foundation for many modern concepts. Raymond de Roover claims that, "The unbridgeable gulf separating modern economic theory from Scholastic economic doctrines was an illusion crafted by apologists, polemicists and ideologues."[12] Economist Joseph Schumpeter, referring to modern economics, notes, "It is all in A[dam] Smith' was a favorite saying of [Alfred] Marshall's. But we may also say: 'It is all in the scholastics.'"[13]

We can extend the same argument to many other fields where much progress was made. In every field of human endeavor, medieval man advanced due to what Rodney Stark calls the "Christian commitment to progress through rationality."[14]

All of these many accomplishments took place in an organic order characterized by healthy localism, intense trade, and impressive dynamism. Had this order further developed without frenetic intemperance or the forces of Revolution that conspired against it, it is not unreasonable to imagine a marvelous civilization that might have been. Nor is it unreasonable to conclude that the same underlying principles of this order can again give rise to a new civilization that could still be.

---

12. Ibid., 19.
13. Schumpeter, *History of Economic Analysis*, 309.
14. Rodney Stark, *The Victory of Reason: How Christianity Led to Freedom, Capitalism, and Western Success* (New York: Random House, 2005), 10. Rodney Stark's book chronicles many of the accomplishments of medieval times. Medieval man conceived, for example, polyphonic music, and the "instruments needed to fully exploit harmonies were perfected: the pipe organ, the clavichord and harpsichord, the violin and bass fiddle among others" (ibid., 51). He especially attributes these and many other accomplishments to a flexible and rational theology that corresponded to reality. He contrasts Christianity with other more rigid systems, especially those of pagan times. Similar comparisons can be found in Mokyr, *Lever of Riches*.

Foundations of an Organic Order

Castle Combe, England.
We are social beings that
normally perfect ourselves
by living together in
community.

A computer circuit board (above) and a hummingbird (below). The best way to show the difference between inorganic and organic society is to compare a machine with a living being.

CHAPTER 21

Organic Society: An Unknown Ideal

S o accustomed are we to living in a mechanistic industrial society
that notions of organic society and its corresponding economy are
not widely known. Thus, we begin by explaining what we mean by
this term.

We employ the concept of "organic society" to mean a social order oriented towards the common good that naturally and spontaneously develops under the guidance of the principles of natural law and the Gospel,
thus allowing man to pursue the perfection of his essentially social nature.

"The term 'organic' comes from a society's resemblance to living or-
ganisms," writes Adolpho Lindenberg. "Just as we find cells, tissues, organs and systems in a living being, in an organic society we find
families, lineages and associations of all kinds, each with its unique
function and scope of activity, and all interrelated and working together towards the common good."[1]

The Most Fundamental Difference

By this definition and description, we can deduce two principles. First,
we recognize the organic living nature of this society that differs sub-
stantially from the mechanistic conception of modern society.

Second, we are social beings that normally perfect ourselves by living in community. Our social nature rejoices in being together with
others where qualities are complemented by others and defects are
counterbalanced. We reject fundamentally the individualistic concept
of Thomas Hobbes, who describes life as a "war of every man against
every man."

Contrasting Living Beings with Machines

Many authors have illustrated the first principle by comparing a living

---

1. Adolpho Lindenberg, *The Free Market in a Christian Society*, trans. Donna H. Sandin (Washington, D.C.: St. Antoninus Institute for Catholic Education in Business, 1999), 200-1.

DEFINING ORGANIC SOCIETY

Organic society is a social order oriented towards the common good that naturally and spontaneously develops, allowing man to pursue the perfection of his essentially social nature. In this society, the family attains the plenitude of its action and influence as the social cell or fundamental unit of society. Professional, social, and other intermediary groups between the individual and the State freely exercise their activities according to their own forms and rights.

The State respects the autonomy of regions and intermediary groups, recognizing in each the right to organize according to its social and economic structure, character, and traditions. The State, acting within its own supreme orbit, exercises its sovereign power with honor, vigor, and efficiency. The Church exercises a hallowing influence upon society, by guiding, teaching, and sanctifying.

being with a machine to show the contrast between an organic society and an individualistic or mechanistic society.[2]

Indeed, compare the two. A living being grows and develops at its own speed according to its own inner dynamism and force that comes from the life of each cell. A machine is inert, operates at a determined speed, and always needs an external force or motor to make each piece move or act. Because they are part of the living organism, individual members or organs grow, change, and continually renew themselves in union with it. A severed arm, for example, cannot long survive separated from the whole body. In contrast, spare parts can exist outside the machine and be used interchangeably with others. No machine part can renew itself from within the mechanism; defective parts must be replaced.

To apply this to social terms: In an organic society, a person is treated as an integral part of society; in a mechanistic society the individual is an interchangeable cog in an organization.

Describing Organic Society

That is to say, *life's processes are very different from mechanical processes.* A mechanistic society is a distortion of our nature since it

---

2. Such comparisons can be found in Rommen, *State in Catholic Thought,* or Wilhelm Schwer, *Catholic Social Theory,* trans. Bartholomew Landheer (St. Louis: B. Herder, 1940).

represents only a narrow application of the rationality of man's soul. As rational beings, we can understand the purely logical processes of machines, which we have designed and set in motion.

However, we are also living and unique beings, and once the element of life enters into the equation, everything becomes more complex. Life brings with it pondered choices, unending creativity, and varied rhythms. Life's spontaneity, unpredictability, and individuality introduce the difficulty of dealing with vitality and moods, nuance and tendencies, poetry and passion.

An organic society is one that is in sync with our nature. This means it is strongly governed by reason but also open to the rich and immense variety of possible human actions that come from the fact that we are living and rational beings. From the exuberant element of life, there springs forth unique systems of art, styles of life, socio-political institutions, and economic models that differ from the rigid and soulless central planning and one-size-fits-all solutions so prized by socialists and bureaucrats.

Mirroring Life's Processes

We are also social beings. Again, we point out that organic society mirrors life's processes. We can extend the single living organism metaphor yet further by comparing our social relationships, albeit imperfectly, with how cells and organs integrate in a living body.

The more developed the life, the more the cell tends to associate. A cell in a complex living organism is not like the individualist who pretends to be a fully self-sufficient, autonomous, and perfect being. Rather, the cell maintains its "individuality" while fully sharing in the body's common purpose.

Thus, each cell follows its own internal ordering principles found in its DNA code, which governs its normal operation and establishes the criteria by which it relates to other cells and organs. The cell, so to speak, finds its perfection, or purpose, by integrating itself into a tissue or organ that has its own ordering principles and in turn finds its perfection in unity with a higher organ or system. Moreover, an organism only functions well when subordinate organs work in harmony and not in rebellion with those performing higher functions. Together they all form that grandiose yet humble, unfathomable yet simple, symphony of organs and tissues we call a living being.

Society Similar to Workings of the Cells

A true organic society works in a similar way. The more developed we become, the more our social nature impels us to seek our perfection in association with others, to help and be helped by others. An organic society is a *true society* oriented towards a common good and not just a mere collection of individual wills. The common good involves the welfare of the whole of society while allowing each person and group to achieve its own perfection.

As Heinrich A. Rommen writes: "Life in community enlarges, exalts, and perfects the individual person, and cures the shortcomings and wants that are connected with mere individuality and isolation."[3]

Like the cell, each person tends to find autonomous expression, meaning, and purpose in families and groups with their own respective inner ordering principles. This manner of expression in conjunction with society does much to explain why Christian civilization produced so many saints, thinkers, artists, and other outstanding individuals that found meaning and thrived in this organic atmosphere.

Not a Perfect Analogy

We must note that the cell is not the perfect analogy since, because cells have definite and unalterable roles in the body, we cannot conclude that man's place is likewise unalterable in society. That is why we emphasize the essential role of reason and free will in organic society and avoid in this way the errors of romantic, biological, or evolutionary views of organicity that would have society being guided by irrational powers or subconscious historical processes. We must recognize that any organic model must have as a premise the fact that, by our free will and our attitude towards responsibility, we can better or worsen our conditions. If this is done, the comparison of society to the organism of the human body may be used with caution since it is still very instructive.

A Notion of Inequality in Our Accidents

Comparisons of society to living beings have circulated since Plato and

---

3. Rommen, *State in Catholic Thought*, 136.

Aristotle and were only abandoned with the rise of the Enlightenment's mechanistic conceptions of the universe. By these comparisons, we see the consistent use of the organic metaphor to convey the idea that society must adapt to our needs as both living individuals and social beings.

This can be observed yet further, for example, in the recognition of inequalities in human society, drawing from the fact that we are all equal in our nature yet unequal in our accidents. These inequalities of talents, abilities, and circumstances result in an ordered hierarchical society where individuals or groups have specific leadership roles, just as members in a body play key roles in our organic metaphor.

Photo/American TFP Archive

Plinio Corrêa de Oliveira (1908-1995)

EQUAL IN OUR HUMAN NATURE, BUT UNEQUAL IN OUR ACCIDENTS

"All men are equal by nature and different only in their accidents. The rights they derive from the mere fact of being human are equal for all: the right to life, honor, sufficient living conditions (and therefore the right to work), property, the setting up of a family, and, above all, the knowledge and practice of the true religion. The inequalities that threaten these rights are contrary to the order of Providence. However, within these limits, the inequalities that arise from accidents such as virtue, talent, beauty, strength, family, tradition, and so forth, are just and according to the order of the universe" (Corrêa de Oliveira, *Revolution and Counter-Revolution*, 51).

Using this metaphor, Leo XIII in his encyclical *Quod Apostolici Muneris* affirms: "He [God] appointed that there should be various orders in civil society, differing in dignity, rights, and power, whereby the State, like the Church, should be one body, consisting of many members, some nobler than others, but all necessary to each other and solicitous for the common good."[4]

---

4. Leo XIII, encyclical *Quod Apostolici Muneris* (1878) in *The Papal Encyclicals*, vol. 2, p. 13, no. 6.

Likewise, citing this encyclical of his predecessor, Pius X in his motu proprio *Fin Dalla Prima* states: "Human society, as established by God, is composed of unequal elements, just as the different parts of the human body are unequal; to make them all equal is impossible, and would mean the destruction of human society."[5]

Application to the Church

So natural is this organic relationship that we find analogies in describing the spiritual ties found in the Church. While the Church as an institution is of an entirely different nature than temporal society, She nevertheless adapts to the organic nature of man. Hence, the faithful form living members of a Mystical Body with Christ as the head. Saint Paul refers to members united to one body.[6] Our Lord uses the image of the vine and the branches.[7]

We see the same organic structures where the individual cell senses itself as an integral part of the whole. Likewise, each social organ, writes historian Christopher Dawson, would "possess a further relation and responsibility to the wider spiritual society of which they also form part."[8] Historian Lewis Mumford comments on how the Church united all in common purpose without the loss of individuality. He found this reflected in medieval cities: "In the most important offices of life, the meanest village stood on the level of a metropolis. The Church Universal gave all communities, big and small, a common purpose; but the unity so achieved fostered rather than suppressed their diversity and individuality."[9]

Thus an organic society respects the fact that we are living and social beings. The society and economy we seek must give free rein to a healthy interplay of maximum individuality and sociability. This or-

---

5. Pius X, motu proprio *Fin Dalla Prima, American Catholic Quarterly Review,* 29, no. 114 (Apr. 1904): 235.
6. See Col 1:18, Eph 1:22-23, 1 Cor 12:12-27.
7. See Jn 15:1-6.
8. Christopher Dawson, *Religion and the Rise of Western Culture* (New York: Sheed and Ward, 1950), 212. Indeed, Fr. Wilhelm Schwer goes so far as to affirm that most of the social order of the Middle Ages "borrowed its social principles of community, organic structure, authority and office … from the ecclesiastical organization." Schwer, *Catholic Social Theory,* 85.
9. Lewis Mumford, *The City in History: Its Origins, Its Transformations, and Its Prospects* (New York: Harcourt Brace Jovanovich, 1961), 266.

ganic society is the basis of a healthy free market economy.

When social and economic models reflect these basic organic principles, as once they did, we will naturally find solutions suited to the perfection of our nature as human beings.

About the organic society, we might conclude:

It is organic, not mechanistic;
Social, not individualistic;
Hierarchical, not egalitarian.
It is all for all, not "every man against every man."

Halles Food Market by Victor Gabriel Gilbert (1847-1933). An organic society avoids mechanistic, rigid planning. Instead, counting upon God's grace and solid rational principles, it recognizes and respects the organic nature of man, full of vivacity, spontaneity, and creativity as might be seen in this vibrant marketplace.

CHAPTER 22

Organic Remedies and Upright Spontaneity

A second element of organic society involves the manner in which remedies are found. In searching for solutions, we must carefully observe the fact that *organic solutions cannot be imposed upon a people as if they were machines*. We must avoid the modern mechanistic systems of order and rigid planning. Instead, counting upon God's grace, we must recognize and respect the organic nature of man, full of vivacity, spontaneity, and unpredictability. This is the essence of a truly organic—that is, living—society.

That is why we *propose*—yet do not aim to *impose*—a model. What we present here is but a sketch, an outline, or a draft of which a final and exact rendering is not possible due to the nature of man and society.

Our intention is like that of loving parents, who, following certain moral principles, strongly guide, nurture, protect, and cultivate their children's growth differently according to their aptitudes and the circumstances. Parents must not determine, force, or program the free will of their children since this is contrary to their nature. And so it must be when we look for organic solutions.

The Nature of Organic Solutions

We must seek to discover basic principles associated with the nature of things and in accordance with the Gospel, and then allow enormous freedom in applying them to the needs of the person or society. Moreover, we need not limit ourselves to a single system but allow an enormous variety of legitimate solutions that adapt to the inequality found in men, peoples, and the differing circumstances of life.

That is to say, there is no single magical system that we can put in place to solve all of our current problems. We can only discern the basic principles of a sound economy and society (which remain the same) and leave it to the ingenuity of each individual or social unit to develop the applications that best suit their needs. This ingenuity is something very much rooted in our own American tradition and con-trary to socialism that always imposes a single unified system with rigid regulations to make sure everything works as centrally planned.

Organic society gives us a few general rules from which come thou-sands of systems. Socialism gives us one system from which comes a thousand rules and regulations. From this we can conclude that it is much more important to have the right general rules and principles than to design a rigid one-size-fits-all system.

Unlike socialism, the organic model of Christian civilization applied principles to concrete circumstances and the nature of things. From the unity of its basic moral principles came an astonishing variety of customs, systems, and solutions wonderfully adapted to the nature of people, places, and things. Such organic solutions give rise to the de-velopment of healthy regionalism where local inhabitants devise their own way of doing things.

Upright Spontaneity

There is a second aspect of organic solutions. This involves the manner by which living things naturally and spontaneously develop without rigid planning. This manner of natural development can be called *up-right spontaneity.*

By upright spontaneity, we do not wish to imply that life should be aimless. It should be purposeful. We do not condone the whimsical or irrational "spontaneity" of the hippies of the sixties or their later in-carnations. At the same time, we do not endorse the blindly evolution-ary and deterministic spontaneity of some modern economists who conjured up the idea of a "spontaneous order."[1]

On the contrary, our spontaneity is upright, rational, purposeful, and moral in accordance with natural law and the law of God. It is founded on firm principles. It should not exclude planning, method, or adaptive systems. Ever mindful of man's rational yet exuberant na-ture, this spontaneity allows man to adapt as he gropes ahead in the general direction of a goal that is often not entirely clear.

---

1. Naturally we disassociate ourselves from the theories of "spontaneous order" or "emergent order" that were circulated by such figures as David Hume, Adam Smith, and other modern economists. Although such theories may appear to be similar to our expression of "upright spontaneity," closer examination shows that they tend to diminish the role of reason and free will. Any such evolutionary, amoral, and individualistic theories do not fit into our proposal.

In the development of healthy traditions, for example, a spontaneous gesture of vague patriotism towards the flag might later solidify into tradition. This might also be seen in the natural development of original schools of art. That is to say, this spontaneous development involves purposeful action towards a perceived *yet not preconceived* goal or perfection. This adaptive process is described very well as applied in medieval cities by historian Lewis Mumford: "Organic planning does not begin with a preconceived goal: it moves from need to need, from opportunity to opportunity, in a series of adaptations that themselves become increasingly coherent and purposeful, so that they generate a complex, final design, hardly less unified than a pre-formed geometric pattern."[2]

In a similar way, a spontaneous society is formed when each person adapts from opportunity to opportunity and from need to need in the general direction of a perceived perfection. In the case of an individual, this process corresponds to a person's purpose, vocation, or calling in life.

Thus, upright spontaneity is a manner of acting according to principles, natural law, and the Gospel, which respects the unplanned development of life and fosters the exercise of free will, creativity, and adaptation.

Many Manifestations

Since life is complex and full of nuance, upright spontaneity can manifest itself in many ways. Indeed, upright spontaneity can be found in acts of decisive leadership, full of energy and initiative. At other times, it can be perceived in acts of lofty contemplation or pondered deliberation. There are also times when upright spontaneity is marked by a strong sense of determination and profound order as might be seen in the building of a Gothic cathedral. This spontaneity can also manifest itself by outbursts of exuberant activity that seem to be chaotic, such as that found in the apparent disorder of a vibrant open-air food market.

---

2. Mumford, *City in History*, 302. Indeed, Mumford explains how medieval towns followed this process to such an extent that although each town was uniquely different, there was a perceived direction that formed a consensus around which all towns formed. "The consensus is so complete as to the purposes of town life that the variations in detail only confirm the pattern. That consensus makes it look, when one views a hundred medieval plans in succession, as if there were in fact a conscious theory that guided this townplanning" (ibid., 303).

Above all, we see the gradual development of things full of delightful nuance and intermediary phases without brutal transitions. Just as a child progresses to adulthood naturally and almost imperceptibly, so also the organic processes advance full of variety and unity.

The Triumph of Common Sense

What makes this principle so attractive is that it represents the triumph of common sense. Upright spontaneity is born of the day-to-day application of principles to concrete reality. It is always oriented towards reality, sensing its heartbeat, constantly gauging whether a situation is legitimate, virtuous, or worth supporting, ready to change if need be.

When the soul is upright and imbued with the four cardinal virtues—prudence, justice, fortitude, and temperance—such a manner of acting exhibits an astonishing ability to find lasting solutions and meaningful traditions. When this spontaneity is carried out in cooperation with the grace of God, it gives rise to great deeds and civilizations.

A Perceived Perfection

In a society of upright spontaneity, each person gradually works out a future. This presupposes a certain introspection whereby the person seeks to discern a purpose or station in life. Each is guided by principles, instincts, inner tendencies, and inclinations, all of which reason must judge. In the silence of one's leisure (so rare in our days), each subtly recollects oneself and perceives a unique calling—God's personal plan for the person—a concept despised by secularists who deny any designs of God in history.

And yet this calling—this discreet discernment of meaning and purpose in self and society and not a direct Divine revelation—is exactly what is lacking in our noisy existential wilderness where we are taught that we have neither place nor purpose in life beyond that of arranging our own pleasure.

"A calling links a person to the larger community, a whole in which the calling of each is a contribution to the good of all,"[3] write Robert Bellah et al. It establishes place and purpose whereby the person senses his part in the whole. At the same time, it is not a tyrannical or

---

3. Bellah et al., *Habits of the Heart*, 66. We might note that the general nature of this calling is clearly different from that of the rigid and fatalistic "callings" proposed by Luther or Calvin.

ordained order that is rigorously imposed upon the person as in a caste. Rather, it is a situation where the person has an enormous freedom to pursue the innumerable options that appear along the path of the ever more coherent development of his calling.

Spontaneity in Society

In a similar way, families, institutions, and nations can freely form, coalesce, and practice this same spontaneity. Governed by Christian principles and upright customs, such human groups can also, so to speak, collectively discern a calling or purpose in history.

Throughout history, innumerable institutions were born in this organic "spontaneous" way—without rigid planning. Historian Léon Gautier, for example, explains that chivalry was not an institution created by decree but by the collective discernment of an ideal. He notes:

> It was born everywhere at once, and has been everywhere at the same time the natural effect of the same aspirations and the same needs. There was a moment . . . when people everywhere felt the necessity of tempering the ardor of old German blood, and of giving to their ill-regulated passions an ideal. Hence chivalry![4]

So it was with the many families, local associations, and religious orders, all of which marvelously melded together towards that perceived perfection that later became Christendom. Virtue, in contact with unforeseen circumstances, gave rise to an unexpected model of a truly organic society without frenetic intemperance. We must also consider the action of grace which moved men to cooperate with God's loving Providence and mold a new civilization. And so it must be for us if we are to find truly organic solutions to the present crisis.

---

4. Léon Gautier, *Chivalry*, trans. Henry Frith (New York: Crescent Books, 1989), 1.

The walls of Ávila, Spain at night. An organic society is a virtuous society. The four cardinal virtues are like castle towers that defend individuals, families, and society against the disordered passions.

CHAPTER 23

A Virtuous Order

A third part of the foundation of an organic society involves acting in accordance with natural law, and therefore calls for a social order where virtue is practiced.

In fact, Saint Thomas Aquinas notes, natural law prescribes "all acts of virtue." As he explains, "There is in every man a natural inclination to act according to reason and this is to act according to virtue." Although the weakness of our fallen nature often makes the practice of virtue difficult, "each one's reason naturally dictates to him to act virtuously."[1]

Thus, *an organic society must be a virtuous society*, and it must be part of the foundation of our proposal.

Opposing Systems of Vice

While this principle should be an obvious conclusion for any society, it runs contrary to modern liberal economic theories and systems.

Such theories hold that man is mainly motivated by self-interest. Rather than insist upon integral virtue, these theories build foolproof systems of checks and balances whereby the selfish vices of men— greed, prodigality, or pride—might be channeled to work for the public good. They hold that by carefully stoking the greed of men, for example, economic growth can be stimulated.

This unholy alliance between virtue and vice abandons the ideal of perfection or personal sanctity as impractical or unobtainable. It creates the illusion that virtue lies in the governmental systems or markets devised by men and not in men themselves. Hence, concludes early American statesman John Taylor, the institutions and "principles of a society may be virtuous, though the individuals composing it are vicious."[2]

---

1. Aquinas, *Summa Theologica*, I-II, q. 94, a. 3.
2. Lasch, *Revolt of the Elites*, 94.

We might also refer to Leo Strauss who summarizes the logic of the advocates of this position as follows: "By building civil society on 'the low but solid ground' of selfishness or of certain 'private vices,' one will achieve much greater 'public benefits' than by futilely appealing to virtue, which is by nature 'unendowed.' One must take one's bearings not by how men should live but by how they do live."[3]

There is no substitute for the practice of virtue. Vice proves to be an unwilling partner to virtuous enterprises. Alas, our sad experience has shown that when we try to turn vice to virtuous ends, vice knows no bounds. We are then doomed to impose mounds of regulations to prevent the crafty abuses of the vicious and burden the honest efforts of the virtuous. When we fan the passions of selfishness in the hope of seeing society prosper, we also awaken those ravaging frenzies that gave rise to the restless spirit of frenetic intemperance.

Towers of the Cardinal Virtues

That is why we must build our society and its economy once more on the solid yet high moral ground of virtue and Christian perfection. We must base our order on the four cardinal virtues—prudence, justice, fortitude, and temperance—since they are the moral virtues upon which all other virtues are hinged and which specifically regulate man's use of material things.

Unlike "selfish virtue," the cardinal virtues stand firm upon this high ground like four towers in a castle. When these virtues are practiced throughout society, everything enters into balance and proper rhythm because we then act in accordance with our nature. This is the true foundation for prosperity.

If, as in our own days, the towers of the cardinal virtues are undefended and abandoned, the disordered passions take over. The walls of the castle are breached, and this delicate balance is upset. Then we can expect the financial turmoil and the frenetic intemperance that so characterize modern economy.

Not Mechanical Virtue

We must emphasize that any mechanical practice of the Ten Commandments without regard for the spirit of the law is not enough. The

---

3. Strauss, *Natural Right and History*, 247.

breath of life that must regenerate our society and economy must come from an ardent and energetic practice of virtue.

We must especially look to the passionate practice of the First Commandment, which is the very soul of the Decalogue and contains all its precepts. One who profoundly loves God with all one's heart and soul, has an instinctive love of the order God put in the universe. By this instinct, the person is gifted with the ability to order society well—including economy.

Far from inhibiting our actions, this love allows man an enormous freedom and facility to act that is found wonderfully expressed in Saint Augustine's counsel for perfection: "Love [God], and [then] do what you will."[4]

The Role of Grace

We should take comfort in the fact that we need not work alone in this endeavor of virtue. What gave special vigor to Christendom was the amazing role of grace whereby God, Who desires our good more than we ourselves, extends to us His Divine assistance for our feeble efforts, so that we might realize our calling or purpose in life.

Through grace, the intelligence is enlightened, the will strengthened, and the senses tempered so that we might turn towards the good. We gain immeasurably from this supernatural life, since we are elevated above the miseries of our fallen nature and even above human nature itself. It is especially through the sacraments administered by the Church that men, thus regenerated, might practice that supernatural virtue, which gave rise to the great feats and true marvels of Christian civilization.

Alas, we must pity those who think only in terms of numbers and formulae. They do not avail themselves of this great gift from God. They do not understand that marvels—including economic marvels—can be worked through grace. Instead they limit themselves to an order of things without grace and, in so doing, refuse to open themselves to the world made possible through this great gift.

Although grace does not alter economic laws, it does help men use them with greater wisdom when faced with complex problems.

---

4. Augustine, *In epistulam Ioannis ad Parthos* (Homily 7 on the First Epistle of John), no. 8, accessed Oct. 16, 2012, http://www.newadvent.org/fathers/170207.htm.

As we have seen, virtue cannot be imposed upon a people. Rather, an organic order creates all the conditions that encourage men to practice it. It sets in place customs, habits, and institutions that allow one to man the towers of the cardinal virtues that keep things in balance. Above all, it introduces a passionate love of God and recourse to His grace that can give us the elements to accomplish true marvels.

CHAPTER 24

A Providential Order

A fourth and final part of the foundation of an organic order is the role of Providence. We have gone to great lengths to describe the vibrant and spontaneous nature of an order that is resistant to rigid planning. The fact that this complex interplay of men and activities does not end in chaos leads us to affirm that *an organic order presupposes the presence of an ordering action found in the Creator and which we call Providence.*

Providence—A Necessary Assumption

Providence is a necessary assumption for any society and the basis of any economy, but especially of an organic society. Human providence involves the foresight of practical reason that allows men to adapt means to an end, as might be seen in parents who save money for their children's education. Yet it is especially the hand of Divine Providence where we see the coordinating of the complex conditions by which men live together in society for a definite end.

Throughout history, men of all times and places have believed in Divine Providence by holding there to be some Intelligent Being who governs the universe and directs the course of the affairs of men with purpose and benevolence. The very term itself reflects this goodness since Providence *provides* for our necessities.

Such a belief is not foreign to our own American tradition since there are abundant references to and invocations of Providence in the literature of our nation's Founders and their public discourse. It is further found in the teachings and works of economists with faith. Fr. Bernard Dempsey, for example, affirms that any order that tends to promote the common good of man naturally "assumes a theory of divine and human providence."[1]

In fact, this ordering action of Providence is so obvious that even

---

1. Dempsey, *Functional Economy,* 81.

secular authors and scholars try to explain it away. Hence, when evolutionists find order coming from disorder they attribute it to a mysterious self-generating evolutionary process. Socialists mistakenly assign the role of Providence to the all-powerful State. Modern economists describe baffling economic ordering processes by employing terms such as an "invisible hand," "animal spirits," or an "emergent order" and, in so doing, fabricate defective theories and what D. Stephen Long calls "a false theology of providence . . . by which vices can be miraculously transubstantiated into virtues."[2]

A True Theology of Providence

A true theology of Providence leads to our organic model. We can see the ordering action of God's Providence at work in society *providing* for men in their complex and unplanned interplay. Providence, for instance, not only cares for our material necessities, but arranges it so that societies always have sufficient farmers, teachers, soldiers, or other professions as we progress together in pursuit of our ultimate end. It is "a most elaborate interdependence that has its basis in the diversity of actual and potential skills with which Providence endows individuals, because they are designed to live in society."[3]

Thus, we can define Divine Providence as "the plan conceived in the mind of God according to which he directs all creatures to their proper end."[4]

Working with Providence

That same Providence that directs the course of the affairs of each man with purpose and benevolence also directs and provides for the affairs of families, societies, and nations. Our task is to work with the action of Divine Providence. Ever mindful of man's free will, God requires the intelligent cooperation of His creatures in carrying out His designs. He expects us to use the resources that He in His Providence puts at our disposal. He assists us in discerning how we might utilize those capacities and talents with which He endowed us—and which society needs from us to function well. He gives us His grace and supernatural gifts to aid in this cooperation.

---

2. Long, *Divine Economy*, 211.
3. Dempsey, *Functional Economy*, 22.
4. Pietro Parente, Antonio Piolanti and Salvatore Garofalo, *Dictionary of Dogmatic Theology* s.v. "Providence, Divine" (Milwaukee: Bruce Publishing, 1951), 234.

It is inconceivable that any economic order should fail to recognize Providence since it is precisely this ordering action of God that aids an economy in fulfilling its end of providing for man's needs. An order that ignores the action of Providence deprives itself of its most precious support and guidance.

Those who govern must, above all, be attuned to the designs of Providence and rule accordingly. There are those who believe that governing consists only of legislation and executive decisions. These things are undoubtedly important. However, we affirm that sound policy consists primarily in discerning the ways of Providence. It is what might be called a prophetic discernment since we strive to see, judge, and act in accordance with God's designs.

If our crisis was built upon the mechanistic framework of an industrial society of frenetic intemperance, then a solution must be found upon a different foundation. For this reason, we have presented an organic order that addresses the nature of man; one in sync with the way we all function. As such, it respects the restraints that our nature imposes upon us.

This order addresses the errors of modernity that we have cited: materialism, individualism, and technological utopianism. It does so with a unity of principles and an immense variety of applications, all exercised with a refreshing upright spontaneity. By insisting on a virtuous and providential order, we depart from the modern narrow-minded conception of a secular society that excludes the sublime from our horizons. By cooperating with God's grace and trusting in His Providence, we not only perfect but surpass our nature.

The Heart and Soul of an Economy

The Departure of the Diligence, Biarritz by Abraham Solomon (1823-1862). The heart and soul of any economy must be embedded with rich and vibrant social relationships that give meaning and context to production and consumption.

The Carpenter's Family by Johann Baptist Reiter (1813-1890). An organic society is full of non-economic influences such as family, community, religion, and other social relationships that are sources of immense material and spiritual wealth that largely go uncompensated and defy quantification.

CHAPTER 25

Reviving the Heart and Soul of an Economy

Given our organic approach to the present crisis, we will not only insist upon the secondary role of economics in a social order, but we will also maintain that the social and economic orders are inextricably intertwined. Any treatment of the present crisis must address both spheres.

Karl Polanyi notes how prior to modern times, "the motives and circumstances of productive activities were embedded in the general organization of society."[1] Thus, we deliberately propose an organic society as a part of the solution to an economic problem because we believe that when economic activities take place inside the context of society, it allows the natural restraining influence of human institutions such as custom, morals, family, or community to calm markets and prevent frenetic intemperance. In fact, this organic social order is so important that we do not hesitate to call it the heart and soul of an economy.

Heart and Soul

This conclusion derives from the fact that, as social beings, it is proper that we associate to produce, exchange, and enjoy together those goods deemed helpful to the common good and the perfection of our nature. As such, it is fitting that something of the living and spontaneous aspects of our free and rational nature and our sentiments enter into these transactions. This is what makes economic actions so unpredictable—they depend on the very nuanced dispositions and free actions of men. Economics can never be an exact science like physics, which deals with matter that always moves according to rigidly determined laws of nature.

In economics, unforeseen factors that stem from the heart and soul of men always enter. Economic science can define norms by which it

---

1. Polanyi, *The Great Transformation*, 73.

is possible to create wealth with the means at hand, but it cannot determine the end of the human actions that can change the outcome of the decisions to create wealth. An economist might, for example, determine if a factory *can* be built given the means in a certain place. Yet the same economist cannot determine if it *should* be built considering all the political, social, and moral factors that might enter into the case. Economists can analyze trends in production and consumption, but they cannot discern the motivation of consumer behavior. They cannot plumb the depths of the human soul; they can only observe the consequences of certain human commercial acts and take limited conclusions. Unlike the laws of the natural sciences, economic laws involve free and rational human beings and are consequently free of determinism.

In vain, modern economists try to minimize or eliminate these unquantifiable factors from their ledger books. It is precisely on these human elements that we will now focus and celebrate.

"A Vast World of Self-Sufficiency"

We must remember that economy in its ancient and even etymological origins was born around the warm hearth of the family home.[2] Aristotle was the first to make the distinction between house-holding on one hand and production for gain on the other.

In pre-modern times, an economy of both sorts was always an accessory absorbed into the social and cultural structures of the day. As sociologist Robert Nisbet affirms, in every successful economy, we find "associations and incentives nourished by the non-economic processes of kinship, religion, and various other forms of social relationships."[3]

Such non-economic processes make up what French historian Fernand Braudel calls "the vast world of self-sufficiency" that long dominated the West and persists to our day.[4] They are sources of immense material and spiritual wealth that largely go uncompensated,

---

2. Economy. "MF *yconomie*, fr. ML *oeconomia*, fr. Gk *oikonomia*, fr. *oikonomos* household manager, fr. *oikos* house + *nemein* to manage 1. archaic: the management of household or private affairs and esp. expenses." *Webster's New Collegiate Dictionary*, 1981 edition, s.v. "economy." It should be noted that in Aristotle's time, the household often referred to an estate and did not exclude some economic surplus production.
3. Nisbet, *Quest for Community*, 212-13.
4. Fernand Braudel, *Afterthoughts on Material Civilization and Capitalism*, trans. Patricia M. Ranum (Baltimore: Johns Hopkins University Press, 1977), 19.

remain unrecorded, or defy quantification. We believe these vast sectors constitute the heart and soul of all economy.

Defining These Areas

These sectors are found everywhere. The first one is the family, which is a dynamic source of uncompensated activity that freely provides its members with shelter, nourishment, education, affection, and health-care. There is also the Church with Her liturgical, moral, and religious acts that communicate untold spiritual benefits to a community. Her moral code secures the nation. She gratuitously bestows culture, charity, and learning upon Her children and society as a whole.

We can refer to local, cultural, or religious associations that generate arts, civic spirit, and works of charity that enrich the community in ways that cannot be quantified. This can also be seen in any kind of organic neighborhood or ethnic community where inhabitants receive the great benefits of solidarity and a distinctive local identity. Common local transactions, barter, or acts of neighborliness are clearly valuable actions that strengthen economy. All of these institutions and activities have an indirect impact upon the formal economy and truly nourish and sustain it. This is especially true in agrarian society where the land, besides freely giving its fruits and creating abundant wealth, also creates a sense of self-sufficiency and a strong attachment to property.

Focus on Property

Before becoming a modern commodity, private property possessed a strong intangible value. Real property, especially land, was a point of anchorage or sanctuary from which a family might develop. Wherever a strong sense of private property exists, a strong family pervades. An intimate link between owner and owned becomes evident when, for example, a house or property becomes identified with a family over years or generations. In such cases, land and property become embedded in social relationships. They are not mere commodities but become part of the social and political organization itself, conferring the intangible qualities of honor, authority, and status upon the owner.

Social Capital

So important are these intangible relationships that there is a growing field of sociological studies that focuses on the value they give to economy. Sociologists claim that intense networks of reciprocal human relationships produce what they call *social capital.*

David Halpern defines social capital as a social network governed by shared norms and values and maintained by sanctions.[5] It is a social fabric that serves as a kind of capital since it creates conditions for trust. Although unquantifiable, it enriches and lubricates social, civic, and economic life, giving it undeniable value. It is also a source of immense security embracing that which is familiar while investigating that which is threatening.

When this trust is gone—and we join Halpern in affirming that it is disappearing—the foundation for commerce and economy is threatened, and the general well-being of society is lost.

Source of Human Warmth and Stability

All of these sectors provide the essential human element that is so important to economy and makes it so nuanced and unpredictable. They provide those essential braking mechanisms inside economy that prevent the rule of frenetic intemperance.

Such spheres are where the drama and poetry of life reside. Like economy, literature was born next to the warm hearth of the family household and has no place in the accountant's ledger. If today this informal economic sphere holds such great attraction for us, it is because we long for that human warmth found in these social institutions and not in our super-rationalized mechanized world and its economy.

These considerations are not nostalgic musings about the past. Rather, all these dynamic elements—church, community, family, personalized property—form an invaluable human infrastructure that actually provides the moral capital, psychological health, and stability upon which even our modern economies must be built. Although scarcely registered in modern economic life and threatened on all sides, their contribution to the economy is incalculable, and their demise will prove catastrophic.

Importance of This Sector

Our focus on this vast "invisible" economy in no way denies the need

---

5. See David Halpern, *Social Capital* (Cambridge: Polity Press, 2005), 10.

or importance of a formal economy in the life of a nation. We only affirm that these two economies are intertwined; the prosperity of one depends upon the other. *Our principal concern should be centered on this vast primary "world of self-sufficiency."*

This is because when these institutions and sectors fail, the nation languishes. This could be seen in the tragic failure of the Soviet experiment, which is patent testimony of a soulless planned economy that deliberately strangled this "invisible" sector and paid the consequences of misery.

If we now wish to return to an economy without frenetic intemperance, a great part of the solution lies in the regeneration of this vast sector that does not appear on the ledger books. It is to this task that we now turn.

In vain do we seek to regenerate an economy if we do not regenerate the family, the community, and so many other institutions that are its heart and soul. Indeed, to what purpose do we prosper if all this withers?

In contrast to the inertia of the modern masses, Pope Pius XII describes the heart and soul of an economy in which a true people manifest that "fullness of life," that "life energy," which "lives and moves" inside a society.

CHAPTER 26

Autonomy, Authority, Vital Flux, and Subsidiarity

There are ordering principles of an organic society that are key to understanding the social structures so important to the heart and soul of economy. They explain the natural processes by which men associate and govern themselves. They make possible the large number of intermediary structures and associations that help to create an atmosphere of trust and solidarity in the pursuit of the common good.

Needless to say, these principles are very different from those of the individualistic and mechanistic society that so favors frenetic intemperance. If we are to regenerate the heart and soul of economy, we must turn to these ordering principles on which an organic society is based. They will provide us with guidance on the road ahead.

A Principle of Autonomy

We begin with the principle of autonomy. Man is a rational being endowed with free will. As such, he naturally enjoys a personal autonomy where he exerts control of himself, his character, and the world immediately around him. The individualist limits this personal autonomy to a mere means to construct a separate little world and further a pursuit of happiness, while in an organic social order, man is a social being that only attains his full development in fellowship with others.

This personal autonomy allows individuals to project the mark of their personalities and talents upon family, profession, and immediate surroundings. A person finds fulfillment in assuming the responsibility for a domain: the father and mother, their family; the farmer, his farm; the teacher, the classroom; the craftsman, a shop; the priest, his parish. Inside the domain, be it large or small, each governs autonomously in a manner that strongly recalls that of a sovereign with little outside interference. Each senses and exults in having a domain and being part of its tradition.

In a similar manner, man freely enters into association with others, forming groups and social units that exercise autonomy and from which rise governing structures and authorities. As a result, the family, parish, local community, occupational group, or cultural or political groupings all form part of man's insatiable appetite for social expression. In an organic order, they are essential supports for the perfection of our social nature that enrich the person and the whole social order.

"Parceled Out Sovereignty"

This great sense of autonomy permeated all Christendom and gave rise to multiple levels of authority. In this order, authority is neither absolute nor centralized since there was a "parceling out of sovereignty" all over society.[1] Each one assumes dominion over a domain while integrating and having recourse to that of higher human groups only when necessary.

Where such autonomy rules, each individual assumes an importance and finds meaning in the context of his community. That is why, as Lewis Mumford explains, "The medieval social order could not be completely mechanized or depersonalized because it was based, fundamentally, upon a recognition of the ultimate value and reality of the individual soul, a value and a reality that related it to equally identifiable groups and corporate associations."[2]

It is an order where everyone knows how to fight for their own legitimate rights with great energy against an intruding higher or lower order. While this fight for rights may seem very intense and even disorderly, it is in reality a superficial fight since it tends to consolidate rather than destroy order in society. A nation where everyone fights for their legitimate rights is a strong nation, not a weak one.

Such a decentralized system creates a healthy society that is layered with personal authority yet bristling with those meaningful and intense associations where an individual belongs to several orders at the same time and is, in the multiple contexts of community, at once both sovereign and subject.

---

1. Marc Bloch, *The Growth of Ties of Dependence,* vol. 1 of *Feudal Society,* trans. L. A. Manyon (Chicago: University of Chicago Press, 1961), xvii. Bloch notes that historian Henri de Boulainvilliers (1658-1722) and the philosopher Montesquieu singled out this decentralized "parceling out of sovereignty" to small and still smaller local authorities as a central characteristic defining feudal society. Such sovereignty would, of course, be limited and relative in smaller social units, following the principle of subsidiarity.
2. Mumford, *Pentagon of Power,* 2:141.

Principle of Authority as Coordinator

This complementary interplay of authority and vital flux differs completely from modern conceptions of authority as being despotic and tyrannical. Leaders must lead based on perceptions of what society needs and where it wants to go. Those manifesting the vital flux have every right to defend themselves should they be forced to act in a contrary manner. Either social bodies have authority that is born of internal coordination of this sort, or order becomes impossible.

Rather than just wielding a firm hand, a ruler's principal function is to be a coordinator of autonomous social groups, a chief of minor rulers. He must not suppress the vital flux of his people but encourage it. He should respect each inferior authority and intervene in their affairs but little. So it was that the medieval monarch, with his limited powers and delegation of authority, knew how to distill the best from the vital flux coming from below and in so doing became himself its most sublime manifestation.

As historian Roland Mousnier confirms: "Normally the king does not interfere in his subjects' affairs. He is content to watch over the observation of the good rules and customs that have become established. If public safety is at stake, he may intervene in the sphere of his subjects' rights, but only temporarily."[8]

"Authority is not a power which is imposed upon a community from the outside; it rests upon the will of the group, represents it, thinks and acts in its place. Through authority society moves toward its goal and strives for development and perfection," writes Fr. Wilhelm Schwer, professor of Christian social theory. He later continues: "Saint Thomas regards authority as the animating and ordering intelligence, the *vis regitiva* which overcomes the resistance of the individual tendencies in the human being and directs his will toward the common good and coordinates it organically into the structure of the universe."[9]

There are times when the harmonizing effort exercised by authority is so intense that the leader must take upon himself the role of a servant of those whom he directs. He must selflessly dedicate himself to serving the common good. It is not without reason that the Pope re-

---

8. Roland Mousnier, *Society and State*, vol. 1 of *The Institutions of France under the Absolute Monarchy 1598-1789*, trans. Brian Pearce (Chicago: University of Chicago Press, 1979), 665.
9. Schwer, *Catholic Social Theory*, 141.

serves for himself the august title *Servus Servorum Dei*—servant of the servants of God.

The Principle of Subsidiarity

A society with authority and vital flux is one of an immensely rich social life. Every family, social group, profession, region, and State tends to gather together under natural leaderships to address the needs so proper to our social nature. Each unit produces by custom and good sense that which it is capable of producing. It makes use of all its riches, beauties, and resources. It is only in this context that we can observe the proper practice of the principle of subsidiarity.

By this principle, a social unit should have recourse to a higher unit or authority only in those matters it is unable to handle. The higher societies are *subsidiary* to the lesser and exist to serve them. "A community of a higher order should not interfere in the internal life of a community of a lower order, depriving the latter of its functions, but rather should support it in case of need and help to coordinate its activity with the activities of the rest of society, always with a view to the common good."[10]

The State should thus leave to the family those tasks that are proper to it. The community should seek help from the State in those matters such as defense that are beyond its capacities. National, state, or local professional organizations should take care of the matters proper to each.

Many, both on the Left and Right, have simplified the principle of subsidiarity to mean that all functions must be reduced almost exclusively to the lowest possible level. They do not consider the role of vital flux and authority and would artificially impose upon all an almost village economy or government. Such a "subsidiarity" without governing layers of intermediary associations is a sterile one where there are but two main players: the primitive social unit and the all-powerful State.

Nation of Vibrant Little Nations

It is only by maintaining the delicate balance between authority and vital flux that small, medium-size, and large human groups form. From those groups, a sovereign would structure a nation of vibrant little na-

---

10. John Paul II, *Centesimus Annus*, no. 48.

tions—a marvelous mosaic of associations, parliaments, and hierarchies.[11] It is from the order of these intermediary groups—vibrant little nations—that the State draws its own powers of order and citizens derive protection from the abuses of government.

This social order is in reality an order of orders. Yet each order of this almost haphazard hierarchical society is similar to the others since each refines that which it receives from the vital flux below and adapts the guiding influence it receives from above. Individuals see in the levels above and below them something of themselves that allows them to belong simultaneously and proudly to a family, clan, region, and nation without surrendering their individuality.

We might even say that it is also a providential order since both authority and vital flux come from God in His Providence Who, while ever mindful of man's free will, disposes things to direct all creatures to their proper end. When men cooperate with the grace of God and respect both authority and vital flux, they come to discern the designs of God and act accordingly.

When society is organized in this manner, it naturally creates ties of solidarity between men. By the vast array of interactions between individuals, men come to sense the common nature that all share and more easily manifest mutual concern and support for others. As a result, this principle of solidarity awakens in souls the fire of charity towards others, and tempers the restless spirit of frenetic intemperance.

Such is the society shaped by Christian civilization.

With autonomy and authority, each individual is not a self-governing grain of sand, but acts like a local sovereign who inserts himself into the community. With vital flux, each person is not a passive participant in society, but a dynamic part of its progress. With subsidiarity, all fits together in harmony. Hence, we seek a decentralized society where each person or association finds its autonomous organic expression in an atmosphere of mutual trust, loyalty, and solidarity that resembles an immense family.

---

11. See Plinio Corrêa de Oliveira, American Studies Commission meeting, Jan. 25, 1988, Corrêa de Oliveira Documents.

The Wedding Meal at Yport by Albert Auguste Fourié (1854-1937). A wedding is more than just a social celebration; it is also a major economic event. It signals the entry of a new entity into economy that naturally favors balanced production and consumption, and sees children as blessings, not burdens.

CHAPTER 27

The Spirit of the Family

I t is only logical that the heart and soul of economy is found first in the family. There can be no organic social order without this most basic unit of society. No institution better applies the ordering principles of autonomy, authority, vital flux, solidarity, and subsidiarity. No social body establishes ties of solidarity that so restrain man's intemperance and prevent him from becoming part of the masses. No other influence extends itself farther throughout society.

The Most Basic Institution

Although the modern world has glorified the individual, we can have no illusions. Isolated man accomplishes very little by himself. It is upon man in association with others that a civilization is built.

That is why the family is so important. The family is the first and most basic social, political, and economic unit without which the State would cease to exist and society would fail to perpetuate itself.

It is to this institution that we now turn. Since both society and economy began around the hearth of the traditional family, it is to the family, with the father as its head and the mother as its heart, that we must return to be regenerated.

The Family Spirit

It is not just the physical existence of the family that we seek. We need the spirit of the family. That is to say, the family is able to communicate an atmosphere of temperance and balance that particularly addresses our present needs.

It does this by creating the ideal psychological conditions for individuals to develop. The family at once limits, yet challenges. It succors, yet makes demands. Inside its climate of intense affinity, affection, and stability, a person can develop a colossal self-sufficiency. At the same time, the individual comes to have a great dependency on the family to provide both support for shortcomings and incentives to excel.

Family members share qualities and appetites, defects and disordered passions. Yet the family, especially the large family, is also rich in solutions since the individual draws upon family traditions, past figures serving as role models, and corrective or counterbalancing traits from the two family lines to hold defects in check. The family is the home of the moral and social virtues. In this way, the family is a veritable school of temperance that provides a practical formation that theoretical teaching cannot supply.

The Marvelous Harp

The family provides temperance. By governing man's natural appetites in accordance with right reason, the family restrains those yearnings for pleasures and delights that most powerfully attract the human heart. It not only bridles the passions, but it allows man to properly enjoy legitimate marvels and delights.

To use the comparison of Plinio Corrêa de Oliveira, we might liken our experience of the world to a harp with a universe of marvelous notes created by God to be enjoyed by men. The quality of the notes depends upon how each of us plays our own harp.[1]

When we practice intemperance, we are dominated by stress, nervousness, or obsessions that distort and warp the sound of the notes. The family introduces elements of temperance and control that allow us to play the notes correctly and hear all the marvels of harmony our harps have to offer. This temperate "playing" of the harp in accordance with the plan of God is where each one discovers the true joys of life and ultimately develops an appetite for Heaven.

The Stability of Generations

We must be very clear as to what we mean by "family." When speaking of the traditional family, we must see it as more than just the sum of living members composed of a father, mother, and children. Throughout history, the family has always been understood to mean the unity of the whole lineage of ancestors and descendants.

It was only with the Enlightenment that this universally held belief

---

1. Plinio Corrêa de Oliveira, American Studies Commission meeting, Mar. 1, 1989, Corrêa de Oliveira Documents.

was called into question. Jean Jacques Rousseau takes his individualism so far that he holds that children "remain attached to the father only so long as they need him for their preservation. As soon as this need ceases, the natural bond is dissolved."[2] Such views form the foundation of modernity where the family is increasingly regarded as a mere convention and the individual is made to reign supreme.

Our model does not refer to this modern mutilation of the family, which dissolves at adulthood or death. Rather, in the words of Msgr. Henri Delassus, the family is "one and continuous," containing the "whole lineage of ancestors and that of the descendants who would come in the future."[3]

Preserving the Continuity of the Family

That is why in pre-modern times, the family took measures to ensure a continuity that spanned the centuries. Family members became trustees who shared not only a common blood of heredity, but a common spiritual and material inheritance that each generation must hold as a sacred trust to be safeguarded and increased.

The Christian family, regardless of social class, naturally developed many variations of institutions such as primogeniture and entail where family goods and property could be preserved undivided. In most cases, the principal heir had the demanding obligation to preserve the family estate, keep alive the memory of the family's past, endow brothers and sisters, care for parents and relatives in misfortune, and guarantee the livelihood of descendants. In this way, the family served as a powerful and affectionate social safety net, providing so many of the services that later fell to the cold detached modern State.

Such concepts make the family more than just a single relationship; it is an institution uniting personalities, property, names, rights, prin-

---

2. Rousseau, "Social Contract," in *Rousseau*, vol. 38 of *Great Books of the Western World*, 387. Such Rousseauan ideas that would seem to reduce family relationships to those of the animals circulated widely at the time of our nation's founding. We find, for example, figures like Thomas Jefferson affirming that every generation must create itself anew since the earth belongs always to the living generation. Reflecting the strong influence of Rousseau, Jefferson asserts: "Every constitution then, and every law, naturally expires at the end of 19 years. If it is to be enforced longer, it is an act of force, and not of right." Richard K. Matthews and Elric M. Kline, "Jefferson Un-Locked: The Rousseauan Moment in American Political Thought," in *History, on Proper Principles: Essays in Honor of Forrest McDonald*, eds. Stephen M. Klugewicz and Lenore T. Ealy (Wilmington, Del.: ISI Books, 2010), 141-42.
3. Henri Delassus, *L'Ésprit Familial dans la Maison, dans la Cité, et dans l'État* (Cadillac, France: Éditions Saint-Remi, 2007), 99. (American TFP translation.)

ciples, and histories. Husband and wife are responsible for each other and their family to such an extent that divorce becomes inconceivable. Because it furthers the well-being of all society, it is in the interest of the State to favor this notion of the family and its continuity—and not burden it with inheritance taxes.[4]

This concept of continuity can also apply to professions that "run in the family." From this, we can also see veritable dynasties of carpenters, teachers, soldiers, doctors, or statesmen who carry on the family tradition and talents towards perfection.

Finally, the continuity and unity transmitted by Christian traditions are expressed in family sentiments, morals, and customs. "Yet of greater import still is spiritual heredity," states Pius XII, "which is transmitted not so much through these mysterious bonds of material generation as by the permanent action of that privileged environment that is the family."[5]

This impressive stability and continuity must be our goal.

The Family as a Factor of Economic Balance

It is only natural that we turn to the family as a remedy for our economic woes. We must recall that a wedding is more than just a social celebration; it is also a major economic event. It signals the entry of a new entity into economy that naturally favors balanced production and consumption. By its very nature, the family expands the economy by celebrating the coming of life since children are seen as blessings, not burdens. The family as an economic entity tends to create patterns of production and consumption different from the individualist patterns of today.

"The central feature of the 'rationality' underlying the family economy is the fact that its productive activity was not governed primarily by the objective of maximizing profit and achieving a monetary surplus," note Peter Kriedte et al.[6] Rather, they affirm of the family that "production was dominated by the producers' desire

---

4. In this regard, Pius XI affirms: "The natural right itself both of owning goods privately and of passing them on by inheritance ought always to remain intact and inviolate, since this indeed is a right that the State cannot take away." Pius XI, *Quadragesimo Anno*, no. 49.
5. Pius XII, "1941 Allocution to the Roman Patriciate and Nobility," in *Discorsi e Radiomessaggi di Sua Santità Pio XII* (Vatican: Tipografia Poliglotta Vaticana, 1941), 363-66. (American TFP translation.)
6. Kriedte, Medick, and Schlumbohm, *Industrialization before Industrialization*, 41.

for consumption and for satisfying their needs."[7]

Thus, the traditional family is at once capable of great acts of labor and leisure. When necessary, the family unites and works arduously to achieve great production. When needs are satisfied, the traditional family knows how to temper its arduous labor with balanced consumption that favors an intense social life. The medieval calendar, for example, was filled with holy days and seasonal work schedules that allowed ample time—often as much as half the year—for leisure, celebration, and worship that foster the whole development of man.[8]

Industrialization quickened the pace of life and undermined the patterns of consumption and production of the family economy. With the breakdown of traditional society and its home-based labors, workers flocked to the new factories for employment. Initially, the factory system (with machines that could not be idle) introduced long work schedules, suppressed religious holidays, and regimented work at subsistence wages. While this system did eventually produce more abundance and increased worker income, it also introduced new patterns of consumption and production that favored the restless spirit of frenetic intemperance.

Family and Money

While a basic social unit, the traditional family is also an economic powerhouse. At the same time, the family economy is best noted for its self-sufficiency and limited use of money. The mother does not charge for the preparation of the family meal; the father is not paid to maintain the family home. Although such tasks have great value, they are not part of the market. Inside the traditional family, money plays a limited role and, in the spirit of subsidiarity, tends to be a means to satisfy those needs that can only be filled outside the family.

Permeation of Family Spirit

When this traditional family as an institution is restored, then we will see its spirit permeate all society. Sir Alexander Gray notes that the implicit motivation for all medieval economic dealings can be found in

---

7. Ibid., 65.
8. See Juliet B. Schor, *The Overworked American: The Unexpected Decline of Leisure* (New York: Basic Books, 1991), 47. Professor Schor reports average work years of 120 days for medieval peasants, 175 days for servile laborers, and 180 days for farmer-miners.

this thought: "We are brothers and should behave as brothers, respecting each other's rights and position in life."[9]

When all are brothers in varying degrees by blood, and spiritual brothers in Baptism, the temperate structures of family tradition protect men from cut-throat competition and the frenzied "process of creative destruction." The predatory influence of usury is lessened since many have recourse to the family in times of need.

The traditional family likewise offers solutions to the problem of the concentration of wealth. It is a unit that produces and concentrates incredible wealth. However, it also constantly distributes wealth directly to its children by inheritance or indirectly to other families by marriage. Such circumstances promote healthy and gradual accumulation of wealth.

Leo XIII speaks of the family as a social matrix when he states that "the family may be regarded as the cradle of civil society, and it is in great measure within the circle of family life that the destiny of the States is fostered."[10] Hence, we see the spirit of the family mirrored in the associations, guilds, and communities, which in fact came from the family. That is why medieval society gave so much importance to these intermediary bodies—they were extensions of the family.

At the French Revolution's National Assembly, one delegate in his rage called for the abolition of guilds and other intermediary societies in favor of the omnipotent State, acknowledging that "the moment one enters a corporation or particular society, one must have it as a family. But the state must retain the monopoly of all affections and all obedience."[11]

These intermediary bodies are not actual families but associations with their proper characteristics and ends. Nevertheless, they are receptive to the temperate spirit of the family, which radiates its benevolent influence outwards in permeating guilds, universities, and other intermediary bodies with loose family-like ties. Even small towns and cities can come to have an extended family-like atmosphere since all become in some way related. Finally, we might say that this same family spirit has such a capacity to absorb and integrate that everyone in a region, even outside elements, eventually shares a common family-like

---

9. Alexander Gray, *The Development of Economic Doctrine* (New York: John Wiley and Sons, 1965), 35.

10. Leo XIII, encyclical *Sapientiae Christianae* (1890) in *The Papal Encyclicals*, vol. 2, p. 221, no. 42.

11. Dempsey, *Functional Economy*, 123. Originally quoted in *Social Justice Review* (Mar. 1941): 383.

mentality, temperament, and affection. We can say that a person from the South, for example, participates in the great "Southern family" or, to extend the analogy further, in our greater American family.

The Family Spirit and the State

This family spirit permeated the truly Christian State, which assumed images and customs by which "people soon began to conceive of the State as a kind of family."[12] The Christian State came to be governed with great family-like affection and even by families themselves.

This sentiment of affection is actually a most important element of union for the State. Constitutions, laws, and institutions may be indispensable unifying elements, but the most vital of all is family-like affection, without which the State is doomed to be divided against itself.

Alas, so many modern states glory in their divisions! They are divided by political parties, factions, or intense economic competition. They should rather seek glory in uniting social groups, factions, and parties. In Christian civilization, from top to bottom, all strove to create family alliances. Marriages united families, industries, regions, and nations. All sought to perpetuate and permeate society with family sentiment. The result was a true patriotism, which was nothing but this family sentiment and common love of native land writ large and applied to all those in the same country.

A Note on the Guilds

Before finishing our treatment of the family spirit, we would like to add a word about guilds or cooperative ventures. There are those who call for the "return of the guilds" or equivalent structures as part of the solution for our labor and general economic problems. They may be surprised not to see this given top priority in our proposal.

We do not, in theory, oppose the idea. But such a restoration presupposes a return to the family spirit. The old guilds were built upon intensely personal relationships like that of the master-apprentice, which can only be understood in the context of the family spirit. A guild or cooperative devoid of this spirit will not regenerate labor or give us the solutions we need.

---

12. Georges Duby, ed., *Revelations of the Medieval World*, vol. 2 of *A History of Private Life*, trans. Arthur Goldhammer (Cambridge: Harvard University Press, Belknap Press, 1988), 17.

The Guild and the Family Spirit

While the guilds were not families per se, they did complement many family functions. They were associations of a providential nature that looked after the spiritual and temporal interests of their members, providing old age and sick pensions, pensions for widows, and burial funds. We see them caring for the children of deceased members while arranging for Masses to be offered for the repose of their souls. They also helped poor members with loans and medical assistance.

In their trades, members worked together as brothers, regulating their crafts, sharing raw materials, establishing ample holidays, and fostering close employee relationships. Guilds were self-governing, making their own rules regulating competition among themselves and setting quality standards to such a point that they prevented intrusion by local or central government. Were it not for their family spirit, this extensive self-regulation could easily have turned into a stifling attack upon free enterprise.

Guilds were also profoundly religious associations forming confraternities that celebrated the patron saint's day with great festivities. They would maintain chapels in their parish churches, perform charitable works, and participate in public ceremonies. Participation in the "town's procession in honor of the patron saint or the Virgin Mary," writes Carlo Cipolla, "was as important as, if not more important than, a discussion of wages and production."[13]

When guilds were filled with the family spirit, they were sources of temperance inside society. They were braking mechanisms that kept in balance the captains of industry of that time. They were buffers against the power of intrusive government.

Loss of Family Spirit

By the end of the Middle Ages, the guilds began to lose this family spirit. They also succumbed to frenetic intemperance. They lost the brotherly solicitude for one another. Religious fervor, so essential to temperance, diminished. They lost the family-like flexibility and adopted rigid and excessive control over members and trade technology.

Historian Joel Mokyr reports that, "It may well be the case that by

---

13. Cipolla, *Before the Industrial Revolution*, 94.

the sixteenth century town guilds had begun to stifle technological progress to protect their monopolistic position and vested interests."[14] Some guilds became extremely rich and entered into the frantic pace of the money economy.

Even in this state, the guilds still retained something of the family spirit. The enemies of Christian order saw in that remnant the embers of a flame that might rise anew. For this reason, the French Revolution and later other governments ruthlessly banned guilds.

In modern times, many have proposed that we repeat the success of the old guilds—yet without family spirit. Some confuse the spirit of Christian charity with that of socialist "fraternity." They propose caricatures of the guild model whereby workers would unite into secular councils to organize production or form self-managing teams. Guild socialism, corporatism (especially its fascist form), and other such movements would end up putting guilds under State control.

Because they are much closer to the worker, such guilds without the family spirit can potentially control the production and lives of their members much more intensely than a remote socialist government. Either a guild master is a father figure, or he easily becomes a tyrant.

That is why any return of the guilds must be done very carefully.

Even in its present state, the family is so important that everything should be done to protect it since it is the seed for a future restoration. At the same time, some might object that a proposal to return to the Christian family spirit is meaningless since it is the work of generations and grace. They might claim that this proposal cannot provide solutions needed right now.

We will readily admit that this regeneration is not immediately possible. The creation of the family itself is a long and continuous process. One cannot instantly create a guild imbued with family spirit. Moreover, the building up of a true family spirit encompassing a whole community would involve an intense melding process of families, mentalities, and temperaments over generations. Without such

---

14. Mokyr, *Lever of Riches*, 77.

groundwork, the mere fact of gathering together families—even very traditionally minded and Christian families—in a locality or village will not guarantee real community.

A much more immediate solution must be found.

CHAPTER 28

The Misunderstood Feudal Bond

A n immediate solution must be found beyond the family. While the family is a tremendously vital force for the individual, it is not a perfect society. It alone will not suffice. A regime of separate and scattered families cannot normally sustain itself in face of life's uncertainties.

To develop themselves fully, families and individuals need to draw upon the talents, services, and protection of others outside the family. They need to reach out beyond the family to engage in intense relationships that broaden horizons and expand their means of action throughout all society.

This is especially true in time of crisis. The inadequacy of the family becomes evident by the mere size of the problems that dwarf the family and its resources. This is compounded in our days by the self-imposed isolation of the individualist who, being alone, is even more limited in finding solutions.

PERFECT AND IMPERFECT SOCIETIES

We say that the family is an imperfect society not in the sense that it is defective. Rather, the family is an imperfect society from a sociological perspective, because it depends upon other social units to exist and function. Thus, the family requires higher bodies to guarantee peace and order, justice and protected rights, or security and defense. Other imperfect societies include municipalities, companies, or professional organizations.

In this sense, the State is a perfect society since it is complete in its own sphere and does not depend upon any other society to fulfill its functions. Likewise, the Church is a supernatural perfect society since She contains within Herself all which is necessary to carry out Her functions. The Church and the State are the only truly perfect societies.

What We Need

At the present juncture, what we need are strong bonds that are similar to, yet go beyond, those of the family. These ties should reach throughout society from top to bottom and create reciprocal social relationships that provide protection, trust, and leadership. They should give rise to numerous intermediary associations. And all this must be done quickly.

We can find these needs filled in a bond that was both the foundation of the medieval Christian social order and the fullest expression of its family spirit. This bond was the feudal bond.

Understanding a Misunderstood Bond

Such an affirmation may appear shocking. Obviously, we neither propose a return to a historical application, nor insinuate that this is the only relationship possible under the circumstances. We merely state that this often misunderstood bond proved extremely useful in similar situations in the past and could prove helpful in finding solutions in our own times.

True to its organic origins, the feudal bond was not a rigid formula but a highly adaptive relationship. Even the concept of "feudal bond" must be understood in a very broad sense. Simply put, it was a mutually beneficial relationship within the rule of law where the stronger sought service and the weaker sought protection inside the context of an intensely family-like relationship.

The feudal bond involved a wide variety of applications that ranged from the more formal bonds of vassalage and fealty down to varying ties of protection, apprenticeship, or tenancy. The diversity of such organic ties was such that it defies the efforts of today's scholars to define them precisely. That is why any general treatment of the topic must deal only with the basic characteristics of the bond itself and not the diverse feudal systems it generated.

At the same time, we cannot idealize this relationship beyond the reality of what actually existed in those hard and turbulent times. Like all things in this vale of tears, we readily admit that the feudal bond had its problems and abuses. It could impose obligations and restrictions upon the parties that were at times heavy.

Nevertheless, we cannot go to the extreme of those who would reduce this bond only to its abuses and equate it with a kind of organized banditry. These critics commonly portray the bond as a unilateral and absolute relationship without foundation in law. They neglect to mention that this bond brought order to society by providing "protection in exchange for service, arranged on a contractual basis," states M. Stanton Evans. "This point is made by all authorities on the era, who note that feudal agreements were reciprocal in nature, and had to be respected on both sides."[1]

Thus, our task is to go beyond such distortions. We will describe the characteristics of this bond and then see if its unifying principles might be adapted to our purposes.

DEFINING THE MISUNDERSTOOD FEUDAL BOND

The feudal bond is any of a broad range of mutually beneficial relationships within the rule of law that bind individuals together in society from top to bottom. It is characterized by one party that seeks protection and another that seeks service. It often involved the distribution of land and offices in return for these services. It is an intensely flexible and personal bond beyond the family yet inside a family-like context. It is a sacred Christian bond permeated by charity and built upon trust and mutual responsibility, generating stable forms of community and leadership. Such bonds give rise to their own structures, protocols, and hierarchies suited to the times.

A Practical and Flexible Bond

The first characteristic was the fact that *the feudal bond was a flexible bond especially in times of crisis*. It arose during a period of chaos and barbarian invasions before the ninth and tenth centuries when families and individuals were overwhelmed by the nearly insurmountable obstacles of surviving amidst the disorder. We might liken the emergence of the feudal bond to the case of a shipwreck. The survivors can no longer function as isolated individuals or families but must forge new relationships to survive.

Born of necessity, desperation, and improvisation, this bond of mu-

---

1. Evans, *The Theme Is Freedom*, 169.

tual dependency suddenly emerged, providing stability, leadership, and direction. It was a tremendously creative bond that got things done quickly and found unimaginable practical solutions on a local level in an age of decaying central authority, social unrest, and economic stagnation. "Feudal government . . . was flexible and adaptable," writes Joseph Strayer, "and under favorable conditions it generated new institutions with surprising rapidity."[2]

A Family-like Relationship

The feudal bond was an extremely personal relationship imbued with the family spirit. In fact, the institution began when desperate families entered the households of local leaders who led them in the fight for survival from barbarian invasion and social strife. Historian Franz Funck-Brentano notes that, in this way, a relationship was formed "whose members are identified one with another, like those of the same family when there is question of joy or sorrow."[3]

Unlike the cold bureaucratic relationships that bind modern man to abstract corporate and governmental structures, the feudal bond was extremely personal. In the widespread feudal bond of vassalage, for example, the vassal freely put himself under his lord whom he treated with all the duties and sentiments of a son to a father to whom he owed affection, counsel, aid, and fidelity. On his part, the lord was like a father obliged to give protection, help, security, and means of support. Each party, in its great need, was forced to appeal for help and resources beyond that of his own family. As a result, this forged bond was so strong that it often "was comparable to, and frequently stronger than, the solidarity of the kinship group."[4]

In the misunderstood feudal bond, there is an extremely practical application of the principle of subsidiarity where one appeals to higher authority for one's needs, and the superior delegates the rule of lands and offices to those in his service. In this way, sovereignty is parceled out at all levels, and a nation of vibrant little nations is formed.

---

2. Joseph R. Strayer, *Western Europe in the Middle Ages: A Short History* (New York: Appleton-Century-Crofts, 1955), 75.
3. Franz Funck-Brentano, *The Middle Ages*, trans. Elizabeth O'Neill (New York: G. P. Putnam and Sons, 1923), 11.
4. David Herlihy, ed., *The History of Feudalism* (New York: Walker, 1971), 69.

Generalized from Top to Bottom

The feudal bond was a generalized bond. We note that this intense family-like and hierarchical relationship existed in varying degrees
throughout all levels of medieval society—not just among feudal lords.
In fact, any individual could be at once both servant and master. These
multiple bonds actually set the standard for unifying society beyond
mere family and clan-like ties.

French historian Marc Bloch affirms that the feudal bond actually
permeated all medieval culture from "the highest to the humblest," embracing all classes and groupings. Moreover, he claims that mention
of this relationship whereby one man became the "man" of another is
among the expressions "more widely used or more comprehensive"
during the medieval period.[5] Likewise, historian Roland Mousnier confirms that bonds of fealty bound men together from top to bottom all
the way to the French Revolution.[6]

Contrary to Hobbes' "war of every man against every man," it was a
society full of associations linking every man to another man.

Establishing Friendship Not Hatred

While there were exceptions, *the feudal bond tended to generate ties of
great friendship.* Those who swore such bonds, Bloch notes, were addressed as "friend" to the point that "friend" and "vassal" were considered synonymous. There was a true linking together of lives, a great
interpenetration of interests and ideas.

In general, feudal bonds were bonds of deep sentiment based on
mutual affection and the free choice of one who put himself under the
protection of the other. It was not a mere economic contract but a giving of self whereby the individual gave devoted service, counsel, and
great dedication. The superior gave affection, trust, livelihood, and advancement. He looked after the other's welfare, helped arrange and
endow marriages, and gave protection. It was a truly paternal relationship where the greater perceived opportunities and sought the growth
and advancement of the lesser. Just as a father does not see his son as
a rival, he does not see the lesser as a competitor.

In this atmosphere of trust and confidence, touching manifestations

---

5. Bloch, *Growth of Ties of Dependence,* 1:145.
6. See Mousnier, *Society and State,* 1:99.

of affection flowed both ways between the two parties, even to the point that both were disposed to die for the other or the family of the other, in this way recalling the teaching of Our Divine Savior: "Greater love than this no man hath, that a man lay down his life for his friends" (Jn 15:13).

This same solicitude can be found in the weaker and more primitive feudal-like bonds like those of servants or tenants. Mousnier relates many cases where the local *seigneur* (lord) appears as a great head of the family and protector of the community. "*Seigneurs* took as godparents for their children their manservants or maidservants, who were drawn from among their peasants. *Seigneurs* signed the marriage contracts of the villagers, stood godfather to the peasants' children, joined in the village festivals."[7] He further explains how they gave advice to local authorities, interceded for the community before the State, protected the communities against invading troops, and gave shelter to the peasants and their cattle in times of danger. They also relieved the hunger of the community in time of dearth.[8]

Mutual Responsibility

It was a bond of mutual responsibility. The strength of this feudal bond leads James Westfall Thompson to observe that "no more intensely personal form of government was ever conceived than that of feudalism, and the cardinal principle of it was mutual responsibility."[9]

That is to say, it was not a unilateral bond of submission, but a highly personal bond in which both parties had to abide by the terms of an agreement as in a partnership with established obligations and limits. From this strong bond, something entirely new was created that integrated ancient barbarian notions of personal loyalty with a Christian order inspired by the Gospel and the desire for Christian charity. The result was a novel yet vast network of personal hierarchical relationships and associations whose intersecting threads wove a formidable social fabric throughout all levels of society.

Above all, it created a class of leaders—true and numerous elites—

---

7. Mousnier, *Society and State*, 1:528.
8. Mousnier concludes, "This is an aspect of life in the *seigneuries* which has necessarily left fewer traces in the records than leases and loans, and it needs systematic study" (ibid., 529).
9. James Westfall Thompson, *Economic and Social History of the Middle Ages: 300-1300* (New York: Frederick Ungar, 1959), 2:705.

who found themselves obliged to govern and seek after the common good. They served to interpret, distill, and direct the impulse of the vital flux of those who solicited their aid. Moreover, this system found a solution for those individuals and families overwhelmed by problems beyond their ability to resolve.

As long as the two parties of this bond remained united, living side by side and sharing life's vicissitudes, this society proved nearly indestructible. Yet, when this bond was broken and the two parties separated, as in the times of the absolutist kings, enmities arose, preparing the ground for revolution and class struggle.

A Social and Sacred Bond

The feudal bond was also a sacred bond. In the ceremony of homage, the two elements of protection and service were symbolically pledged by the superior placing his hands over the other's folded hands. An act of fealty was added whereby the parties swore on the Gospels or relics of the saints to be faithful to one another. Christ and His saints served as witnesses to guarantee its fulfillment.

Hence, these acts transcended mere material advantages since the very salvation of the parties' souls depended upon fulfilling the feudal obligations. In that age of Faith, both parties took the act of fidelity seriously, understanding that a commitment was established that had to be executed with all honesty. By this agreement, each gave to the other the rights and elements to defend themselves against abuses and breach of contract. To break the feudal bond on either part was considered a felony and a dishonorable act, freeing the parties from their oaths of fealty and giving them the right and even the duty to resist.

Such a bonding of mutual trust is inconceivable without the virtues of the Faith. This explains why it is so misunderstood in our secular age. This spiritual bond can only come from a population imbued with the cardinal virtues and the theological virtues of faith, hope, and charity.

Finding Solutions to Problems

In the broad sense, this is the feudal bond reduced to its most basic characteristics. Notwithstanding its human shortcomings, it is a flexible and creative bond inside a family-like relationship. It is a bond that permeated all society from top to bottom generating ties of friendship and mutual responsibility. It is a sacred bond founded upon roots of a religious unity. We find in it the balanced application of autonomy, authority, vital flux, solidarity, and subsidiarity so essential to an organic order. In this bond is found that human element missing from the modern economy of frenetic intemperance.

We might also judge this bond by its fruits. Europe arose from the ruins of antiquity and barbarian invasions with a spontaneously developed, highly decentralized, self-financed, social, military, and economic infrastructure born of a strong family-like bond and religious union that could adapt quickly amid chaos.

One might ask: Does our solution lie in the feudal bond? It would depend upon how these basic characteristics could be adapted to the present circumstances.

We definitely are experiencing the same type of abrupt disintegration of our social fabric that calls for some kind of unifying relationship. We hear the complaint that our society is coming apart with a growing gap between those who succeed and those with less. And yet we have nothing similar to the feudal bond to bridge this gap and unite all in common cause to resolve our problems.

Likewise, if families were overwhelmed by the disintegration of their society in pre-feudal times, how much more are today's isolated individualists vulnerable to being overwhelmed by the multiple crises of our times. In face of the social disintegration that threatens us, we might well look for a "feudal" solution to call us back to order.

CHAPTER 29

A Nation of Heroes

At first glance, it would appear that we do not have the elements to put together a "feudal" solution in face of the impending crisis. As we have already seen, individualism has done much to isolate modern man, who is told he need not depend upon others in the pursuit of happiness. Yet another obstacle is the fact that those who show leadership in society are encouraged in the name of a misguided populism to deny their role as elites. We might also mention the diminished sense of community where reciprocal family-like relationships might take place. The unraveling of our cooperative union has created a state of paralysis that discourages social bonding.

Moreover, we face the seemingly impossible task of seeking not a few leaders but cohorts of leaders and heroes inside society from top to bottom who would take upon themselves the arduous task of seeking the common good. Hence, the circumstances could not be more contrary to our designs. While these obstacles may seem insurmountable, we must recall that a similar breakdown of leadership and community in the past called forth the flexible feudal bonds by which men united, improvised, and dared to find organic solutions.

Calling Forth "Feudal Bonds"

We believe our own lack of leadership, community, and direction can also call forth "feudal bonds." This can happen if, as the intensity of our present crisis increases, we admit our own shortcomings and abandon our individualist notions. Then, our social nature and concrete needs will compel us to look beyond ourselves and our immediate circles and seek others with whom we might unite to address the problems that threaten to engulf us.

When our individualist myths collapse, we will discover the raw materials for our "feudal solution." As in pre-feudal times, we will open our eyes to the surviving structures that still exist. We will find support

A representative character is a person who translates ideals into action and sets the tone for a social group. One example is that of Venerable Pierre Toussaint (1766-1853), a hairdresser whose wisdom and sanctity set a tone for the ladies of New York City's high society whom he served. Another is Col. John W. Ripley, USMC (1939-2008) whose feats and character made him a living legend to his fellow Marines and to all Americans.

in the battered remnants of community that still linger in our culture. More importantly, we will find support in those remaining figures, pacesetters, and true elites with the experience, wherewithal, and skills to get things done, and who already play some social leadership roles.

At the same time, we will see the emergence of new groups of select persons, at all levels in society, who stand out and excel. They will be asked to realize their duty to go beyond self-interest and seek to represent the best of their communities or social groups.

When in the midst of the present crisis all these factors come together, the beginnings of a feudal solution, unlike any of the past, could well be born. But simply having recourse to feudal figures and community structures, whether new or old, is not enough. We do not want the social contract called forth from our cooperative union. Rather, we want those intense family-like bonds that will lead the nation to unite in sacrifice and fuse together in society to face the great challenges that threaten the commonweal.

Representative Characters

Our needs are different from those of feudal times. We do not seek the military chieftains who, in the face of barbarian invasions, took upon themselves the task of resisting barbarian hordes. Instead we seek those figures who take upon themselves the more subtle task of becoming what some sociologists call "representative characters" who, not unlike past feudal figures, are as much a product of society as their own efforts.

As Alasdair MacIntyre writes, such characters "are, so to speak, the moral representatives of their culture and they are so because of the way in which moral and metaphysical ideas and theories assume through them an embodied existence in the social world."[1]

Representative characters take the principles, moral qualities, and virtues desired and needed by their communities and translate them into concrete programs of life and culture. They quickly transform thought into action, doctrine into reality, and tendencies into fashions. That is to say, in our concrete case, these figures must engage themselves in our society in crisis and draw and fuse society together to for-

---

1. MacIntyre, *After Virtue*, 28.

mulate the very essence of a rich social life.

"A representative character is a kind of symbol," write Robert N. Bellah et al. "It is a way by which we can bring together in one concentrated image the way people in a given social environment organize and give meaning and direction to their lives."[2]

WHAT IS A REPRESENTATIVE CHARACTER?

A representative character is a person who perceives the ideals, principles, and qualities that are desired and admired by a community or nation, and translates them into concrete programs of life and culture.

We might point to famous figures like General George Patton or those lesser known people such as self-sacrificing clergy, devoted teachers, or selfless community leaders who draw and fuse society together and set the tone for their communities. Modern culture discourages the idea of representative characters and proposes false and unrepresentative characters that correspond to our mass society.

None Dare Call It Feudal

We believe this can be done since these characters have always naturally arisen in society. Indeed, this has *already been done* because our own history is full of "Washingtonian" figures born of great sacrifice, often in times of crisis.

On a national scale, we can identify those famous statesmen, generals, soldiers, religious figures, artists, professors, businessmen, and so many others who embodied and distilled those admired and sturdy virtues that built our great nation. We might also observe local figures such as extraordinary city leaders, farmers, merchants, police chiefs, and others who made the great sacrifice of entering into authentic public service, treating their employees like family, or taking upon themselves the problems of others.

And why not affirm it? We see not only individuals but families that, over the course of generations, have contributed much to the glory of

---

2. Bellah et al., *Habits of the Heart*, 39.

our nation and its communities and formed what none dare call a framework of traditional elites that is vaguely feudal.[3] Even today some of their family names ring out in positions of leadership and trust.

From Top to Bottom

In face of the present crisis, there are plenty of people who have leadership qualities and succeed fabulously in what they do. There are also plenty of people who need help and direction in dealing with the huge problems we face. What is missing is a way to unite the two groups. We need to regenerate a culture that encourages reciprocal bonds and representative figures to unify the nation and confront the crisis. We need natural leadership rather than the modern obsession for a culture of entitlement turned towards the State.

If such representative figures flourished in our past, we should again desire and encourage these self-sacrificing figures to arise everywhere from top to bottom. Such a society of heroes would reintroduce into the economy those human elements that temper and quell the restless spirit of frenetic intemperance. Each in their field would represent "an ideal, a point of reference and focus, that gives living expression to a vision of life."[4]

Such a recognition would create conditions whereby every family or association could have "legendary" members. That is to say, each would come to have great personages who, by their extraordinary deeds, perfections, or works, would elevate the whole family or group. Their feats would then be told and retold to succeeding generations. We would then see the formation of veritable cohorts of legendary figures at all levels of society. Such heroes are like leaven that rises without special planning, the incredibly fecund product of minds turned heavenward towards perfection.

Some might object that an encouragement of these "heroes" might also lead to bad elites and leaders. As in all things human, this can happen. But one must not forget that, in an organic system, such leaders are much more a product of the society that calls them forth than an imposition of an isolated class or caste. There is an organic connection

---

3. It is what has been called the American paradox of an aristocratic nation inside a democratic State. See Corrêa de Oliveira, *Nobility.*
4. Bellah et al., *Habits of the Heart*, 39.

between leaders and society that forms a whole. Truly representative characters share life's vicissitudes side by side with those whom they represent. When people are virtuous, society generally brings forth virtuous elites.

Beyond Mere Virtue

For these characters to be truly representative, they cannot be just good administrators. They must practice not only common virtue but the extraordinary valor found in those who sacrifice for the common good. It is especially found in those who love their neighbor for the love of God when practicing Christian charity.

We might use the comparison of the Ten Commandments that all must practice and the voluntary evangelical counsels of poverty, chastity, and obedience only for those who seek greater perfection. Our representative characters must practice not just common civic virtue, but a higher degree of civic virtue with the same spirit of detachment, self-sacrifice, and perfection as those who follow the counsels. Society has a natural intuition for these authentic figures, which helps explain their ability to attract. That is why figures like dedicated military officers, self-sacrificing religious leaders, devoted teachers, or selfless statesmen are the stuff of which heroes and legends are made.

Above all, these representative figures serve to set the tone and harmonize society. By their influence, they shape the demand, fashions, and trends of the day—even more effectively than advertising.

Plinio Corrêa de Oliveira likened society to a carillon.[5] The carillon is a large musical instrument consisting of at least twenty-three cast bronze bells often suspended in bell towers and arranged to play music. To apply his metaphor, the carillon is a society or social unit, and each person is a different bell. The representative character can be compared to the *bourdon* or principal bell with the lowest note that sets the tone for the other secondary bells and keeps the carillon on key. From the initial ringing of the *bourdon*, the smaller bells resonate and find their own tone.

---

5. See Plinio Corrêa de Oliveira, American Studies Commission meeting, July 31, 1989, Corrêa de Oliveira Documents.

> ## THE ROLE OF TRUE ELITES IN EVERY SOCIETY
> "Mankind would never have reached the present state of civilization without heroism and self-sacrifice on the part of an elite. Every step forward on the way toward an improvement of moral conditions has been an achievement of men who were ready to sacrifice their own well-being, their health, and their lives for the sake of a cause that they considered just and beneficial. They did what they considered their duty without bothering whether they themselves would not be victimized. These people did not work for the sake of reward, they served their cause unto death" (Ludwig von Mises, *Bureaucracy*, [New Haven: Yale University Press, 1944], 78).

Bourdon Souls

"Setting the tone" means that these representative figures use their insight into the aspirations and vital flux of their social groups to orient and harmonize those around them with advice, direction, and leadership. Their principal function is to create resonance and great harmony inside given social groups. So it is that families, groups, regions, and even historic epochs have their *bourdon* souls who harmonize society and whose note when sounded causes others to resonate and ring out with joy in this great concert known as history.

Thus, in fulfilling their roles at all levels in society, these representative characters manage to fuse "their individual personalities with the public requirements of those roles," an accomplishment that allows them to "demarcate specific societies and historical eras."[6]

The role of being a *bourdon* soul carries a great responsibility. If taken seriously, these figures can be like saving angels succoring others. If they fail to set the right tone, others will find it especially difficult to overcome their challenges and trials, and so the course of history might well change.

Finding Such Souls

Again we emphasize that *bourdon* souls naturally arise and are found all over society. Their role does not necessarily depend upon great

---

6. Bellah et al., *Habits of the Heart*, 40.

virtue or high office. Sometimes through their capacity to influence others, people without any public office or status are able to perceive the model that Providence wants for a family, town, or region and can inspire others in this direction. Such was the case, for example, of Venerable Pierre Toussaint (1766-1853), a slave hairdresser whose wisdom and sanctity set a tone for all the ladies in New York City's high society whom he served. More often than not, they are actual figures of authority such as Saint Louis IX the King of France or Sir Winston Churchill, who, although not a saint, did inspire the best from the English nation and thus set the tone for a whole historical epoch.

Such a telling of history—so irritating to modern egalitarian ears—leads us to conclude that a relatively small number of *bourdon* souls can lead to the flourishing or decadence of societies. We can ask fascinating questions about history by looking back at past figures and pondering their role in the rise or fall of nations. In our time of crisis, we must ask questions no less fascinating.

In our industrial age, the great carillons have been silenced and replaced with the artificial sound of electronic bells, horns, or sirens. So many fake and dissonant "bells" ring out. Where are those who should set the tone for our society today? Can we not awaken the *bourdon* souls to help us in our search for solutions?

How This Might Be Done

It is possible to reawaken these *bourdon* souls. However, we must first re-emphasize that what we desire is these figures in the context of the "feudal bond" discussed earlier—those reciprocal social relationships that generate stability and leadership. We do not seek to impose the feudal structures or hierarchies of the past. By their nature, feudal bonds generate their own structures, protocols, and hierarchies suited to the times. We must also discover our own.

Secondly, let us recall that, historically, representative characters have always existed and played their essential role, especially in troubled times like ours. Such characters do exist today, but a hostile culture prevents them from taking center stage. It is not for us to create them but to recognize and support them. It is not for these figures to deny their role but to embrace it by making sacrifices for the common good. For when this is not done, counterfeits and opportunists take their place. Part of our problem is that we have embraced those *unrepresentative characters* that so dominate our mass culture: media stars, celebrities, and unprincipled politicians.

CALLING FORTH OUR HEROES

1. We must find our own "feudal" formulas, not those of the past.
2. We must reject today's unrepresentative figures: celebrities, media stars, and unprincipled politicians.
3. We must connect with and call forth the heroes among us.

We should connect instead with the heroes that are among us. We need to break out of the individualist model that so isolates us in our own little self-absorbing worlds. We must be open to the re-emergence of reciprocal social relationships (that need not be contractual or commercial) whereby we might have recourse to the influence of those truly representative figures, be they statesmen, employers, teachers, or religious leaders, who, on their part, must have the courage to rise to the occasion. We must be attentive to the sound of the *bourdon* bell to set the tone. Let us once again dare to desire a society with cohorts of legendary figures that come from all ranks to create a nation of heroes.

Such simple measures will prepare the climate for our representative characters—some who are remnants of traditional elites embedded in our own communities, others still to come from the ranks of society—to step forth and help harmonize our nation and improvise with the elements at hand to provide organic solutions. If our society is coming apart, as some claim, it is because no representative characters have come forth to bring us together.

In our materialistic society, we have called forth great technicians, businessmen, and engineers to meet our needs. In our celebrity culture, we have called forth actors, rock stars, and sports figures to entertain us. It is not unreasonable to think that in our hour of great need, we can call forth our representative figures. If we desire them, they will come.

And if these figures be not forthcoming, then we must fall on our knees and beseech God in His Providence to send us saints and holy heroes to deliver us from the present calamities. Just as He in His mercy sent the prophets and His only begotten Son to heed the sighs of Israel, He will send those Charlemagnes, Joans of Arc, and other providential figures to save His people.

CHAPTER 30

A True Idea of the Christian State

I t might seem strange that in a time when all speak out against crushing and intrusive big government that we might propose the State, although a Christian one, as a part of our organic remedy. Popular wisdom has decreed that "the State is the problem, not the solution." At most, some claim, we must tolerate the State as a necessary evil from which we can expect little good.

Such hostile attitudes come from the fact that many see only today's bloated and dysfunctional State and consequently have confused notions of what constitutes society, nation, State, and government.

Making Distinctions

Thus we will begin by clarifying these notions. Society starts with informal groupings of individuals, families, and intermediary associations mostly dedicated to furthering their own individual good. When this collection of social units coalesces into a clearly distinctive whole, a nation is born. The nation forms a cultural, social, economic, and political unity unable to be included or federated into any other one. The goal of this new social unit is no longer only furthering the individual good of each member, but the common good of all. This common good ensures the peace of the community, allows virtuous co-existence, and favors the material and spiritual good of all in the community.

The State is the political organization and order of the nation; its role is to safeguard the common good and facilitate virtuous life in common. The State, therefore, presupposes a people, intermediary associations, territory, and organized political power. The government is the political system and institutions by which the State is administered and regulated.

The end of the State—the ordering of the common good—is qualitatively different from the sum of the goods of the individuals. This is why the State as the form of political life has "a supremacy of mission, power, and, therefore, intrinsic dignity, which is adequately expressed

by the word *majesty*."[1] There is no more perfect *natural* society than
the State, which is a necessary element for the proper functioning of
society. However, the organic State of our proposal could not be more
contrary to the modern State.

Contrast Between the Modern and Organic States

The modern State accomplishes its role by instituting an all-powerful
bureaucratic system of legal norms to safeguard and regulate the private interests of its citizens. The modern State, notes Pius XI, has assumed the overwhelming functions and tasks that were once borne by
intermediary associations. The result was that through the "overthrow
and near extinction of that rich social life which was once highly developed through associations of various kinds, there remain virtually
only individuals and the State."[2]

In contrast, the organic State accomplishes its role by safeguarding
the fundamental principles of morals, civilization, and public order
that are normally lived and defended by its many social units—family,
guild, town, university, or any of a number of privately-formed associations that make up the rich social life of a nation.

A Subsidiary Order

Our proposal of a State is one where the principle of subsidiarity is
practiced to a high degree. As a result, the State respects individual social units oriented towards the common good and recognizes certain
rights, functions, and privileges that allow them their own autonomy,
or even quasi-sovereign rights.

Thus each region develops its own customary laws and traditions.
Each guild, university, or religious association maintains its own way
of self-government and self-regulation. The result is a patchwork of
local authorities at all levels exercising unique powers proper to them.
David Herlihy writes that it is a "kind of partnership in the exercise of
power," a "shared jurisdiction and authority,"[3] which made of the me-

---

1. Corrêa de Oliveira, *Nobility*, 89. "Majesty" comes from the Latin "*major*" meaning "greater." We
use the term to mean the State's greater mission of exercising sovereign power, authority, and
its corresponding dignity, and not in the sense of an absolutist and all-powerful State so idealized in modern times.
2. Pius XI, *Quadragesimo Anno*, no. 78.
3. Herlihy, ed., *History of Feudalism*, 207. "The nature of feudal government," Herlihy states, "excluded all possibility of a true absolutism" (ibid).

dieval State a federation of autonomous social entities—each suited to its own needs, each with immense cultural and social richness, each generating veritable cohorts of legendary figures.

The State—the Protector of the General Order

As the supreme power of last appeal, this organic State gives unity and a framework to this federation. Far from assuming the modern State's monopoly of supreme power, the organic State does not smash or reduce these lesser groups to subservience. Rather, it is the preserver and protector of the overall order upon which they depend. Far from concentrating authority, this State encourages its wide distribution by recognizing authority as it exists in lesser groups so each might accomplish its proper functions more easily.

"The supreme authority of the State ought, therefore, to let subordinate groups handle matters and concerns of lesser importance, which would otherwise dissipate its efforts greatly," writes Pius XI of subsidiarity. "Thereby the State will more freely, powerfully, and effectively do all those things that belong to it alone because it alone can do them: directing, watching, urging, restraining, as occasion requires and necessity demands."[4]

As a result of this "parceling out of sovereignty," there can be no modern masses since there is no single monolithic authority. Each individual conserves a unique character, subject to those overlapping levels of authority that both define and correspond to a special identity, function, and position in society.

Thus, explains Joseph Strayer, "This [medieval] division of authority made absolutism impossible; neither the unlimited power of the Roman emperor nor the equally unlimited power of the modern sovereign state could exist under such circumstances."[5]

Referring to this organic medieval State, M. Stanton Evans notes that "as an abundant record demonstrates, *it was the era of the Middle Ages that nourished the institutions of free government, in contrast to the ideas and customs of the ancients.* Conversely, it was the rejection of medieval doctrine at the Renaissance that put all Western liberties at hazard, leading to autocracy in Europe and despotic practice in the modern era."[6]

---

4. Pius XI, *Quadragesimo Anno*, no. 80.
5. Strayer, *Western Europe in the Middle Ages*, 4-5.
6. Evans, *The Theme Is Freedom*, 150.

Staying within Limits

When the State's sovereign power stays within its limits, less force and money are needed to maintain it. There is, for example, little need for huge budgets, since much of this federation of autonomous associations is in private or quasi-private hands. "Perhaps the most striking character of the feudal State was its almost absolute lack of finances," writes noted medievalist Henri Pirenne of its self-financing character. "In it, money played no role."[7]

Carlo Cipolla notes that administrative expenses of the State in medieval Europe were few and simple. This was because "many administrative tasks continued to be performed by noblemen who—in deference to the principle of *noblesse oblige*—received no salary for their activity."[8]

Striking examples of such self-governance include England's Justices of the Peace who are called even today the "great unpaids," because for nearly 600 years they have undertaken the greater part of the judicial work in England and Wales without compensation.

"Thus, the sworn crafts, like the other corporations of the kingdom, collaborated with the king in legislation, government and administration," writes historian Roland Mousnier about pre-Revolutionary France. "Besides their particular economic function, they fulfilled an increasing number of public functions on behalf of the state, in its place, on its initiative, and under its supervision."[9]

The same author records the existence in France of 70,000–80,000 seigniorial courts that administered public (yet not supreme) justice *at the expense of the local lord*. He reports that on the whole, these courts "provided justice that was equitable, inexpensive, easily accessible, and rapid."[10]

We might also mention that village communities, ruled by their own customs, relieved the State of an important part of the task of local administration by assuming considerable self-governing functions, especially those connected to communal privileges. All of this came at no cost to the State and without the heavy burden of bureaucracy.

---

7. Henri Pirenne, *Medieval Cities: Their Origins and the Revival of Trade*, trans. Frank D. Halsey (Princeton: Princeton University Press, 1952), 225.
8. Cipolla, *Before the Industrial Revolution*, 48.
9. Mousnier, *Society and State*, 1: 472.
10. Ibid., 528.

"All in all, one must admit that the portion of income drawn by the public sector most certainly increased from the eleventh century onwards all over Europe," Cipolla notes, "but it is difficult to imagine that, apart from particular times and places, the public power ever managed to draw more than 5 to 8 percent of national income."[11]

Representative Figures and the State

Likewise, there is little need for big government in the organic State since shared authority is expressed everywhere. In such an atmosphere, representative figures at all social levels play their important role.

In fact, this model of the State relies much more on human relationships than on money contracts. It governs more by influence than by command. It penetrates deeply into society by drawing on the prestige and moral standing of those to whom it delegates its powers. It integrates into the culture, expressing itself in the very human terms of ceremony, pageantry, and legend.

This intensely personal form of government confers a great unity upon society, which rests upon the broad shoulders and prestige of its representative figures and its parceled-out authority. Thus, a State like this becomes not a necessary evil but a great good since it unites and protects individuals and groups so that they might live together with great autonomy and liberty.

The Highest Good

Since the State deals with the common good of all its members, Aristotle and Catholic authors from Saint Augustine onward have long regarded the State as the highest and most important *earthly* form of social union. That is why so many go even to the point of sacrificing their lives for its continuance. A State like this facilitates the practice of the social and political virtues of justice, devotion, allegiance, and sacrifice for the common good. It is, properly speaking, this governing framework that makes it a key part of the heart and soul of economy.

---

11. Cipolla, *Before the Industrial Revolution*, 47. The author further explains: "At the middle of the nineteenth century in most European states, public expenditure still represented only 2 to 6 percent of national income" (ibid., n).

The organic State then gives unity, direction, and purpose to society—embracing but never absorbing, delegating but never concentrating, encouraging but never stifling.

So conceived, this State is a blessing for a community and a guardian of its prosperity and well-being. Since men can only reach their moral perfection in organic connection with a community, it is man's legal and moral duty to belong to the community governed by the organic State. It is to this idea of State that we should return.

CHAPTER 31

The Role of the Church

U pon defining the State as a structure at the heart and soul of economy, we do not hesitate to address the essential role of the Church in this organic order. From our avowedly Catholic perspective, it is natural that we will refer specifically to the role of the Catholic Church. This is all the more so since it was the Church that originally embraced this organic order and inspired organic structures. Thus, by describing how the Church actually fulfilled this role, we make clear why She should be part of the heart and soul of a socio-economic order—an affirmation denied by the radical secularists of our days.

Again, as with the idea of the State, we find popular misconceptions about religion's role in society. There are those who would completely exile religion from social and economic affairs by turning it into the private matter of isolated individuals. To others, the Church as an institution is (or at least should be) a purely spiritual community of love, full of sacramental mystery and fellowship but without projection in the workaday world of economic production and consumption. Still others imagine the Church as a power-seeking institution that wishes to absorb the State and must therefore be contained inside its own sphere.

This confusion over how to resolve the roles of Church and State lies at the root of the Cultural War that so divides America. It is essential, then, that we address this matter directly since it is of utmost importance in any organic order.

Specific Ends and Goals

We must first understand that the Church and the State are both independent perfect societies with specific ends and goals. Each is juridically competent to provide all the necessary and sufficient means to carry out its purpose; each is sovereign in its own sphere.

The Church has as Her immediate and specific purpose the promotion of the supernatural life and the salvation of souls, and, as a secondary and indirect goal, to help the common good of temporal society. And the State has as its specific and immediate end the promotion of the common good and, indirectly and secondarily, to help men to practice virtue and thus attain eternal happiness.

The Church fulfills its purpose by safeguarding the moral order of right and wrong, maintaining Divine worship, and administering the supernatural means of grace to man. The State reaches its end by securing internal and external harmony and peace of society through the use of an external juridical order, favoring conditions for the creation of wealth, and providing for the common defense.

Clearly Defined Roles

With such clearly defined roles, it is evident that the Church does not seek to dominate or absorb the State as some liberals might claim. Actually, more often than not, it has been the State that has sought to absorb or dominate the Church. Tyrannical rulers of all types have tried to subject the Church to their power by establishing state-controlled churches that are turned into subservient departments of the State with their ministers turned into court chaplains.[1]

Throughout its long and glorious history, the Catholic Church has always resisted such attempts by insisting upon Her liberty and independence. She has refused to renounce Her spiritual mission of sanctification, worship, and preaching the Gospel—even to the point of enduring persecution.

A Visible Community of the Faithful

While we acknowledge that the Church's sphere is essentially spiritual, this fact does not change the reality that the Church is a visible community of the faithful. She is a living force, an organized hierarchical institution, and a public forum that projects Her immense influence into society and history.

She is found in the world, the professions, the family, and the State,

---

1. We can cite the present example of Communist China, which tried without success to install the Chinese Patriotic Catholic Association to replace the Catholic Church. We might also mention historic examples such as Henry VIII's establishment of the Church of England, the French Revolution's attempt to subject the Church to its Civil Constitution, and the Russian Orthodox Church's subservience to the czars.

where the Christian works out his salvation by obeying God's laws. By drawing upon twenty centuries of wisdom, the Church must play an active role in the world as She applies moral norms to the concrete historic circumstances that help to orient the spiritual and social life of Christians.

Thus, the Church cannot retreat into an abstract and empty corner of society, a mere psychological support for weak souls with no connection to our industrialized and globalized world.

A Universal Message

No, the Church is ever ancient, ever new. She is older than the nations yet not limited to or under the jurisdiction of any single people. She is both supranational and supernatural, uniting human and divine. She is both Mystical Body of Christ and hierarchical institution; She is in the world, yet not of the world. She has a universal message and mission applicable for all times and places that far outstrips the poor extent of the globalism of our days.

It is this universal Church that insists upon Her role in society to promote the worship of God and teach the moral law and dogmas necessary for sanctification.

Defining Roles

In this way, the Church clearly recognizes as proper to the temporal sphere an enormous range of activities and customs that belong to the natural development of man in society. Among these are the functions of government, the juridical order, the common defense, the mechanics of economy, and the general welfare of the nation. In all matters purely temporal, the jurisdiction of the State over its citizens is supreme.

Yet in moral matters where sin is involved, the Church affirms Her right to intervene in temporal affairs. It is proper for the Church to speak out against injustice and immorality, which is detrimental to all in society. She also engages in charitable activities and works of mercy to alleviate suffering, especially among the poor.

In addition, we must recognize that some activities are shared by both spheres since they involve moral acts that affect both sanctification and the temporal common good. It is inevitable that they should have mutual relations in the juridical order. It is, for example, to the benefit of both societies that the institution of the family be safeguarded. It is natural that in these shared areas the two spheres should work together. Contrary to the modern liberal doctrine, there should be bridges of cooperation instead of Iron Curtains of separation between the two.

Part of the Heart and Soul of Economy

It is in these shared areas that the Church becomes a most important part of the heart and soul of economy. By safeguarding the moral law, the Church provides immeasurable social capital for the free practice of commerce. Her charity binds men together in a higher union hindering them from following only secular ends where they might easily succumb to the lust for power and riches.

The Church has a hallowing influence upon the structures of society and economy. She establishes a high degree of justice so as to prevent the State from abusing its authority and descending to the level of organized banditry. As guardian of the natural and Divine law, the Church helps the State fulfill its functions more perfectly. Where the Church's influence is present in society, there is a beneficent action upon all that prevents the ruin of a nation. Giving a historical example of this positive influence, M. Stanton Evans writes that, "On net balance, it is fair to say, *the Catholic Church of the Middle Ages was the institution in Western history that did the most to advance the cause of constitutional statecraft.* This resulted from its constant readiness, in the spirit of the Hebrew prophets, to challenge the might of kings and emperors if they transgressed the teachings of religion."[2]

The State best fulfills its role when permeated by the Christian spirit, and when the two work together for the common good. This is especially true of the Christian State we have just described.

Leo XIII spoke of this respectful cooperation of Church and State in this way:

> There was a time when the *philosophy* of the Gospel governed the states. In that epoch, the *influence of Christian wisdom* and its divine virtue *permeated* the laws, in-

---

2. Evans, *The Theme Is Freedom*, 152.

stitutions, and customs of the peoples, all categories and all relations of civil society. Then the religion instituted by Jesus Christ, solidly established in the degree of dignity due to it, flourished everywhere thanks to the *favor* of princes and the legitimate protection of magistrates. Then the Priesthood and the Empire were united in a *happy concord* and by *the friendly interchange of good offices*. So organized, civil society gave fruits superior to all expectations, whose memory subsists, and will subsist, registered as it is in innumerable documents that no artifice of the adversaries can destroy or obscure.[3]

CHRISTIANITY GREATLY FAVORS THE WELFARE OF THE STATE

This beneficent action is described by Saint Augustine, who comments:

"Let those who say that the teachings of Christ are harmful to the State find armies with soldiers who live up to the standards of the teachings of Jesus. Let them provide governors, husbands and wives, parents and children, masters and servants, kings, judges, taxpayers and tax collectors who can compare to those who take Christian teachings to heart. Then let them dare to say that such teaching is contrary to the welfare of the State! Indeed, under no circumstances can they fail to realize that this teaching is the greatest safeguard of the State when faithfully observed." ("Epist. 138 ad Marcellinum," [Chap. 2, no. 15]) in *Opera Omnia*, vol. 2, in J.P. Migne, *Patrologia Latina*, col. 532). (American TFP translation.)

Liberal Antagonism

Someone might object that such a happy concord is not possible given the history of our secular State.

To this, we would reply that we find vague echoes of a desire for concord in the writings of the Founding Fathers who, despite their personal beliefs (heavily influenced by deism and the Enlightenment), understood the indispensable role of religion for the nation to prosper.

"Of all the dispositions and habits which lead to political prosperity,

---

3. Leo XIII, encyclical *Immortale Dei* (1885), no. 21. (Emphasis added. American TFP translation.)

religion and morality are indispensable supports," writes George Washington in his Farewell Address.[4] "Religion and virtue are the only foundations, not only of republicanism and of all free government, but of social felicity under all governments and in all the combinations of human society," wrote John Adams to Dr. Benjamin Rush in 1811.[5]

Such patriotic pleas run counter to today's tragic antagonism between Church and State. This hostility is a product of a liberal attitude that refuses to recognize the Church as a perfect society. In its more extreme form, it is based on the Rousseauan idea that all rights come from the people who delegate them to the State, and consequently the Church has no rights, save those conceded to Her by the State. As such, the State has no obligations towards the Church, which must live a separate subordinate existence. And while its more moderate form may be less intolerant of the Church, the logical course of this liberal attitude eventually leads to the hostility and confrontation of our days.

A truly balanced position is that each perfect society should recognize the rights and autonomy of the other, and each should render to the other those obligations that arise from this recognition. Such an association should lead to opportunities for cooperation and not exclusion.

The Crisis in the Church

Someone might further object that the crisis that affects modern society has also had its effect upon the Church, which impedes our having recourse to Her. To support this claim, we need only recall the words of Benedict XVI who, while still Prefect of the Congregation for the Doctrine of the Faith, reminded us of Paul VI's somber pronouncement that the dissent inside the Church had gone "from self-criticism to self-destruction."[6]

This crisis, grave as it is, does not diminish or change the Church's doctrine in these matters. It does not prevent us from drawing upon

---

4. George Washington, "Farewell Address," in *A Compilation of the Messages and Papers of the Presidents*, ed. James D. Richardson (New York: Bureau of National Literature, 1897), 1:205.
5. William J. Federer, *The Ten Commandments & Their Influence on American Law: A Study in History* (St. Louis: Amerisearch, 2003), 20.
6. Joseph Cardinal Ratzinger and Vittorio Messori, *The Ratzinger Report: An Exclusive Interview on the State of the Church*, trans. Salvator Attanasio and Graham Harrison (San Francisco: Ignatius Press, 1986), 29. We might also cite Paul VI's June 29, 1972 allocution *Resistite Fortes in Fide* warning that "the smoke of Satan has entered into the temple of God." *Insegnamenti di Paolo VI*, 10:707-9. (American TFP translation.)

the rich treasures of the traditional Magisterium of the Church to find solutions for today's problems—as we are now doing. It calls us to be cautious when dealing with those who espouse modern errors. Above all, we must confide in God and His Providence because the Church has weathered many storms. Calling upon our Blessed Mother to guide us maternally, the Church will also weather the present storm.[7]

Especially in the present hour of affliction, we would do well to turn to this spiritual sphere. How foolish it is to claim that the Church is detrimental to our development! Economy should regard religion as a great ally. All society benefits when the Church serves as a moral guide, a hallowing influence, and guardian of the law. Above all, we find in the Church a loving Mother, ever provident, ever solicitous, and ever caring.

---

7. See TFP Committee on American Issues, *I Have Weathered Other Storms: A Response to the Scandals and Democratic Reforms That Threaten the Catholic Church* (York, Pa.: Western Hemisphere Cultural Society, 2002).

A Passion for Justice

Stained glass, Notre Dame la Grande Church, Poitiers, France. Saint Louis IX of France became known for his wisdom and fairness while administering justice to all who brought cases to him as he held court at the foot of a great oak tree in Vincennes.

The scales at a marketplace from a fifteenth-century stained glass window, Tournai Cathedral, France. A passion for justice whereby each receives his due helps economy by creating conditions for trust and temperance.

CHAPTER 32

An Organic Economic Order: A Passion for Justice

T he organic social order we have described serves as the foundation for any organic economic model. Inside these social units and relationships, we find those essential constraints that serve to temper the passions that lead to the frenetic intemperance that so burdens us. There is that human element that is missing from the mechanistic mind-set introduced by the Industrial Revolution.

We now turn to the organic economic order itself. We will look at the institutions and unifying principles of this order as they existed in Christendom. Consistent with our organic approach, it is an economic model that adapts to the nature of things. That is to say, it considers man not as *homo economicus*, the man who lives in function of money; rather he is *homo sapiens*, from which comes the English word "sapient" meaning "possessing or expressing wisdom."

A Passion for Justice

Central to our position is the idea that the foundation of any organic economic model is a passion for justice. It is the search for this justice that prevents economics from becoming a means for man to feed his selfish or unbridled passions—or engage in business with frenetic intemperance.

To the medieval mind, economics was not the mere mechanics of commodity exchange where ledgers indifferently registered transactions of need and greed, necessity and luxury, virtue and vice. As we have seen, economic transactions generate relationships that involve moral and ethical actions.

"The subject matter of economics," observes Odd Langholm, "is properly the habits, customs, and ways of thinking of producers, consumers, buyers, sellers, borrowers, lenders, and all who engage in economic transactions."[1] Hence, medieval economic thought was

---

1. Odd Langholm, *The Legacy of Scholasticism in Economic Thought: Antecedents of Choice and Power* (Cambridge: Cambridge University Press, 1998), 183.

especially absorbed with a passion for the cardinal virtue that should govern transactions—justice. "If one word were sought to cover all phases of medieval economic teaching," writes Sir Alexander Gray, "it would probably be found in the idea of 'justice.'"[2]

The Demands of Justice in Economy

Saint Thomas Aquinas defines the virtue of justice as "to render to each one his own."[3] In economic matters, commutative justice is the particular kind of justice that assures that one party will render to another in transactions what is due in strict equality as, for example, when the price one pays for an apple corresponds to its worth.[4]

It is by this justice that we own property. Although the earth was made to be shared by all, because of our fallen nature there arose the need for private property, so that by caring for that which is strictly ours, we preserve the peace and harmony of society. For as Aristotle points out, if property is commonly owned, "complaints are bound to arise between those who enjoy or take much but work little and those who take less but work more."[5]

It is this justice by which we own the fruits of our labor, whether it be wages, fees, profits, or property. This is the basis of free enterprise since each tends to make the most efficient use of his own resources when properly compensated for those efforts. This, in turn, benefits the common good. Saint Albert the Great affirms that "everybody is by nature inclined to pay more attention to what is his own than to what is common; so that if this will be better cultivated it will also grow to good fruition where all are concerned."[6]

Just Price and Markets

This search for justice was the reason why the idea of the just price for essential commodities was one of the central concepts of medieval economy. It held that things had value based on a standard of justice. It is by acting in accordance with this standard that we avoid cheating and taking advantage of others in transactions. Likewise, we see the

---

2. Gray, *Development of Economic Doctrine*, 35.
3. Aquinas, *Summa Theologica*, II-II, q. 58, a. 11.
4. See ibid., II-II, q. 61.
5. Odd Langholm, *Economics in the Medieval Schools: Wealth, Exchange, Value, Money and Usury According to the Paris Theological Tradition 1200-1350* (Leiden: E. J. Brill, 1992), 172.
6. Ibid., 174.

great solicitude to provide a just wage so that those who labor might be rightly compensated for "the laborer is worthy of his hire" (Lk 10:7).

Justice ensures the free flow of markets by protecting them from their great enemies: monopoly, speculation, usury, false advertising, induced scarcity, and other practices that produce fraud or obstructions in commerce. As a result, the Christian State protects the markets with clear rules and severe laws so that healthy competition, free consent in contracts, and transparency in exchange might naturally take place. At the same time, the State avoids undue interference in the markets or excessive taxation. All of this must be governed by a great sense of justice.

"The modern mechanistic conception of the market as a suprapersonal force setting the terms to which an individual exchanger must submit was foreign to the medieval masters," Langholm writes. "Their frame of reference was a moral universe that obliged any buyer or seller to act for the common good and agree to terms of exchange accordingly, regardless of the advantage granted him by the forces of the market."[7]

The Benefits and Dangers of Commerce

While this idea of justice may sound utterly utopian to modern ears, such a concept, as we will see, does not inhibit commerce but greatly favors it.

Commerce is a great good to society since it distributes goods from areas of abundance to those of scarcity, and stores supplies in times of plenty so that they might be sold in times of dearth. It facilitates consumption by bringing goods to convenient markets. Therefore, it is fitting that merchants justly profit from their efforts and skills.

Medieval man recognized that, as in all professions, the merchant's work also presents its dangers. While the merchant's services are indispensable to the welfare of society, he often faces the special temptation of fraud and avarice. He is placed in situations where he can falsify weights and measures, sell defective goods, charge excessive prices to strangers, and a host of other deceptive practices that imperil the merchant's soul, destroy trust, and drag down an economy.

---

7. Langholm, *Legacy of Scholasticism*, 85.

The practice of justice is therefore necessary, so that the merchant, in addition to looking amply after his own welfare, might also be a voluntary servant of the public good, as should be everyone in their various professions. "The purpose of the merchant's profession," medieval moralist Alexander Ariosto states, "should not be the accumulation of wealth, but the support of his household, aid to the poor, or service to the community."[8]

Thus, it is justice and not the market that keeps commerce in check. It demands obligatory restitution in cases of fraud. It creates mutual trust and security, which reduces transaction costs. We will find its mark everywhere in our considerations of organic economy. Justice ties trade to moral actions in favor of the common good and away from exaggerated self-interest and short-term gain. It becomes a braking mechanism that brings equilibrium wherever it is found and prevents unbridled markets from developing into what could later become frenetic intemperance.

The Hand of Prudence

While this passion for justice is the foundation of a good economy, it alone does not suffice. Justice can often become rigid and harsh. Another cardinal virtue must be brought into play to mitigate the demands of justice and rationally apply them to daily life. This virtue is prudence.

Prudence is the virtue whereby man applies right reason to actions.[9] In its natural form, it introduces into economy those norms of experience, common sense, and balance that make economy human, flexible, and practical. For this reason, prudence is also called practical wisdom.

Contrary to modern misconceptions, medieval economy was not bound by a rigid set of moral and dogmatic rules. Rather, there was a refreshing set of balanced and reasonable norms ever respectful of the demands of justice, yet ever mindful of the fragility of our human nature.

---

8. Odd Langholm, *The Merchant in the Confessional: Trade and Price in the Pre-Reformation Penitential Handbooks* (Leiden: Brill, 2003), 192.
9. See Aquinas, *Summa Theologica*, II-II, q. 47, a. 4. "Prudence consists not in thought merely, but in its application to action, which is the end of the practical reason" (ibid., a. 1, ad. 3).

Jewels of Wisdom

In the theological and moral manuals and summas that oriented economic acts of that time, there are jewels of wisdom and prudence that calmly considered man's flexible needs.

For example, the concept of the just price was generally defined by justice as the price for which a good is commonly sold in the market at the time of sale. By the practice of prudence, moralists adjusted this theoretical definition to the concrete circumstances.

It was generally held that just price could not be based upon the intrinsic value of an item since items of immense value to us such as air or water, are abundant yet sell for little. Prudence held that the commercial value of something depends upon a multitude of factors. In fact, it was already generally recognized in medieval times that the just price could not be a precise amount but only an approximation based on wage, risk, utility, custom, and especially demand.[10]

The purpose of determining just price *was not* to serve as an absolute price control system imposed upon merchants. Rather, it was a standard of justice by which transactions might be judged by authorities in case of doubt or fraud. Using this standard, disputes could be resolved; restitution for wrongful gains might be made. It allowed each factor affecting price to be considered and weighed to ensure the health of the market.[11]

Moreover, the just price did not destroy the nature of the free market by depriving man of his ability to bargain. Actually, the norms left merchants free to haggle and bargain within one-half of the just price without offending the demands of justice. Furthermore, necessities enjoyed the protection of just price while luxuries received no such protection.

Moralists dealt with the obligations of the merchant to point out major defects in merchandise to avoid fraud. On the other hand, the merchant was not required to highlight *obvious* defects since by his

---

10. The confessional manual of Godescalc Rosemondt lists eight ways by which just price might be determined: "First, by reference to the common estimate by merchants who deal in the same good or in similar goods; second, to what the good in question is usually sold for; third, to labor, industry, care and expenses incurred in transport; fourth, to risk; fifth, to the volume and variety of such goods or their scarcity; sixth, to improvement and storage; seventh, to their usefulness to the community; and eighth, to legal statutes and custom." Langholm, *Merchant in the Confessional*, 98.

11. Alejandro Chafuen observes that the just price was always much more a rigorous moral judgment than a legal standard. The range of the legal just price was much wider than that of the moral just price. This is yet one more proof that the just price theory was not rigid and inflexible. See Alejandro A. Chafuen, *Faith and Liberty: The Economic Thought of the Late Scholastics* (Lanham, Md.: Lexington Books, 2003), 86.

emphasis he might deprive himself of its just price. In another case, he might sell a product at today's price knowing well that a new shipment would be arriving tomorrow and therefore make the price lower. He did not need to inform the buyer since he commits no injustice in charging the current price. When there was no usual price for a product, the seller was to ask a wise man, an experienced merchant, or a priest for advice as to what the just price might be. At other times, custom established just price as that which had always been.

Such flexible and simple norms found their way into a thousand economic customs and laws that bowed to our frail human nature and the local circumstances, so that man might more easily practice justice. Such prudence leads to markets with little outside interference. Langholm concludes: "A local market, functioning more or less normally, provides its own justice, even as prices vary."[12]

This self-regulating market still required effort, as Fr. Bernard Dempsey notes:

> The chief difference between Scholastic *just price* and classical *natural price* is that the liberals believed their deistic Providence constituted fair markets automatically through the magic of competition, no matter how hard men tried to make them unfair. The guildsmen believed that men were sons of Adam as well as of God and that the accomplishment of the designs of Providence required the sedulous application of human reason as well as cooperation with divine grace.[13]

This intense search and effort for balance characterized every aspect of medieval economy and thought. Historian Diana Wood claims that this "mean, in the sense of the balance of justice, was based not on precision but on more flexible reason and common sense. It was a question of virtue rather than econometrics."[14]

Obviously for our more complex economy, we would have to develop our own norms of prudence. In this way, prudence becomes a flexible and ever present component of organic economy and serves as a moderating influence. It prevents frenetic intemperance while freely promoting and facilitating commerce.

---

12. Langholm, *Economics in the Medieval Schools*, 582.
13. Dempsey, *Functional Economy*, 100.
14. Diana Wood, *Medieval Economic Thought* (Cambridge: Cambridge University Press, 2002), 209.

The Quality of Mercy

Finally, charity is a moderating influence on economy. Naturally, charity cannot govern economic transactions since, for an economy to function justly, each party must be strictly given its due. To insist that charity be made part of economic theory would put the charitable at a disadvantage and leave the marketplace in the hands of the hardhearted or dishonest.

However, we find the constant admonition of moralists and theologians that the fires of avarice might be extinguished with the practice of charity towards one's neighbor. While never mandating how it must be done, the merchant was always urged to practice his Christian duty to engage in almsgiving by spending some of his honest gains to relieve the suffering of the poor. Sometimes merchants made God their partner and would fix His name in their ledgers together with "the percent of net profits to which 'the Lord God,' as representative of the poor, was entitled."[15]

Moreover, we note that in the midst of purely economic transactions, there was a persistent concern to provide justice, especially for the poor. The just price and just wage had the poor especially in mind. There was the condemnation of merchants that cornered the market, thereby exploiting the vulnerability of the poor who must buy from them.

In his simple wisdom, Saint Bonaventure says that charitable mercy is somehow contained in the cardinal virtue of justice. "If one does not love one's neighbor, it is not easy to do him justice."[16]

Necessity of Charity

Furthermore, charity is necessary because it perfects and secures the practice of justice in society. For, although justice can diminish strife and disunity, only charity can bring about a true union of hearts and minds. "Without charity," writes William Thomas Gaughan, "all of the finest regulations made by well-intentioned men in the interests of the common good come to nothing."[17]

This was the view of Saint Antoninus who taught that charity

---

15. Raymond de Roover, *San Bernardino of Siena and Sant'Antonino of Florence: The Two Great Economic Thinkers of the Middle Ages* (Cambridge: Harvard University Printing Office, 1967), 15.
16. Langholm, *Economics in the Medieval Schools*, 155.
17. William Thomas Gaughan, *Social Theories of Saint Antoninus from His Summa Theologica* (Washington, D.C.: Catholic University of America Press, 1950), 104.

regulated the affections and will of man and "binds men together in a brotherhood that is a true and perfect oneness. The entrance of charity into the social order makes it possible for men to be self-sacrificing in favor of the common good. Charity helps us love our neighbor as ourselves. It recalls to mind our common origin, our redemption by Christ, our sanctification through the Holy Spirit."[18]

Thus, although it is not an economic principle in itself, charity easily serves as ballast amid the turmoil of frenetic intemperance.

These virtues are found in all the institutions governing organic economy. The question remains as to how this justice and its associated virtues might be manifested, enforced, and put into practice. To this we reply that it is done by custom, law, and conscience, which will now be seen.

18. Ibid., 109.

CHAPTER 33

"Finding" Law Once Again

Among the institutions brought forth by the medieval passion for justice is that of the rule of law. It is legal justice that inclines men to render to society what is due in view of the common good.

The rule of law is also a major component of our organic economic order. We cannot conceive of economy or order without law. At the same time, we must not think in terms of modern laws and regulations, but instead of those customs and laws that spring forth from an organic order. Ours is the task to return to sound law based on this passion for justice. A sound economy calls us to go back to our roots and "find" law once again.

Custom, Unwritten and Handed Down

Historically, we are heirs to a system developed from medieval customary and common law.[1] We can trace it back to long accepted usages and the customs of the people that were handed down by tradition.

Customs are those often unwritten rules that are the result of the gradual accumulation of knowledge, experience, and wisdom. In economy, it was custom, not state regulation, that governed simple transactions and united farmer, artisan, and merchant to work for the common good. These tried-and-true unwritten rules were so intertwined in the very social and economic fabric of society that it turned the people into true legislators.

Saint Thomas Aquinas considered custom superior to statute "because it regulated men's conduct by their own habits of mind," therefore requiring less compulsion from outside authority.[2]

---

1. Russell Kirk claims that "actually the basis of American law, still applied in countless cases, is the common laws which began to develop in England nine hundred years ago." Kirk, *Roots of American Order*, 371.
2. Thomas Gilby, *The Political Thought of Thomas Aquinas* (Chicago: University of Chicago Press, 1958), 173.

Customary Law—Not Made but Found

At times, unwritten custom was not sufficient; law was needed to take care of more complex situations. All law requires a legislator, an enforcing authority, and recognition by the governed. In this case, the people still made the customs, but custom became law when the ruler fulfilled his role of "finding" rather than making law. His was the task of inquiring, articulating, and uncovering what "the law had been discovered to mean."[3]

To medieval man, law was found among the many places where God had planted it—in public opinion, the common conscience, the testimony of custom, the ancient charters, and the legal sense of the people. It was all part of the same unchangeable law, yet it manifested itself in many different ways as all fought to "preserve the law proper to their order, their town or their house."[4]

That is not to say that this "unchangeable" law was stagnant. When new situations and facts called for innovation, the law was adjusted, but this was not done through upheaval and novelty. Rather, without contradiction, the one true law was constantly being "rediscovered," clarified, and purified against injustice, obscurity, misunderstanding, and forgetfulness. In its unity, medieval law progressed by neither revolution nor evolution, but by constant regeneration.

The Law Changed by Consent

The ruler was obliged to "find" law, give it his sanction, and enforce that law that came from time immemorial. The law did not belong to him. To aid in this discovery process, he had to seek the assent of those affected; he often was bound to have recourse to assemblies or councilors. As a result, one of the most original medieval institutions was born: representative government.

Unknown to either ancient Greece or Rome, representation occurred because medieval law required consultation between ruler and people. Important decisions had to be made collectively, and public consent and recognition be given to any change of custom following

---

3. Frederick B. Artz, *The Mind of the Middle Ages, A.D. 200-1500: An Historical Survey* (Chicago: University of Chicago Press, 1980), 278.
4. Friedrich Heer, *The Medieval World, Europe 1100-1350*, trans. Janet Sondheimer (New York: Praeger Publishers, 1969), 12.

the maxim "what touches all, must be approved by all."[5] True to this consultative spirit, medieval jurisprudence later gave rise at all levels to representative bodies like the British Parliament, which continues to our present day.

Law Was Sovereign

All were subject to this unchangeable law whether they were rulers or the ruled. In the Middle Ages, the king was a creature of law, which he swore to safeguard. It was held that "the law makes the king" (*lex facit regem*). He was not the creator of law; his power was not above the law, and consequently he could not arbitrarily change it. Indeed, Robert Nisbet writes that, "No legal understanding was more widespread in the medieval period than that which declared the ruler to be *under* the law."[6]

In fact, subjects had the right to resist and were freed from their oaths of fealty when the law was violated by the ruler. They might even resort to force since "to oppose force to the king's use of force was, according to the common legal creed of the Middle Ages, not only permissible but even in certain circumstances obligatory."[7]

This bottom-up legislative process of "discovering law" that was sovereign over both ruler and ruled gave protection to the people, who knew they could constantly invoke it and hold authority accountable. This equality under the law is the basis of the rule of law and limited government that gave the West its great advantage over other civilizations.

Natural Development of Customary Law

There was also common law, a body of court precedents and customs where abstract rules were drawn from specific cases, custom, decrees of parliament, charters, and other sources over the course of cen-

---

5. The old adage, "*quod omnes tangit ab omnibus probetur*," was part of the Justinian code and introduced into canon law by Gratian. It was amply applied in medieval society: "During the thirteenth century it was the general conviction that the realm was preserved by customary and constitutional law. The king was a kind of trustee whose duty it was to safeguard the laws. There was scarcely any important statute in which he omitted to claim that he had consulted advice and received assent, in other words, that he was in agreement with the legal convictions of the community." Gilby, *Political Thought of Thomas Aquinas*, 285.
6. Nisbet, *Twilight of Authority*, 154.
7. Fritz Kern, *Kingship and Law in the Middle Ages: The Divine Right of Kings and the Right of Resistance in the Early Middle Ages; Law and Constitution in the Middle Ages*, trans. S. B. Chrimes (Oxford: Basil Blackwell, 1968), 83.

turies. Common law preserved the continuity of tradition while adapting to the fresh conditions in the life of the community. M. Stanton Evans notes that "common law created a tremendous obstacle to the *workings of unchecked power in the state*. For if the law grew up by way of custom and tradition, over great periods of time, then it was not the work of any individual and could not be changed at anyone's discretion."[8]

We might also mention the revival of Roman law, which established universal legal principles, gave order to common law, and vigorously defined individual and property rights. The medieval adaptations of Roman law often defined explicitly that which custom held implicitly, by furnishing "a set of categories into which new ideas could be fitted and a vocabulary by which they could be described."[9]

Roman law, while at times abused by the legists, never completely dominated medieval European law. The Church played a leading role in its revival by adopting Roman law in its own canon law. Within the same organic spirit of customary law, what prevailed in temporal society was the harmonic, though at times contentious, co-existence of Roman, customary, canon, and merchant law that was called the *jus commune* or "the law of the land." This flexible arrangement gradually weakened and was finally swept away by the widespread imposition of codified civil law after the French Revolution.

A Higher Law

What made all law so binding and unchanging was the fact that a sacred trust bound it to a higher law. It was conceived in the conviction that the source of all law—whether customary, common, or Roman—was God and His eternal law.[10]

"Eternal law," "divine law," "moral law," or "natural law" are all terms used to describe an objective moral compass that makes social order possible. It is the same for all peoples, places, and times.[11]

---

8. Evans, *The Theme Is Freedom*, 80.
9. Joseph R. Strayer, *On the Medieval Origins of the Modern State* (Princeton: Princeton University Press, 1973), 25.
10. "The only 'sovereign' of the high Middle Ages was God Himself, and all men stood under Him and His law." Ellis Sandoz, *A Government of Laws: Political Theory, Religion, and the American Founding* (Baton Rouge: Louisiana State University Press, 1990), 35.
11. Proof of the universal character of natural law can be found in Cicero's expressions, *lex naturae, non scripta sed nata lex, lex caelestis, lex divina* ("natural law, inborn or unwritten law, heavenly law, divine law") that were adopted by Christian philosophers and canonists.

Saint Thomas Aquinas affirms that eternal law is that rational plan by which all creation is ordered by God's Wisdom. This can be perceived in society by unaided reason through natural law, which is so well summarized in the Ten Commandments.[12]

In fact, for the Middle Ages, all law was literally linked to objective moral law, which made all subjective rights equally sacred and valuable.[13] The maxim, "unjust law is not law" (*lex injusta non est lex*), was universally accepted. On its part, the Church saw divine or natural law as universally obligatory law that was binding in conscience, and She insisted that rulers put it in practice even when in conflict with customary law.

> ## NATURAL LAW IS THE SAME EVERYWHERE, AND BINDS ALL MEN IN ALL TIMES
> American law's attachment to higher law dates back before independence as can be seen in this reference from renowned English jurist Sir William Blackstone: "This law of nature, being coeval with mankind, and dictated by God himself, is of course superior in obligation to any other. It is binding over all the globe, in all countries, and at all times: no human laws are of any validity, if contrary to this; and such of them as are valid derive all their force, and all their authority, mediately or immediately, from this original" (*Commentaries on the Laws of England* [Oxford: Clarendon Press, 1765], 1:41).

Thus, all were bound together in an objective legal order with ample means of protection. Appealing to the Church, higher law, and God's name, anyone might claim the right of opposition to unjust laws or edicts. For both subjects and ruler were subject to this higher order and could appeal to its precepts.

Thus, higher law was always embedded in early medieval docu-

---

12. Aquinas, *Summa Theologica*, I-II, q. 91, a. 1-2.
13. Medieval man saw no need to separate any specific fundamental rights into a constitution beyond the power of the ruler since all law was considered sacred and untouchable. Indeed, until the late eighteenth century, the term "constitution" was understood to be the assemblage of laws, institutions, and customs which were held from time immemorial. "Only the activities of the absolutist States which succeeded the medieval and representative States, and which ruthlessly encroached upon private rights, explain the demand for constitutionally protected fundamental rights." Kern, *Kingship and Law*, 186. We might also refer to Viscount Bolingbroke's well-known definition of a constitution written in 1735: "By Constitution we mean, whenever we speak with propriety and exactness, that assemblage of laws, institutions, and customs, derived from certain *fixed* principles of reason ... that compose the general system, according to which the community hath agreed to be governed." C. Bradley Thompson, "The Revolutionary Origins of American Constitutionalism," in *History, on Proper Principles*, eds., Klugewicz and Ealy, 5.

ments and discourses. This can be seen, for example, in King Alfred the Great's *Liber Judicialis*, which began with the Ten Commandments and was followed by other Mosaic precepts.

Our American legal system inherited a strong higher law tradition. We find numerous documents and laws in which the mark of the Ten Commandments is so deeply entrenched that separation becomes almost impossible.[14] Even though tainted by Enlightenment errors and distortions of the Thomist notion of natural law, American legal tradition was nevertheless firmly attached to the idea of higher law.[15]

Like an ancient forest constantly rejuvenating itself, the law was ever old yet constantly new. Born from the customs and habits of the people, it was found, not made. Once established, it could be changed only with the consent of the people. Restraining the power of government, the law bound all and held all accountable. Guided by a higher unchangeable law, the law preserved an objective moral order.

Born of a passion for justice, this law can be restored. The key is to return to a higher law, valid for all times, peoples, and places. Indeed, this law is easily found since it is written upon our hearts (Cf. Rom 2:15). Indeed, it is easier to wrench out our hearts than to erase that universal law that is written upon them.

Thus, if we could but return to our higher law tradition, we would once again "find" law and that economic order that we so need.

---

14. William J. Federer's *The Ten Commandments & Their Influence on American Law* is an exhaustive compilation of texts that show how each of the Commandments historically impacted the development of law in America as might be seen, for example, in laws forbidding perjury or polygamy.
15. Sir William Blackstone (1723-1780), whose *Commentaries on the Laws of England* (1765–69) is the ultimate authority on both American and English common law, unequivocally defends higher law. Such opinions can also be found in the works of Sir Edward Coke (1552-1634), who strongly influenced American law.

CHAPTER 34

The Two Tribunals

I t can easily be seen that the medieval passion for justice found in law was the basis for both economic and political order. Although not perfect, the firm attachment to higher law helped diminish fraud and guarantee the security of property and future transactions. The medieval concept of the supremacy of law binding ruler and ruled protected the people and their dealings against arbitrary government.

Thus, a tribunal of justice, based on custom and "found" law, was established unlike any other. Permeated as it was by prudence and charity, it made economy more flexible and human. We no longer see the savage nature of the ancient markets that led the Romans to exclaim: "Man is a wolf to his fellow man" (*homo homini lupus*).

The Tribunal of Justice

This tribunal led to an atmosphere of trust and security unknown to many peoples. This was seen, for example, when the Catholic fleet defeated the Turks at Lepanto (1571). The victors were surprised to discover several captured ships laden with treasure. It appears the Muslim admirals took their assets with them since they had no place of trust to deposit them.[1]

Above all, this tribunal adopted moral guidelines that frontally addressed the dangers of the merchant trade: avarice, fraud, monopoly, and speculation. It not only insisted upon the efficient operation of an enterprise, but a just one as well.

The Assistance of the Church

It was considered normal, then, that the Church as guardian of the moral law might assist the tribunal of justice by issuing objective

---

1. See Stark, *Victory of Reason*, 72.

norms that would concretely help identify and denounce injustice in economy. It was natural that Her charity, by which all Christians become brothers in Christ, would serve to quell the divisive passions of avarice so common to the merchant trade.

The result was an atmosphere of justice tempered with prudence and crowned with charity that helped create conditions for the impressive rise of the West. This atmosphere also helps explain the exponential growth of creativity and industry that marked the Middle Ages and only slowed down with the economic downturn of the Renaissance. Such an atmosphere, however, is not entirely explained by the tribunal of justice.

A Second Tribunal

We can observe that laws and customs alone did not satisfy the medieval passion for the perfection of justice. The public tribunal of justice is rightly limited to those external acts that threaten the common good. The private and sinful acts of men must lie outside its legal jurisdiction.

However, there is a second tribunal of which few historians speak. This tribunal worked the wonder of judging the private conscience of man without destroying his freedom or reputation. In his voluntary quest for perfection, man accuses himself in this tribunal before a Divine judge.

Thus, Odd Langholm notes, the medieval theologian William of Rennes made the distinction between the external court of law and the internal court of conscience where "the Church, represented by the priest in the confessional, held the keys that also gave it the power to judge and to absolve its members secretly according to the more severe norms of God's law."[2]

A Perfection of Justice

While oriented towards all sin, this court also addressed those sins which hindered economic progress such as the smooth clearing and settlement of accounts. That is to say, men realized the perils of sin that lay in these matters and brought them before confessors. They

---

2. Langholm, *Merchant in the Confessional*, 43.

freely submitted themselves to a stricter code of justice, so that even those private acts rightly outside the jurisdiction of the law might be judged. In doing this, they created an even greater climate of virtue where transactions were more secure, restitution was better made, and the peace of conscience was more completely restored.

In appearing before the court of conscience to judge these economic acts, the penitent submitted himself to Divine justice. He freed himself from the slavery of avarice. For although avarice led to sins against one's neighbor, it also had a corrosive effect upon character, wrought great disorder in affections, and disturbed one's peace of mind. Avarice led men to scorn the things of God and turn from His loving Providence.

A Penitential Doctrine

The Church responded to the needs of this court with a wealth of economic literature that developed the prudential norms and criteria for judging just exchange, theft, restitution, and other such matters in this second court. For this reason, medieval economic thought is often found in scholastic theological treatises, popular sermons, and handbooks for confessors. There were literally hundreds of confessional manuals with successive reprintings that defined a penitential doctrine and tradition that dealt with these personal economic matters focused on justice.[3]

Obviously we cannot affirm that all medieval men submitted themselves to this second tribunal. Yet, while we cannot quantify the concrete effects of such a penitential tradition on medieval economy, we can say that the fact that such manuals were widely used and often reissued attests to a climate that produced trust and security on one hand and temperance and restraint on the other. As long as this second court remained in session, it served as ballast to keep economy, markets, and society in equilibrium.

The Loss of Balance

There was a waning of this passion for justice during the Renaissance.

---

3. Norwegian economist Odd Langholm analyzes ninety of these confession manuals in his book, *The Merchant in the Confessional: Trade and Price in the Pre-Reformation Penitential Handbooks.* From this brilliant analysis he deduces a practical economic doctrine found in Scholastic thought.

Later, certain currents inside the Reformation (and especially those inside Calvinism), helped open the floodgates of avarice by holding that the perils of the accumulation of riches no longer presented obstacles to salvation. These currents, together with commercial interests, began to recognize the vice of avarice as the social and economic virtue of self-interest. With this breakdown, frenetic intemperance became almost inevitable.

"This doctrine," notes Odd Langholm, "led, among other things, to a search for confirmation through an unceasing, frenzied accumulation of wealth for its own sake which, as though unintentionally, provided the basis of modern capitalism."[4]

Thus, the structures of prudence and charity that so tempered the demands of justice fell away. Justice itself was reduced to the security of property and contracts—which was truly the basis for incredible material prosperity. But economy returned to its savage ways with the Hobbesian idea of a "war of every man against every man" or its modern equivalent of "dog-eat-dog."

We must return to the passion for justice. This passion should lead us to look after our own self-interest for that which is our due. Legal justice demands that, through good customs and law, we render to the common good that which is its due.

But there is a special perfection of justice found in this second tribunal where man subjects himself to a stricter code of justice before the Divine Judge. It is here that justice shines with a special brilliance. Frenetic intemperance becomes impossible. In this climate of impressive honesty, trust, and consideration of neighbor, we find the foundations of true prosperity.

---

4. Langholm, *Merchant in the Confessional*, 263.

Photo/American TFP Archive

**Saint John Bosco
(1815-1888)**

THE FEAR OF GOD AND JUST PRICE

We find a concern for the second tribunal reflected in the following conversation between Saint John Bosco and a simple blacksmith who supported the saint's works:

"Do you know what my biggest worry is?"

"Surely it must be to live and die in the grace of God."

"No, I'm not worried about death. I take care, though, to be prepared for it when it comes. My biggest worry is this: I am a blacksmith, and I am very much troubled when after finishing a job I have to decide on the price I must charge. As I enter the charge in my book I ask myself: Will the good Lord write down the same amount? If I charge more, won't that be a charge against me? To play it safe, I always charge 20% less than the ordinary rate" (Giovanni Battista Lemoyne, *The Biographical Memoirs of St. John Bosco*, ed. Diego Borgatello [New Rochelle, N.Y.: Salesiana Publishers, 1965], 1:230).

Obviously not all tradesmen can or should take such a position. However, the fact that this simple and successful blacksmith and many others like him showed such a great concern for justice can only have created an atmosphere favoring commerce in general.

Spanish, Portuguese, Venetian, Florentine, and Moorish coins found in the coffers of a Portuguese trading vessel. Pre-modern money varied greatly according to the needs of the people. Money must always keep its natural functions as a measure of value, a convenient means of exchange, and a store of wealth.

CHAPTER 35

The Matter of Money

As justice calls forth law, so also it serves as the basis for money. By making it easier for each to receive more exactly his due in transactions, money facilitates the practice of commutative justice.

Thus, if we are to return to a sound and organic economy, we must define the simple conditions whereby money best fulfills its end and purpose. To do this, we turn to a basic definition of money given by Saint Thomas Aquinas, who says money is that which is "invented by the art of man, for the convenience of exchange, and as a measure of things salable."[1]

A Creation of Law

Money is truly an invention. What makes it universally accepted is an agreement or convention established by usage and custom for the purpose of the exchange of goods and services.

A monetary system is established when it is recognized by law. That is why money is termed *numisma* (from which we get *numismatics*), meaning law; it is a creation of law. Currency becomes money by the authority of the State or ruler, who enforces its acceptance, and takes it as payment for taxes. By law, currency can be issued or changed; old currency and coinage can be made useless and demonetized.[2]

Like a stable legal system, a stable monetary framework is an extremely important component in a market economy. Hence, it falls upon responsible government, which exists for the common good, to limit money and currency supply, prevent counterfeiting, and keep money's value stable. This responsibility of government in monetary systems has been universally recognized throughout history. Our own

---

1. Aquinas, *Summa Theologica*, I-II, q. 2, a. 1.
2. Saint Thomas holds this view when he states: "But if the situation of the human beings who use wealth is altered (e.g., if it should please a king or community that coins have no value), money is of no value and offers nothing for the necessities of life." Aquinas, *Commentary on Aristotle's Politics*, trans. Richard J. Regan (Indianapolis: Hackett Publishing, 2007), 53.

American Constitution explicitly grants Congress the power to "coin money, regulate the value thereof, and of foreign coin."[3]

A Measure of Value

Money is a "measure of things salable." That is to say, it is the manner by which we gauge value. We look at things, for example, in terms of dollars, our local money of account. The money of account serves as a yardstick. To the degree possible, it is the duty of the State, which also maintains standards of weights and measures, to maintain money as a stable measure of value. This is because when a money of account changes, the terms of all contracts change to the detriment of just trade and the common good. To this effect, the State must especially safeguard political stability, which assures the value of money over time since commerce needs the assurance of future stability to plan and prosper. In addition, it should secure for itself the functions of the determining and issuance of its money of account since these are attributes of sovereignty, and whoever exercises them directs not only all economic operations but those of the nation. Any surrender of these powers would easily risk putting the country in the hands of a shadow government of manipulators.

Money as Medium of Exchange

The primary purpose of money is to serve as a medium of exchange. Once the value of goods can be determined in terms of dollars, for example, trade can begin. Money then becomes an immaterial and legal claim and a socially recognized and transferable right-to-buy.[4]

One way this is done is when goods are interchanged and accounts are then cancelled out as was done in medieval trade fairs and is presently done in modern banking. Such practices diminish the need for large amounts of cash.

Money as a medium of exchange is more commonly expressed by a

---

3. U.S. Constitution, Article I, Section 8. In quoting the American Constitution, Milton Friedman notes: "There is probably no other area of economic activity with respect to which government intervention has been so uniformly accepted." Milton Friedman, *A Program for Monetary Stability* (New York: Fordham University Press, 1980), 8.
4. Money represents a claim on the economic community. It is created and issued in the same way that a person makes a promise or creates a contractual relationship. We are also reminded of the definition of Georg Simmel, who writes: "All other objects have a specific content from which they derive their value. Money derives its content from its value; it is value turned into a substance, the value of things without the things themselves." Simmel, *Philosophy of Money*, 121.

physical currency to facilitate commerce. Since ancient times, states have issued currency and it has taken on various forms established by convention and fixed by law. It is proper that this currency should be of good quality, durability, and beauty to make it more desirable, respected, and therefore more trusted. That is why authorities have always used superior design or quality materials like noble metals in the manufacture of currency. Nevertheless, we believe that money should not monopolize such metals to the extent that it deprives society of their use as artistic symbols of excellence.

Money Must Be Trusted

An organic concept of money cannot be based upon authority alone. Something of the vital flux of the people must enter into its use. Money's value may be found in its legal face value, but without the trust of the public, it will easily fail or fall into disuse. That is to say, the value of a money is especially found in its extrinsic value based on the customs and conventions of the public. As a result, a dollar has the same face value everywhere, but the valuation people give it will vary greatly and confer different buying power depending on time and place.

The Late-Scholastic writer Fr. Luis de Molina notes that "in money exchanges we must take into account not the value that is in its nature but the estimation of that value." Likewise, fellow Late-Scholastic Friar Tomas de Mercado specifies that, in the exchange of money, what matters most is not its metal value or legal standard, but "the extrinsic value that is accidental and depends on esteem."[5]

Money Must Be Convenient

Sound money must be practical, serving man for the convenience of exchange. It is invented to facilitate and preserve community life by making transactions easier and more just. It solves the awkward problem of barter by replacing large commodities with much smaller tokens of value and measure put at the service of the community.

Money becomes a burden on the community when it is over- or under-valued; when there is too much or too little of it. Then it loses its quality of ease of exchange and the trust of the public. Such money

---

5. Chafuen, *Faith and Liberty*, 63.

becomes onerous since the community is then made to serve money when its nature is to serve men.

Hence, many currencies were born precisely to resolve problems in the ease of exchange. In the line of innovation, we can refer to our own eighteenth-century Pennsylvania "colonial scrip" money born of a major dearth of silver and gold coins. Issued by colonial officials, this well-regulated paper money, the "Pennsylvania pound," circulated with great stability and ease.[6] We also read of imaginative ways of canceling debt, like the split tally stick money that was especially popular in England. Used extensively in medieval times, the split Hazelwood stick was notched to signify money amounts, and served as a tool of the Exchequer in the collection of taxes and was in continuous use until 1826.

Responding to Local Needs

In the line of medieval organic solutions, there was no single unified monetary system. Most money consisted of local monetary systems where money adjusted to the locality and its needs. Some national coinages with international projection were used to facilitate large foreign transactions. For their convenience, people would even use multiple currencies for purchases. Money was extremely flexible and practical.

It is not surprising that medieval money exhibited this flexible organic character. Just as sovereignty was "parceled out" to form a nation of vibrant little nations, it was not uncommon in medieval times for a sovereign to authorize other local authorities to mint separate coinage for the convenience of their populations.

Medieval France, for example, had many independent coinages spread throughout the land, all differing in weights, denominations, alloys, and types.[7] Even in countries with only one unit of account, money naturally tends to adapt itself to the needs of the community when in contact with the concrete economic reality.[8] Economy functions best when currency is allowed to adapt to the money rates,

---

6. Richard Lester claims that during the fifty-two years Pennsylvania was on the paper standard prior to the American Revolution, it was "more stable than the American price level has been during any succeeding fifty year period." Richard A. Lester, "Currency Issues to Overcome Depressions in Pennsylvania, 1723 and 1729," *Journal of Political Economy* 46 (June 1938): 325.
7. See A. M. Innes, "What Is Money?" *Banking Law Journal* (May 1913): 377-408.
8. We might also cite our own colonial unit of account, the pound, where its worth in shillings varied greatly among the colonies.

labor scales, and price levels peculiar to places and cultures without outside interference.

Unity and Diversity

It is very characteristic of medieval times that, from an immense diversity of coinages, there would appear a stable source of unity. There were two types of medieval money. The first was an extremely stable money of account that was called abstract, or "ghost" money, since it had no physical form. This unit was usually not minted, but existed in the mind as a measure of value or as transactions in ledger books for large international trade. The most common of these moneys in medieval Europe were various versions of a pound unit.

The second type of money was the great array of local and national currencies that existed as media of exchange in function of a money of account. To put it in our terms, it would be as if there were to exist an array of stable and valuable dollars that would almost never be minted and whose value would rarely change. There would also be a variety of corresponding pennies, nickels, dimes, or other fractional coins that varied in value in accordance to the local conditions, so that 120 pennies might equal a dollar in one place and 80 pennies in another.

Freedom to Develop and Adapt

While such a bewildering variety of monetary systems may seem impractical to modern minds, it did have its advantages. The first was that, by reducing money to reasonable proportions, it eliminated the need for complex systems of regulation and control by the State or central banks. In this decentralized system favoring subsidiarity, each monetary system—international, national, or local—took care of its own markets. It also reduced the danger of manipulation and inefficiency of currencies since, if a system became onerous and unworkable to a population, it could always be seamlessly replaced by a competing one operating nearby.

Secondly and more importantly, it allowed for people, in their passion for commutative justice, to express themselves freely in their own currency or monetary systems. Through custom and usage, currency acquired the content, form, quantity, and value that best served the people of an area.[9] In addition, that same custom relegated money to its proper secondary place inside a regime of services, obligations, and benefits.

Forcing nations to abide by a single monetary standard in a world economy imposes a system that cannot adjust to local needs. It is like forcing people to speak badly a more universally spoken language different from the language or dialect with which they express themselves best. Moreover, when one member of such monetary unions falters, all suffer, which then causes unjust hardships upon poorer nations and undeserved burdens upon richer ones.[10]

At the same time, medieval currency remained adaptive, yet stable. In times of great crisis or emergency, it could be inflated or deflated to distribute the cost burden of the crisis over the whole population. In normal times, as the economy developed, money also adapted accordingly, yet ever so slowly and incrementally, adding to or altering an existing system that was deeply ingrained in the customs of the people, so that the change was almost imperceptible.

By describing medieval money, our purpose is not to apply identical formulas for our times, but rather to point out the means by which money can return to order. We seek a concept of money in which it no longer rules society but again becomes the servant of man, finding ways to facilitate the convenience of exchange. Money must once again be stable as a measure of value of things salable and not an instrument to be manipulated. In the context of organic society, it should be an adaptive expression of the culture of a people in their passionate search for justice.

---

9. We can see this great variety of money in pre-modern Japan. In 1871, the yen was officially adopted as the basic monetary unit. The government suspended the exchange of clan notes which consisted of paper money that feudal lords had issued and used since the late sixteenth century. At the time, there were estimated to be a total of 1,694 denominations of clan money. These were issued by 244 clans, 14 magistrates' offices, and 9 shogunate retainers during the Tokugawa period (1603-1867). See *Encyclopædia Britannica 2009 Deluxe Edition*, s.v. "yen."
10. This can be seen in the dissatisfaction of many European nations that want to return to their own currency since the euro has led to abuse by some and become an undue burden to others.

CHAPTER 36

Money and Credit

T here is another function of money that Aristotle calls "a store of wealth" that we have yet to discuss. It involves money's ability to hold value over time and therefore ensure the stability of trade. It is perhaps the most problematic of all money's functions.

The fact that some pre-modern money had precious metal content gave it enough value to insure its future worth. Individuals naturally sought to accumulate and even hoard it. Yet as money gained stability over time, all monies, even those with lesser or no intrinsic value, began to take on the function of storing wealth. The benefits of turning such accumulated savings into capital for extending credit became evident.

A Factor of Imbalance

In itself, there is nothing wrong with the saving of money, the formation of capital, or its extension as credit. What is a problem is the massive expansion of credit that helps turn money from a means to an end, which can easily throw the economy out of balance.

Then money, which should naturally serve as a middle term to purchase the final term of a commodity, serves the opposite purpose. The obsessive trader easily enters into speculation by using any commodities as a middle term to reach a final term of accumulating ever more money.

We can see this same imbalance in the leveraging of capital, resulting in a system that thrives on easy credit and the issuing of debt. This, in turn, facilitates risk and the throwing off of restraint. Money, which should be a stable store of value, becomes a tool of frenetic intemperance.

A Universal Hostility to Interest

Throughout history, we find the extension of credit and the charging of interest entering as factors of imbalance. It is not without reason that, in all times and societies, there has been a universal hostility to the taking of *any interest*, which in ancient times was classified as usury. Cato and Seneca compared usury to murder since it ravaged the civilizations of antiquity. We also note widespread opposition to usury in medieval times, led especially by the Catholic Church. Nor was the Church alone in this opposition, since as Max Weber notes, "The canonical prohibition on interest . . . has a parallel in almost every religious ethic in the world."[1]

Much has been written about this pre-modern opposition to the taking of any interest, an opposition that many falsely claim hinders economic progress. Such critics fail to recognize that the thrust of this opposition was turned to high-interest, high-risk, consumer loans that preyed upon the most vulnerable in society. These critics do not see usury through the eyes of the medieval saints who denounced this scourge as that which "ever breaks and consumes the bones of the poor."[2]

Remnants of this hostility even extended into modern times. To cite one example, we mention the surprising commentary of founding father John Adams, who denounces credit as the cause of so much folly that the person who could discover a way to abolish credit forever "would deserve a statue to his memory."[3] Beginning in the early twentieth century, popular resistance to consumer credit was gradually overcome by installment buying, credit cards, and other consumer schemes that helped create our present credit culture.

Wisdom of the Church's Ruling on Credit

The long and bitter debate over credit in pre-industrial times was largely dominated by the Church's ban on usury. Suffice it to say that the Church recognized the developing economic conditions of the times and defined the ample opportunities for investment and the generous extrinsic titles by which moderate interest might be charged.[4]

---

1. Weber, *Spirit of Capitalism*, 201.
2. John T. Noonan, Jr., *The Scholastic Analysis of Usury* (Cambridge: Harvard University Press, 1957), 78. Noonan also notes that throughout the Middle Ages, capital was scarce in general and, even with all the moral pressure on lenders, authorities had generally been unable to bring below 35 percent the rate of interest charged by the public usurers. See ibid., 294.
3. Forrest McDonald, "The Founding Fathers and the Economic Order," in *History, on Proper Principles*, eds. Klugewicz and Ealy, 265.
4. While the Church rigorously condemned the exacting of anything over and above capital, She did define circumstances when it could be allowed. These are called the extrinsic titles for the charging of interest. The most common titles are when the lender is in danger of losing a profit on his capital loaned (*lucrum cessans*) or cannot advance his loan of money without exposing himself to a loss or to deprivation of a gain (*damnum emergens*). Other titles include loaning to enemies, interest as a gift, interest as a penalty (*poena conventionali*), interest in case of delay, and similar cases.

The result was a credit policy that actually helped, not hindered, economic development. "The rule, as applied, did not choke commerce. It regulated, in some measure, the course of credit," writes John Noonan. In addition, the same author notes that it even stimulated "a greater use of risk-sharing investments than might otherwise have occurred."[5]

The Church's position also receives the unexpected support of John Maynard Keynes, who once dismissed the Church's attitude towards credit as absurd and found the extrinsic titles to interest to be "a practical escape from a foolish theory." Upon later consideration, Keynes changed his view and saw the wisdom in the efforts of the Scholastics regarding interest, since their formulations allowed "the schedule of the marginal efficiency of capital to be high, whilst using rule and custom and the moral law to keep down the rate of interest."[6]

We might also add that the Church's attitude towards usury was largely supported by most people who were not clamoring for credit in the pre-industrial medieval order. "There was no sharp collision between the doctrine of the Church and the public policy of the world of business," notes historian R. H. Tawney.[7] Pre-modern economy was not a money economy and needed no huge outlays of capital.

"Before the Industrial Revolution," writes historian Charles Beard, "the communities were more self-sufficing, and competition among the home workers was very limited. Vast fortunes accumulated from manufacturing industries were unknown, and *there was little demand for capital before the rise of the factory system.*"[8]

We also note that this same attitude towards money and credit prevented huge speculative bubbles. Edward Chancellor, in his extensive history of financial speculation and bubbles, skips over the Middle Ages since he had nothing to report, observing that the "culture of medieval Europe *was inimical to financial speculation* for both practical and ideological reasons."[9]

---

5. Noonan, *Scholastic Analysis of Usury*, 195.
6. John Maynard Keynes, *The General Theory of Employment, Interest and Money* (Amherst, N.Y.: Prometheus Books, 1997), 351-52.
7. R. H. Tawney, *Religion and the Rise of Capitalism: A Historical Study* (New York: Harcourt, Brace, 1926), 38.
8. Charles Beard, *The Industrial Revolution* (Westport, Conn.: Greenwood Press Publishers, 1975), 48. (Emphasis added.)
9. Chancellor, *Devil Take the Hindmost*, 6. (Emphasis added.)

An Aggressive Campaign

All this changed with the coming of the Industrial Revolution. It is curious that while many have seen fit to condemn the Church severely for its ban, few have criticized the promoters of an increasingly commercial society driven by frenetic intemperance, which favored an enormous expansion of credit to fund ever greater risks that often had tragic consequences.

In fact, the nineteenth-century Industrial Revolution produced a financial system with an explosion of credit opportunities so great that the new money markets essentially made all money interest-bearing, according to the extrinsic titles allowed by the Church.[10]

These same money markets created by the Industrial Revolution also facilitated the official establishment of fractional reserve banking, where money could be multiplied by lending more than existed in a bank's cash reserves. In this way, unbridled and easy credit became a fixture in modern economies. This fuels the speculation, inflation, and profiteering that leads to the leveraging of credit to absurd extremes to the ultimate detriment of the economy. We can trace the aftermath of this credit explosion not only through financial successes, but also from the debris of bubbles, busts, and bankruptcies that litter the pages of modern economic history with billion-dollar, and now trillion-dollar, losses. It is this same credit that makes possible the mountain of consumer debt and mortgages that lead so many to live beyond their means. This credit naturally facilitates the massive deficit spending of governments.

Facing a Dilemma

In our quest to discover a solution in the area of credit, we are faced with the following dilemma: If we admit that modern money markets should allow moderate interest under certain extrinsic titles, then there is no reasonable argument to prevent the present explosion of credit and massive debt from recurring. On the other hand, if we condemn the charging of all interest, then we face the prospect of stifling the legitimate needs of our complex and developed economies.

---

10. Since money markets put any person not utilizing interest-bearing deposits "in danger of losing a gain"—*lucrum cessans*, one of the extrinsic titles to interest—this was judged a special reason among others to authorize the charging of moderate interest.

Photo/American TFP Archive

Easy credit fuels frenetic intemperance in modern economy.

Here we can easily see that the problem is not the credit itself, but the frenetic intemperance by which credit is used to break away from normal restraints or go headlong into the pursuit of some quick and easy gain or dream of consumer happiness. Either this restless spirit of frenetic intemperance be addressed, or all effort will be in vain.

A System of Justice

This is why we insist upon an economy that is guided by justice and not by money and markets. The rule of money makes the present system of money and credit inevitable; the rule of justice makes it impossible.

There are certain things that a society ruled by justice does not permit. It does not live beyond its means. Saddling future generations with the expense of the present offends its most basic precepts. It does not permit the deliberate overextension or acceptance of credit to and by those who have no means to pay. Justice tempers credit and spending since we do not desire that which is not proper to us. Justice demands that one does not leverage money to issue loans or fund certain types of speculation and money manipulation with funds that do not actually exist.

That is to say, justice creates the conditions for an orderly and temperate economy, which will then be free to operate according to its own norms of prudence.

Usury and Charity Do Not Mix

This is also why we insist upon an economy influenced by charity—that habit which disposes us to love God above all creatures, and to love ourselves and our neighbor for the sake of God. Saint Antoninus teaches that, by putting the greater good over the lesser, charity regulates the affections and will of man by giving him a true hierarchy of values. In this way, the fires of charity serve to quell the passion for unbridled profits and unrestrained consumption.

This is especially applicable to a consumer society that multiplies both credit opportunities and the occasions of ruin and bankruptcy. Where charity prevails, we do not encounter the dog-eat-dog atmosphere of the markets that use credit to increase their profits at all costs and above all things. Inside a true hierarchy of values, we do not find the aimless pursuit of material happiness that prompts so many consumers to live beyond their means. There is no offering or accepting of large amounts of credit that saddles people of limited means with massive debt.

Thus, the medieval mind found it difficult to reconcile usury—such a great cause of suffering—to the idea of Christian charity and brotherhood that should prevail in Christendom. It is not right that citizens devour one another, cried Saint Antoninus of the moneylenders. Saint Albert the Great, Saint Bernardine, and so many others all argued that under no circumstances should a Christian take advantage of his neighbor. Saint Thomas Aquinas calls usury evil because "we ought to treat every man as our neighbor and brother, especially in the state of the Gospel, whereto all are called."[11]

Loans to Brothers and Neighbors

Such thinking does not deny the need for occasional loans, especially in times of hardship. It does not even forbid other loans with moderate interest, as, for example, those that involve commercial activities, according to the aforementioned extrinsic titles allowed by the Church.

---

11. Aquinas, *Summa Theologica*, II-II, q. 78, a. 1, ad. 2.

Such an attitude goes yet further by searching for alternatives based on models of charity that moderate the conditions whereby loans become onerous to brothers, and by which they are not saddled with constant debt. Thus, Christian families come to the aid of other family members in need. Innumerable intermediary associations, such as guilds, extended interest-free loans to members or to the poor. The Church set up Her own financial aid organizations, such as the *Montes Pietatis* that lent money upon the security of objects left in pawn, with a view to protecting poor persons in great need from usurers.

"The scourge of debts, which in Greek and Roman antiquity so sorely afflicted the people," writes historian Henri Pirenne, "was spared the social order of the Middle Ages, and it may well be that the Church contributed largely to that happy result."[12]

Unhappily, we cannot make the same claim today.

Charity Towards All

Above all, acts of charity proved the greatest shield from usury. The Church led the way and encouraged all to extend gifts of monies and goods to those in great need. We read how the rich distributed vast sums to the poor. Attached to the bylaws of countless medieval associations and guilds are the constant admonitions to give alms to the poor. Services are to be given freely to the needy.

"Thus is seen to develop the great virtue of the Middle Ages: *love*," writes Franz Funck-Brentano. "Never has the divine and human precept, 'Love one another,' penetrated hearts more profoundly. . . . And the chief result of this love is generosity in giving."[13]

If we are to have a sound economy, we must oppose the abuse of money's function as a storage of value, which makes possible our world of unbridled credit. We do not deny the need for credit to help build economies. What we criticize is the explosion of credit that facilitates the spirit of frenetic intemperance.

It is an explosion that no regulation or law can contain, for unre-

---

12. Pirenne, *Medieval Cities*, 125.
13. Funck-Brentano, *Middle Ages*, 164.

CHAPTER 37

The Backing of Money

Money cannot be created arbitrarily. The State's consent can only be given to create money when based on a real need for it. In an economy dominated by a passion for justice, any money should be "backed" by the goods and services in an economy. One way money generally remains stable is when the quantity of money in circulation is kept in proportion to the value of goods and services in the economy. As Fr. Bernard Dempsey writes, "A fixed money supply, or a supply altered only in accord with objective and calculable criteria, is a necessary condition to a meaningful just price of money."[1]

Determining Money Supply

In an organic economy, there is no precise formula for determining the correct quantity of money supply since it depends upon many factors. The rate at which the money circulates must be considered. The public may also prefer to hold a large portion of its wealth in personal or real property rather than cash, which in turn diminishes the need for money. There are certain money extenders, such as bills of credit, checks, clearinghouses, barter, or other money substitutes, that likewise diminish the need for issuing currency.

Money supply is maintained when the government issues currency to replace that which has been lost through wear and tear. It can also increase the money stock to "back" growth in the economy. Such money draws upon the prestige of the State to impart some of its value and can exact seignorage, that is, a small profit as payment for supplying an exchange medium to the public. This is especially true of currencies of small value, like our own American coinage, that the State mints as a service to the public and to the profit of the Treasury.

---

1. Bernard W. Dempsey, *Interest and Usury* (London: Dennis Dobson, 1948), 210.

Backing of Money

When large infusions of money are needed in times of crisis, great investments, or rebuilding, money must find "backing" to guarantee the confidence of the public. It must prevent the inflating of the currency by tying the new money to a future value.

Historically, such money has been backed by many things. At times we find land, government assets, metals, and commodities used to back the issue of this new money. Other money has relied upon future tax revenues, bonds, and loans. In times of war, fiat currencies have circulated and retained surprising value backed solely upon the touching patriotism of the people.

All this forms part of the flexibility of money born of the ingenuity of men who call it forth for the better practice of justice and the service of the common good.

Establishing Norms of Justice

From these considerations, one might ask in the final analysis what monetary plan do we offer in our present time of crisis. Rather than propose a concrete scheme, let us first outline the norms of justice that would characterize the system we desire. Hence, let us have sound money, ample in supply, stable in value. Let us spurn the temptation of leveraging money that so favors unbridled credit, expansion, and speculation.

Money must fulfill once again its primary functions as a measure of value, a stable exchange medium, and a temperate store of wealth. Let the State issue money once again, and let it not originate or thrive on debt. Let money serve as a convenient means of exchange. Let it enjoy the trust of the people and be a true expression of their culture.

No monetary system can suppress greed since there will always be greed in this vale of tears. If we let the two tribunals of justice function, we will not see the manipulation of money, frenetic intemperance, and the restless probing for profit opportunities that so destroy the integrity of money and men.

When justice rules, prudence naturally puts in place systems of simple norms full of common sense, wisdom, and flexibility. Charity is then better able to perfect justice and serve man in his needs.

Which System?

To those who would insist and ask us what specific system we might favor, we would reply that many systems have worked in the past—local, national, and international currencies, ghost monies, tally sticks, and seignorage systems. Many media have successfully recorded money's value—metals, leather, paper, ledgers, and even electronic systems. Many things have served to back money and keep it stable.

As long as the above norms of justice are met, it matters little which system or systems are used. Such decisions are best left to the diverse customs and usages from which men have always called forth money for the better practice of justice.

One might finally object that this is hardly an economic solution. It does not offer practical systems and monetary theories needed to give us sound money. It is merely a ploy to escape giving a real solution.

Basis of Good Money

To this, we would reply that there is one important consideration that goes beyond monetary theory and which many economists deliberately ignore. It is a fact that, in the stormy history of money, bad money most often appears not from bad monetary theory but from the despotic or manipulative acts of men.

While good monetary theory is essential, we must insist on what should be an obvious fact: the good or bad actions of men in society are what really determine the course of the economy and the soundness of money. In the final analysis, man, who calls forth money from society for the better practice of justice, must also call forth the accompanying virtues that this justice demands.

In fact, the integrity of any currency is based on the trust in the authority that issues it. When authority pursues justice, money enjoys the power and prestige of office put at the service of the common good. We do not hesitate to affirm that our own "capitalist" system would not have prospered if not for the natural "bourgeois" virtues of men and authorities.

When authority governs with injustice, betrays the trust of the people, and ignores the rule of law, there is no monetary system that cannot be circumvented, or monetary theory perverted, in the pursuit of ill-gotten gains. We have no doubt that the present crisis is born not only from unsound monetary policy, but the intemperate acts of countless men and authorities whose frenetic intemperance has brought our system to ruin.

In vain do we speak about a sound monetary policy outside of virtue. The lessons of history do not fail to record that where virtuous leaders and saintly kings rule, sound money—and sound monetary theory— flourishes. We read that when money suffered debasement from the wars and policies of fourteenth-century French kings, the people clamored and longed for the "strong money" of good King Saint Louis. In this sense, all virtue, including and especially supernatural virtue, is the best backing of money, one that far outshines the brilliance of gold.

If we are to search for a general rule to guide us in the present crisis, then let it be this one: Every people constructs the monetary system that reflects its values. Our present system reflects the rule of money and the set of values that frenetic intemperance imposes upon us. If we wish to return to order, we must replace today's rule of money with another rule. We must adopt a whole new set of values from which will come an organic monetary remedy.

The gros tournois coin from the time of King Saint Louis IX (1266-1270).
When justice rules, it creates the ideal conditions for sound money. The
French long remembered the "strong money" of the saintly king.

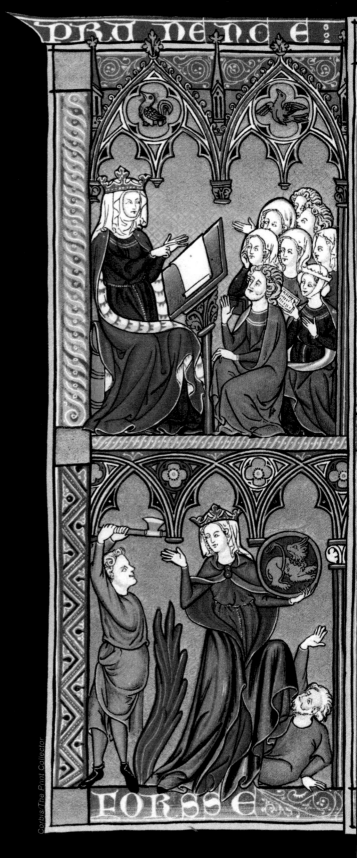

PRU NE N·C E ::

FOR SS E

A Corresponding Temperance

Representation of the Four Cardinal Virtues . When temperance and the three other cardinal virtues rule in society, frenetic intemperance can be held in check.

Illuminated manuscript. When society is filled with principles, ideas, and moral values, the influence of the rule of money is greatly diminished. A new set of values, ruled by honor, is reflected in the arts, society and economy.

CHAPTER 38

A Different Set of Values

To combat frenetic intemperance, there must be a corresponding temperance. The purpose and goal of this temperance is the establishment of an inner order in man and society from which comes forth serenity and harmony.[1]

Such a solution runs contrary to that of the socialists or progressives who affirm that the only way to restrain a "savage" economy is with equally savage regulation, which would restrain all commerce. It is the equivalent of curing a persistent itch with a straitjacket instead of a soothing balm.

We must address the real problem of the itch. It does us little good to establish a monetary system based on justice or charity if the temperamental state of men is to engage in frenetic ventures where money is made to play the dominant role in our lives. This rule of money and its set of values fuel frenetic intemperance. The only way to challenge this intemperate rule is with a contrary rule that promotes temperance.

A Return to the Rule of Honor

This clash of rules is hardly new. Throughout history, two sides, two economic outlooks, two lifestyles have long opposed each other as if engaged in constant combat.

On the one side, there is the rule of money with a set of secular values, which include quantity, function, efficiency, and utility. This rule tends to reduce everything to terms of self-interest, matter, and production.

On the other side is another rule with its own set of values that opposes that of money. We experience some difficulty in naming this op-

---

1. Saint Thomas discusses this restraining characteristic of temperance saying it "withdraws man from things which seduce the appetite from obeying reason" (Aquinas, *Summa Theologica*, II-II, q. 141, a. 2).

posing rule. Many authors have written about it using words like "moral," "status," or "humane" to describe it. They list virtue, tradition, or prestige as its attributes. However, the overwhelming tide of change wrought by our industrial society has so undermined the meaning of these terms as to render difficult the task of finding a word that characterizes this rule entirely.

We think *honor* best describes this rule since the word survives less sullied from modernity's brutal egalitarianism. Honor conveys the definition of an authentic esteem given to all that is excellent in a social atmosphere of respect, affection, and courtesy. It towers above that which is strictly material, functional, and practical.

By using the word honor instead of prestige, for example, we avoid the misunderstanding of those who would confuse our order with vainglory, vanity, or pride. Rather, honor conveys the idea of values that cannot be bought and sold. It spreads the atmosphere of tranquility and temperance that we desire.

Most Effective Against Rule of Money

The rule of honor is a fitting response to the rule of money because it defines a lifestyle that naturally leads men to esteem and seek after those things that are excellent. It introduces into the market square a set of values that includes quality, beauty, goodness, and charity. This rule is open to the calming influence of the cardinal virtues, which inject balance and psychological well-being into society and economy.

So powerful is this rule that we can observe that when honor is spread throughout all levels of society, the rule of money loses its attraction. Certain professions, for example, are sustained much more by true honor than money, as can be seen in the university professor or military officer. When honor reigns, money's influence wanes, institutions are zealous of their reputation, families uphold their names, and culture flourishes.

Riches and Honor

By affirming the rule of honor, we do not in any way disparage riches, goods, or money. All we are saying is that they should not dominate a culture.

Nor do we advocate a primitive or impoverished economy devoid of luxury and splendor. Where honor rules, men make abundant use of material goods as a means to make life in society dignified, upright, and agreeable to body and soul. Wealth tends to be held more in accumulated goods and less in money. Luxury becomes a tasteful expression and not the measure of honor.

By contrast, where the rule of money holds sway, riches become the supreme measure of life. We see the decay of principles and convictions, which allows the media to reign supreme and makes gaudy luxuries sought and displayed. This rule cultivates a shallow and insipid cosmopolitanism that is characterized by a decay of both culture and good taste.

Transcending Modern Economy

Perhaps the greatest advantage of a rule of honor is that many modern problems regarding money and credit are simply sidestepped or transcended.

A rule of honor, for example, favors calm accumulation of wealth and orderly growth. As a result, we do not see the artificial speeds of the Industrial Revolution that incite society to produce frantically or consume madly. Accordingly, such an economy no longer presupposes massive injections of loans, capital, and other financial instruments that so dominate modern economy.

In a similar way, the rule of honor profoundly changes economy by modifying the demand for goods. Its set of values effectively undermines today's consumerism. Production would tend to be less standardized in a society that values relationships over money, quality over quantity, beauty over utility. This society's patterns of demand would give producers every incentive to make goods of greater durability, lasting value, and craftsmanship. The natural advertising of the producer's good reputation means much more to the consumer than the commercial advertising of created dissatisfaction.

Character Not Capital

The greatest product of the rule of honor is the building of character. Man himself is the focal point of production where the unfathomable riches inside each soul can be developed. When the rule of honor dominates economy, it produces inside each soul what Richard Weaver lists as "the formation of character, the perfection of style, the attainment of distinction in intellect and imagination."[2]

By this set of values, man is defined by who he truly is and not by what he has. His patterns of production and consumption are determined by a clear sense of identity of one who has found that place, that calling, where he feels he belongs in society. He is not the "mass man" constantly looking to others for directions. Rather he feels so secure in his convictions that he comes to have "station" or "standing" in society, which means that he is not easily intimidated by public opinion, taken up by fads, or lured by fast fortune. That is to say, the rule of honor favors a different type of economy defined much more by character than capital.

In the rule of honor, each cultivates a profession which enhances the person's dignity by emphasizing the respectability and not the profitability of his profession. Then the traditional farmer, for example, is seen much more as a man of good sense and judgment than the efficient land manager. The craftsman is much more an artist than a mere maker of goods. In the lawyer or doctor, we value the man of wisdom much more than the competent and money-making specialist.[3]

Embedding Honor in Society

One might ask how a rule of honor can be restored. To this we would reply: Fill society with principles, ideas, and moral values and the influence of the rule of money will greatly diminish.

When guiding principles govern conduct, money cannot buy loyalty. When society is blessed with a rich and balanced intellectual life, it shows "far greater esteem for all that has to do with true religion, philosophy, art and literature than for what has to do with the good of the body and the exploitation of matter"—the reign of money.[4] When society has morals, money's ability to facilitate sin falls upon deaf ears.

We might also highlight the role of true elites in this task. By their concern for the common good, these representative figures are in a natural position to preserve, defend, and spread Christian principles, ideas, and moral values. If faithful to the virtue, culture, refinement,

---

2. Weaver, *Visions of Order*, 29.
3. See Plinio Corrêa de Oliveira, "Money Is Not the Supreme Value," *Folha de São Paulo*, May 9, 1971.
4. Corrêa de Oliveira, *Revolution and Counter-Revolution*, 80.

and education that naturally come from their traditions, they can serve as models for all society. If society at all levels is filled with representative figures who value and embody all these things contrary to the harsh rule of money, their influence will greatly favor the return of the benevolent rule of honor.

A Moral Restoration

In short, the overthrow of the rule of money requires a moral regeneration centered on the highest set of values—those of Christian civilization. Indeed, through Her teachings, liturgy, and moral example, the Church embeds principles, ideas, and moral values inside the social fabric, inspiring men not to profits, but to an ardent love of God where all things revolve around the First Commandment.

Under the shadow of the Cross, the Church overcame the harsh rule of money and laid the foundation for the rule of honor.

———————————————————— · ————————————————————

Our task will now be to describe the proportion and order of the rule of honor and then the ideals that must inspire this rule. Without a change of values, all our efforts will be in vain, and we will not see the corresponding temperance needed to combat frenetic intemperance. The consequences of not returning to the rule of honor are dire.

As Edmund Burke remarks: "Where trade and manufactures are wanting to a people, and the spirit of nobility and religion remains, sentiment supplies, and not always ill supplies, their place."[5]

Should the sole rule of money finally prevail, we will find ourselves in moral destitution. "But if commerce and the arts should be lost in an experiment to try how well a state may stand without these old fundamental principles," Burke continues, "what sort of a thing must be a nation of gross, stupid, ferocious, and, at the same time, poor and sordid barbarians, destitute of religion, honor, or manly pride, possessing nothing at present, and hoping for nothing hereafter?"[6]

The choice is clearly ours.

———————————————

5. Burke, "Reflections on the Revolution in France," in *The Works of Edmund Burke*, 1:490.
6. Ibid.

A winemaker evaluating his wine. Products are true expressions of a people and culture when there is a close interrelationship between producers, inhabitants, and the locality.

CHAPTER 39

Tending Towards Self-Sufficiency

B y returning to a rule of honor, we set the stage for a great temperance to descend like a gentle rain over the economy. It could not be otherwise since temperance is the virtue whereby man governs his natural appetites and passions in accordance with the norms prescribed by reason and Faith.

Thus, we can say that temperance naturally gives rise to an organic economy since it teaches us to desire that which is proper for us and naturally leads to balance, proportion, and especially a tendency to self-sufficiency, which we will now describe.

A Turning Inward

In tracing this economy back to its roots, we note a prevailing concern: there is a turning inward whereby one provides for one's own. This tendency begins with the individual and extends to the family, community, and nation.

The origin of this turning inward comes from man's natural desire to express his personality and originality. To do this, he draws from and vigorously develops those God-given qualities and possibilities that make him unique and unmistakable in the order of creation.[1]

This turning inward contrasts sharply with the modern notion of individualism in which individuals close themselves up in the world of their own self-interest and then turn outward, becoming part of the masses to avoid complete isolation.

On the contrary, when individuals express their individuality in an organic order, they delve deeply within themselves as a means of developing a self-assurance, which allows them to stand out and define themselves unambiguously in society. They have principles, certainty, independence, and dignity. They are not part of the masses or slaves of public opinion.

---

1. See Aquinas, *Summa Contra Gentiles*, II, 45; Aquinas, *Summa Theologica*, I, q. 47, a. 2; I, q. 50, a. 4.

Such persons have the means to perceive the meaning of their lives and how they fit into society. They make use of small social units, especially the family, to help properly develop their personality and, in turn, they impart something of their own character on the social groups to which they belong.

Extending this notion of turning inward yet further, we can say that social groups, as moral entities, can also seek a similar expression of their unique character. Villages, parishes, institutions, academies, and families all have the capacity to draw from and develop their own qualities springing from the vibrant richness of their members. From this development, each social group finds its own path, which later can give rise to the birth of cultures and civilizations.

An Economic Application

This notion cannot help but have economic applications. Being naturally endowed with intelligence and free will, man tends, by his own spiritual faculties, to draw from himself all the necessary qualities to provide for his welfare. This in turn gives rise to unique expressions of self-sufficiency.

From the very beginning of economy around the hearth of the home, man turned vigorously inward seeking to sustain the family. Likewise, he developed intermediary associations of kinship, community, and Faith by turning inward, seeking to advance the material and spiritual well-being of members. Larger associations such as cities, regions, and even nations, forming concentric circles of concern, shared in this inward development and self-expression where each group took care of its own and, by the *principle of subsidiarity*, had recourse to a higher order only when necessary.

Astonishing Self-Sufficiency

This great tendency to develop and take care of one's own, results in an astonishing degree of self-sufficiency that filters up to all levels of society. It gives rise to the temperance and joy of living within one's own means at both the individual and community levels.

In medieval times, for example, families, intermediary groups, and states not only amply provided for themselves, but safeguarded the future with stocks of food, necessities, and arms.[2] It is a self-sufficiency allowing for great independence and individual creativity without either jeopardizing the richness and unity of the whole or resulting in isolation and discord.

Lewis Mumford illustrates this principle well by describing the neighborhoods and precincts of the medieval city, as "a congeries of little cities, each with a certain degree of autonomy and self-sufficiency, each formed so naturally out of common needs and purposes that it only enriched and supplemented the whole."[3]

At the same time, it must be observed that this economic self-sufficiency is a relative one. Since the family and intermediary associations are not perfect societies, they are still in need of others to obtain their end. Even the State, which is a perfect society in the sense that it is sufficient unto itself, enjoys only a relative self-sufficiency, since it also needs to participate in the community of nations. Inside this context, balanced trade becomes necessary.

Formation of Regions

This economic self-sufficiency easily leads to healthy localism since these inward movements come to be tied to a community and place. It necessarily leads to the formation of regions inside of which people come together and practice the temperance of living with the resources at hand.

Hence, a region is formed by the intimate relationship between a people and a place. Each region has its own vegetation, lay of the land, natural wonders, hinterland, and mysteries. Sometimes it seems that there are places that Providence has blessed with harmonic features, as if awaiting inhabitants. Other wilder areas require more effort to inhabit and develop.

---

2. "Throughout the whole of the Middle Ages every person who was not a pauper stored in his own house substantial reserves of grain, salted meat, salt, candles, etc. What the private individuals did the state did also. In the feudal period, it was the unfailing policy to keep ample reserves for emergencies on the manors. In the following period, the communal authorities, while concerned not to allow excessive hoarding on the part of private speculators, built up stocks, especially of grain, to be resold in times of emergency at a low price." C. M. Cipolla, "The Italian and Iberian Peninsulas," in *Economic Organization and Policies in the Middle Ages*, vol. 3 of *The Cambridge Economic History of Europe*, ed. M. M. Postan (London: Cambridge University Press, 1963), 402. Cipolla also notes "the armory in the hands of the private citizens and the weaponry owned by the public powers ... represented quite a sizable amount of wealth" (Cipolla, *Before the Industrial Revolution*, 104).
3. Mumford, *City in History*, 310.

When families settle on lands, they gradually discover the area's features. They curiously take on some characteristics of the area, and it might be said that the region comes to reflect a bit of the mentality of the families. A rugged land often leads to the forming of a hardy people, whereas a sunny Mediterranean climate might result in inhabitants with cheerful dispositions. A disciplined people tend to organize their region accordingly. True communities and regions form in the fortuitous circumstances where families feel the happiness of being at home, anchored in a particular place, be it a rural area, city, or neighborhood.

Thus, the region becomes the true home of their homes. So great is this relationship that there are even those who figuratively affirm that the irregular physical limits of a region are defined much more by the extension of the common love for the region by a family, clan, or people than by its mere geographic designation.

The Human Element: A Natural Preference

Hence, inhabitants become sensitive to a place and develop natural preferences for the setting where they were born or raised: its panorama, land, climate, or foods. They come to prefer their own region even over other places with better resources.

Accordingly, they come to understand that their region is made for them and they for their region. For them, the region has a wide variety of supreme delights that no other place can offer. Regions come to have indefinite possibilities of development for those who make the effort to discover their hidden potential.

REGIONAL FOODS EXPRESS LOCAL CULTURE

Regional varieties of foods flourished and a very wide range of flavors could be distinguished before the standardization of so many food commodities. Local consumers might, for example, enjoy the subtle differences of flavor between grass butter and hay butter or May cheese and Michaelmas cheese which could be found only in their small region. (See Joan Thirsk, "The Rural Economy," in *Our Forgotten Past: Seven Centuries of Life on the Land*, ed. Jerome Blum [London: Thames and Hudson, 1982], 89.)

The region is like a tower that provides inhabitants with a perspective to see the things of this world better and, by comparison, estimate their value. Such a vision does not exclude the appreciation, use, or esteem of things outside the region. Nevertheless, the natural preference for one's own leads a person not to covet the excellent products of other regions even if they be greater.

The Debate over "Local" Production

Just as we naturally prefer our native land that is known to us, so also our human nature tends to take comfort in those goods we know. "Homemade," "handcrafted," or "local" products are those "known things" that allow us to sense that personal and human touch stamped with the familiar mark of the place and people who produce them. So strong is this preference that the advertising industry, even today, uses imagery of the "homemade" to sell its factory-made goods.

Inside the context of self-sufficiency and a healthy regionalism, production becomes more than just the mechanical manufacturing of goods, reflecting instead the expression of a people, culture, and locality. Those reassuring human touches so enhance markets that we are left to wonder if perhaps the world would be much richer in quality and culture if it were much more local, and much less global, in its production and markets.

Obviously not everything can be locally produced, nor do we suggest that there be only artisan production. Many things (such as planes or electronics, for example) by their very size or complexity are better suited to manufacturing on a larger scale. There is a great variety of goods today that we cannot imagine outside the framework of present production methods. But this fact should not lead us to take the unbalanced position that almost everything must be mass produced on a global scale and that local production be reduced to quaint artisan production of little economic importance.

We might also note that local production is not always limited to a small area but rather extends itself in concentric circles outward, depending on markets and resources. We cannot, for example, expect a small village to support the manufacturing of pianos. In this case, the "local" market would correspond more to a region, a state, or even a whole nation.

When the rule of honor prevails, it creates the conditions for the appreciation of and demand for these local products. It provides for their ample and efficient production. Consumers come to see with great pride and loyalty those products which are an expression of their full development and identity.

Presuppositions of Local Production

We must clearly define what we mean by local production since "local" production has come to mean different things to different people. There are those who have turned "local" production into an ecological cause, a healthy alternative, or a political statement. Such "local" initiatives have little to do with healthy localism. In fact, without a special set of circumstances, even handcrafted goods or homegrown crops will not necessarily enrich a local culture.

The principal presupposition of authentic local production is a close interrelationship between producers, inhabitants, and the locality. There must be that turning inward by which a people use their own local resources to make products suited to their tastes and oriented towards the perfection of their society.

In this sense, *demand should influence production much more than production should determine demand.* By constantly adjusting available materials to local tastes, producer and consumer should become the "co-creators" of goods. For example, a farmer might plant crops he perceives are both suited to his soil and prized by his customers. A local cuisine develops when chefs constantly adjust local dishes and native ingredients to reflect what local people like.

We might mention as an example certain sheep cheeses from the wild and brambly regions of Corsica that are coated with rosemary, thyme, fern leaves, fennel seeds, savory, or juniper berries.[4] In the profoundly Christian souls of the artisans who make these fine cheeses, we encounter a passion for perfection that leads to the search for the ideal cheese through the constant interaction between the cheese makers and the local population over the course of generations. Hence, local production is a distilling process where the people experience the spiritual joy of seeing the product of their

---

4. See, for example, these Corsican cheeses: Pecurinu, A Filetta, Montatimu, Brin d'Amour, and Fleur du Maquis.

joint creativity with the materials at hand.

Local production is enriched even more when families refine their products over generations and the good word of their quality provides natural advertising and makes such products a source of local pride. In this way, an area becomes "known" for its particular wines, fruits, or handicrafts.

Special Role of Local Resources

The locality also plays a special role in the richness of products. God endowed each place with a great diversity of riches and resources, many of which are hidden. In His Providence, He put those things there principally for the discovery and use of those who live in the locality and to aid them in their quest for perfection.

Thus, it is proper that regions discover and use their own local resources to produce an astonishing array of products. In this way, presenting everything that the region has of its best becomes truly a work of art. Contrary to modern economy and its law of comparative advantage, we should not automatically assume that a locality cannot fulfill a specific need. The Corsican cheese makers cited above were not resigned to import the "best" cheese from the French mainland as might happen today. Instead they sought out the seemingly meager resources of the area to produce the finest of cheeses.

Of course, local products will not always be able to provide for all our needs, but necessity is often the mother of ingenious invention. Local needs can force man to make great efforts to use his creativity and skills to extract those resources and produce items of extraordinary originality that confer cultural richness and diversity upon an area. In this sense, the possibilities for local production are practically limitless.

Locals used the fragrant juniper berry, for example, to flavor gin. They further distilled juniper oil from the wood and leaves of several species and used it in perfumes and medicines. So it is that local and distinctive foods, fabrics, arts, and architectural styles are created. Even when better and well-established alternatives are available elsewhere, it should not prevent local producers from challenging these products with their own original creations, and local consumers from preferring—and therefore buying—their region's very own.

Even the locality itself can enter into products. For example, medieval craftsmen would often include in their artwork local animals, plants, and scenes culled from daily life, which gave their works a distinctively picturesque, familiar, and warm human quality. "The worker who had walked through the nearby fields or woods on a holiday," writes Lewis Mumford, "came back to his stone carving, his wood working, his weaving or gold-smithing, with a rich harvest of impressions to be transferred to his work."[5] The potter might perceive local colors and use them when glazing his dishes, or the stone carver might observe a field mouse and sculpt it on his column. Their products were truly local.

This mutual interpenetration of people and place creates the conditions for a rich culture. Just as the bee takes the local flowers' nectar to produce its unique honey, so also the creativity of a people takes from the locality those materials that result in products that are custom-made expressions of their own creativity, culture, and mentality—and not those of others.

Need for Stability

We must again emphasize that this localism presupposes a stable family life, which supports a love of reflection, tradition, and local identity. It presupposes a desire for full development that leads men to seek after production, refined over time, where demand is not regulated by advertising but by people zealous for products that reflect their own identity. It presupposes ample and even large-scale production to ensure adequate supplies. There should be thriving and stable elites who can distill the best from an area.

That is why we affirm there is a temperate and delightful richness in this kind of local production that we do not find in anonymous globalized trade and massive production. At the same time, we note that this same richness cannot be found in many modern "local" or "organic" goods (even when produced by local farmers and artisans). While we welcome and encourage the renewed interest in local and organic production of recent years, it will only bear fruit if there are stable links between producer, customer, and locality, and especially

---

5. Mumford, *City in History*, 297-98.

if such production extends beyond a single generation.

With mass production and the Industrial Revolution, intemperance threw markets out of sync, breaking down the intense relationships between producer, consumer, and locality. People were induced to desire cheap and plentiful goods from around the world while disregarding their own goods formed by their own temperament and mentality. Modern men threw themselves frenetically into this global consumption, coveting goods designed by others while showing little appreciation for their own.

In these times when global consumption patterns are failing, we should seek the temperance of a healthy self-sufficiency. We should hold as an ideal that "turning inward" whereby we opt for the qualitative richness of providing for our own and reject the quantitative poverty of global mass production.

Tapestry based on a painting by Francesco Guardi (1712-1793). Merchants sell their wares in Venice. Church doctors are clear in affirming the need for international trade.

CHAPTER 40

Protective Trade and Free Markets

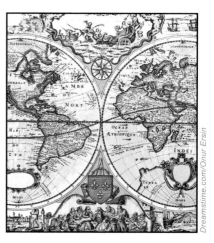

Dreamstime.com/Onur Ersin

S omeone might object to our concept of self-sufficiency on the grounds that it naturally becomes protective. In fact, it is undeniable that pre-modern economies tended to protect local markets. In their zeal for material independence, local rulers and towns took measures to discourage outside competition, exercising a kind of mild medieval "protectionism" that targeted regional as well as foreign competitors.

Before answering this objection, we would like to note that such "protectionism" was generally not excessive, and some scholars claim its effects were exaggerated. Fernand Braudel, for example, reports that while numerous tolls are often cited as protective obstacles that discouraged trade and slowed down transport, they seldom exceeded on a single river, for example, significantly less than a half-percent of merchandise value.[1]

Officials tended to welcome and facilitate the importation of necessities and discourage the export of valuable local resources without need. They never entirely blocked off markets. Moreover, tolls put the expense of transport infrastructure on those who used it and not on the general population. "Protectionism certainly was not yet born," Raymond de Roover notes. Citing examples, he declares the supposedly "crushing burden of tolls in the Middle Ages" to be "far from excessive."[2]

1. See Fernand Braudel, *The Perspective of the World*, vol. 3 of *Civilization and Capitalism 15th-18th Century*, trans. Siân Reynolds (New York: Harper and Row, 1984), 290-291.
2. Raymond de Roover, *The Rise and Decline of the Medici Bank 1397-1494* (New York: W. W. Norton, 1966), 145.

The Need for International Trade

By defending healthy localism and its protective consequences, it might seem we are condemning international trade. Quite the contrary.

Church doctors are clear in demonstrating that natural and positive law support the need for trade, whether national or international, since denying necessities to people would violate the Golden Rule of doing unto others what you would have them do unto you. There would seem to be a certain intemperance in asserting that all communities must survive only on the resources at hand. Reason indicates that trade is a benefit to a society that suffers from various wants.

In addition, the fact that God did not distribute all resources equally makes trade necessary. Raw materials such as precious stones or rare minerals are universally sought yet concentrated in particular regions. Certain local medicines or goods are needed for the health and general welfare of peoples. Above all, scarcity of basic foodstuffs and other vital commodities in times of crisis makes international trade essential for relieving suffering and furthering the common good.

International trade can also further cultural ends. Trade involving fine arts, crafts, or luxury items is wholesome since it facilitates the healthy interpenetration of cultures. Such items are also helpful to those in leadership positions or elites who, by force of their functions, need to understand the distinct mentality of those in other nations. Adopting a calculated cosmopolitan attitude facilitates this process without harming the distinctive local character of the person.

Thus, international trade should and must exist. It should be both ample and common, especially when satisfying basic needs. However, it should not dominate or destroy local culture and production.

Natural Protectionism

Church doctors recognize that just as rulers have the right to tax populations for the common good, they may also levy moderate import taxes to protect the local economy.

Communities and nations should have the right to take an attitude of self-defense of their own culture and economy when confronted with intrusive and especially unfair trade practices. Out of love for its own identity, a local population can have a reasonable and healthy suspicion towards the invasion of global or outside products.

Such attitudes need not take on a coercive character, as in tariffs or duties. A much more effective means of defense is a natural protectionism—respectful of free markets—that in the past was born of a zeal whereby the population simply preferred the local product out of the joy of consuming that which was specific to it and a natural wariness for that which was not. Supported by healthy customs and local elites, people had the temperance of staying within the limits of that which was an expression of their souls, culture, and mentality.

It would be understandable, for example, that the population of a region, which has had its own distinctive drink for over 500 years, might reject the entrance of a commercialized drink that has nothing in common with their culture. We can sympathize with the attitude of residents sipping their native Scotch while a ship full of cheap vodka lies rejected in the harbor . . .

A Balanced Defense

Any defense must be balanced and flexible enough to encourage the importation of outside products when local items are unavailable or inadequate. It should be realistic enough to understand that some local products may disappear through competition. In their enthusiastic preference for their own, members of a local community and their representative figures should be open-minded enough to appreciate occasional products from the outside that can provide legitimate diversity that helps give a bit of spice to life.

At the same time, a community should avoid a false cosmopolitanism where world-class products are automatically adopted without regard for the local culture or tastes as a sign of "higher culture." For example, the systematic adoption of truly fine quality French wines to the exclusion of local wines, even very good ones, would put a society in the position of seeking to better itself inorganically, artificially, and inauthentically.

Such a delicate balance is not found in the indiscriminate interplay of market forces but rather in the rule of honor and its set of values. A truly free market is not found in a total interdependency, but in an economy where individuals and families can develop their own personalities and potential.

CHAPTER 41

The Restoration of Dependency

While temperance teaches us to see the reality that each man is capable of colossal self-sufficiency, it also reveals to us that we are contingent beings.

The fact that we are dependent upon others helps, not hinders, our full development. Hence, the same person who develops admirable habits of self-reliance also takes the initiative to evaluate his own insufficiencies and has the courage to seek out the aid of others. It is this acknowledgment of dependency that binds us together in community and makes trade necessary.

The Dependent Individual

Such dependency is an important part of our personal development since we cannot perfect ourselves alone. We depend on community—especially the family, intermediary associations, and the Christian State—to supply our deficiencies and thus reach the perfection of our essentially social nature. So important is community that Heinrich A. Rommen emphatically writes, "Any kind of seclusion from the fullness of community life ultimately means for the individual a personal loss, a self-mutilation, an atrophy, a defect in self-realization."[1]

Thus, we are by nature dependent. As medieval English writer Ralph of Acton notes, "When God could have made all men strong, wise, and rich, He was unwilling to do so. He wished instead that these men should be strong, those weak; these wise, those foolish; these rich and those poor. For if all were strong, wise and wealthy, one would not be in need of the other."[2]

Finding the Balance

Such a concept differs greatly from that of the individualist man

---

1. Rommen, *State in Catholic Thought*, 136-37.
2. G. R. Owst, *Literature and Pulpit in Medieval England: A Neglected Chapter in the History of English Letters & of the English People*, 2nd ed. (Oxford: Basil Blackwell, 1961), 561.

whose autonomy prevents him from recognizing his natural limits and the weaknesses of his fallen nature. He is a self-made man beholden to no other. This is well expressed in the ravings of Jean-Paul Sartre, who wrote that "no man should have to be dependent on another man."[3] Ironically, this same "autonomous" man is totally dependent, not on men, but on the modern interdependent systems into which he is inserted.

In an organic society, this dependency is limited and complementary. We can return to the imperfect analogy of the living being with interrelated cells, tissues, organs, and systems working together for the common good. Likewise in society, this dependency aids us in our quest for self-sufficiency by providing comfort, aid, and guidance. It makes allowances for individual strengths and weaknesses that can be counterbalanced and complemented in others, thereby creating the sensation of wholeness, security, and well-being for the entire community or social group. We have already cited the feudal and family bonds that serve as examples of how this dependency enriches society yet protects individuality.

Economically, dependency has a similar effect. This harmonic interplay of self-sufficiency with dependency creates an economy where skills are complementary rather than set in competition. In fact, such dependency often involves great sacrifice, especially in those cases where parties must constantly adjust to human weaknesses. We might cite as an extreme example the dependency of those who are mentally impaired. Those who care for them must practice great patience and virtue and temper their own desires. Such virtue benefits all society and introduces a human element in social and economic relationships. Such an attitude is contrary to the mechanistic vision of society, where any defects or dependencies are judged inefficient and efforts are made to eliminate them at all costs.

The ability to deal with dependencies involves a love of neighbor as self that requires religious fervor. When this fervor decays in the family and community, mutual dependency is replaced by rivalries which lead to friction and later hatred. This finds economic expression in cutthroat competition and a desire to command that could be

---

3. Braudel, *The Wheels of Commerce,* vol. 2 of *Civilization and Capitalism 15th -18th Century*, 514.

seen in the rival Italian Renaissance cities and later in the practice of frenetic intemperance.

Dependency and Charity

When this dependency is practiced with the fervor of Christian charity, we witness an excellence in the love of neighbors that goes beyond that of exercising patience and forbearance towards them. It also means admiring in others that which we ourselves lack. Charity includes taking delight in the qualities and richness of others, even experiencing joy in the very qualities in others that complement our own shortcomings. These qualities are but reflections of the Divine Perfection in God, and our joy is analogous to what we will possess when contemplating God, who satisfies all our shortcomings. Ultimately, admiration of others leads us to a greater love of God.

When dependency unites with charity, there is not only the joy of giving but also the joy of receiving from others. Christian civilization was full of enriching dependencies allowing all to receive help without humiliation and to give aid with humility.

This gives rise to temperate relationships free of self-interest. It leads to an objective judgment of people since all came to admire and pay homage to those who deserve it, pity and help those who need it, and rejoice together with those of similar circumstance. Within the limits of our fallen nature, this objective vision makes human society delightful because such relationships create an atmosphere of trust. Such temperate souls are like brother souls—next to which the *fraternité* of the French Revolution is but a worthless parody.

Thus, the needy receive alms without shame. The craftsman receives the apprentice like a family member. And the king solicits advice from his council with earnest attention. All seek God's grace with humble yet loving supplication.

Jeans for sale. Mass standardization cannot fully satisfy an individual's material and spiritual needs. Consumers often sacrifice their personal tastes to products made for mass markets.

CHAPTER 42

Addressing Production and Standardization

I t remains for us to address several issues related to frenetic intemperance that we criticized earlier. One of these is mass standardization, which we characterized as a factor in the creation of a mass society.

As we have seen, a certain standardization is needed to ensure adequate production. To insist that all production be adapted to the individual is not realistic. We must also avoid the opposite extreme of affirming that all products can be standardized indifferently without harming the individual.

The Limits of Standardization

How standardization affects us differs as each individual is unique. We naturally tend to express ourselves in terms of consumption that corresponds to our psychological, moral, and physical development. Hence, some people might have a problem in using a particular standardized product while others experience none. To use a very simple example, a ready-to-wear coat might feel comfortable on some because of their particular build but uncomfortable on many others.

We note that, when exposed to large amounts of mass-produced products, there is a point where we ourselves feel "standardized" and "massified." That is to say, we need to assess the degree of standardization that we can accept and still retain our personality. We need to determine that measure beyond which we cannot cede an inch lest it harm our development. This can be seen in the case of fads and fashions that become obsessive or lead many to act in a manner contrary to their well-being or personality. One should have sufficient love and self-respect so that, when sensing a loss of personality, steps can be taken towards diminishing the standardizing influence.

The Goal of Production

To understand this problem better, let us look at the goal of production. We produce to fill a need. While this can be done by simply supplying the minimum necessary to fill a physical necessity, it will not necessarily satisfy certain human desires that vary from person to person, or address spiritual appetites for beauty, excellence, or refinement. Such desires correspond to man's constant desire to discover ways to better his situation.

We need to eat, for example, yet any food can fill our stomachs. However, we experience a special joy when we are given delicious or well-presented food that suits our tastes. We need clothes to protect our bodies. We experience a special delight in wearing tasteful clothes that fit us well instead of ill-fitting or ugly garments. This delight corresponds to the higher spiritual element of production, which gives to the product those intangible things that please the soul and aid in the practice of virtue.

That is to say, generally speaking there is a physical and spiritual dimension to any need that varies in intensity from person to person. To the degree that both dimensions are satisfied, production accomplishes its purpose.

The Emphasis of Modern Production

We note that modern mass production places most of its emphasis on the physical dimension to the detriment of the spiritual. We do not affirm that it completely ignores the spiritual since it will often add elements of taste and beauty to products.

Nevertheless, the spiritual aspect tends to diminish as standardization increases. Art, beauty, or quality are all elements that are most likely to be sacrificed on the altar of efficiency. The principal goals of mass production are maximum efficiency, broadest appeal, and economy of scale. The machine becomes the choice means of production since it can endlessly replicate the production process. The result is mass standardization where, writes Tibor Scitovsky, "the monotony of mass-production work is fully matched by the monotony of its product."[1]

Through this mass standardization, we have put in place a vast market system that is undoubtedly convenient, plentiful, and inexpensive.

---

1. Tibor Scitovsky, *The Joyless Economy: An Inquiry into Human Satisfaction and Consumer Dissatisfaction* (New York: Oxford University Press, 1976), 249.

Yet, in the process, we have sacrificed that human touch that so delights and enriches the soul. There are certain things that money cannot buy that are lost in the standardization process. While there are custom products outside this system, mass-minded consumers usually adjust their tastes to products made for these convenient mass markets, thus deadening their own spiritual appetites by accepting only what is offered.

The Spiritual Dimension and Technology

We believe that this did not have to happen. Had frenetic intemperance not entered into the markets, the spiritual and material could have remained united. In fact, when the spiritual dimension becomes the primary element of production, it can also end up satisfying and putting in order our material necessities.

This can be seen, for example, in the development of technology. It is simply false to say that technology calls for greater standardization. In pre-modern production, we note that the emphasis on the spiritual dimension curiously did not work to the detriment of the physical. On the contrary, it challenged the development of technology to meet both physical and spiritual needs.

Take, for example, the development of the Gothic arch, flying buttress, and stained-glass window. All of these are the practical inventions developed to aid in the primarily spiritual pursuit of beauty, symbolism, and meaning that would be expressed in the higher, better illuminated, and acoustically-designed cathedral. They also involve feats of incredible technological daring specifically developed by medieval ingenuity to meet these esthetic needs.

"The technicians of the twelfth and thirteenth centuries, far from being traditionalists, were creating an entirely new concept of architecture, dynamic rather than static," writes Lynn White. "In their cathedrals we see a sublime fusion of high spirituality and advanced technology."[2]

The Spiritual Dimension in Everyday Life

This same union of material and spiritual dimensions is not limited to highly specialized projects like cathedrals; it can also be seen in prod-

---

2. White, *Machina Ex Deo*, 63.

ucts found in everyday life. The spiritual dimension introduced added value, culture, and warmth to the most common things. About such production, Lewis Mumford writes, "No article, even of vulgar daily use, was regarded as finished, unless it bore some unmistakable stamp, by its painting or modeling or shaping, of the human spirit."[3]

Historian Carlo Cipolla notes how simple products became veritable works of art because "the beauty and perfection of many products of European pre-industrial craftsmanship give the inescapable impression that the craftsman of the time found in his work a satisfaction and a sense of dignity which are, alas, foreign to the alienating assembly lines of the modern industrial complex."[4]

THE CULTURAL RICHNESS OF A HIGHLY DEVELOPED LOCAL PRODUCTION

The concept of satisfying material and spiritual needs extended into all fields in pre-industrial times. James J. Walsh writes: "This mingling of the useful and the beautiful is of itself a supreme difference between the thirteenth century generations and our own. Mr. Yeats, the well known Irish poet, in bidding farewell to America some years ago said to a party of friends, that no country could consider itself to be making real progress in culture until the very utensils in the kitchen were beautiful as well as useful. Anything that is merely useful is hideous, and anyone who can handle such things with impunity has not true culture" (*The Thirteenth, Greatest of Centuries* [New York: Fordham University Press, 1946], 113).

Integrated Production

We must emphasize that all this was done without jeopardizing the efficiencies of markets of the time. By focusing on the more important spiritual dimension, pre-modern production with the means available maintained an admirable balance between primary spiritual needs and the need for quantity, efficiency, economy, and technology so necessary for production.

This was possible because, as Richard Stivers notes, "technological

---

3. Mumford, *Technics and Human Development*, 1:253. We might also note that, for example, antique collecting purists consider 1830 as the latest date that defines the antique since pieces after that date were increasingly mass-produced by machines and thus without that warm human stamp.
4. Cipolla, *Before the Industrial Revolution*, 91.

innovations were integrated into the extant culture" and "situated in aesthetical, ethical, and religious relationships."[5] That is to say, pre-industrial production was integrated into exactly those cultural institutions that temper economy and prevent frenetic intemperance—and mass standardization.

Balanced Consumerism

These same "aesthetical, ethical, and religious relationships" reflected in production also form the basis of balanced consumption. They help form a culture where the virtue of temperance is nurtured and the consumer has a sense of proportionality that causes a desire for what is reasonable and balanced.

More importantly, individuals develop virtuous habits that find their expression in a demand for goods that fortifies their personalities and creativity. A hardy and thrifty person, for example, might seek or adapt durable products that reflect hardiness and thrift. A more artistic individual might find expression of a habitual appreciation of beautiful things in items of greater brilliance or luxury.

Balanced consumerism gains even more richness when the individual develops habits of consumption inside the protective framework of the family, associations, and community. With the elements at hand, one can develop a demand for products that expand horizons and enrich tastes. In this way, an intense social life creates patterns of demand that find their expression in regional cuisine, architectural styles, music, and arts.

By returning to balanced consumption, we would reconnect the broken link between producer and consumer. These temperate markets would be driven much more by the consumer than the producer and give rise to a demand that governs both the quantity and quality of production. Since consumption would no longer be massified, it would impede mass standardization.

Our present problem is not the fact that we have developed a highly

5. Stivers, *Illusion of Freedom*, 30.

efficient, plentiful, and inexpensive system—the most advanced in the world. Rather, our problem is that we have developed this system without proper balance. With the Industrial Revolution, we unnecessarily broke the long tradition of developing an economic system inside the broader context of our culture. By concentrating on standards of efficiency, we separated producer and consumer, quantity and quality, function and beauty. By resorting to mass standardization, we sacrificed those intangible values of culture and human warmth that money cannot buy.

Our challenge is not to return to some primitive economy but to develop an advanced, inexpensive, and efficient system with balanced production and consumption. As we have seen in pre-industrial times, such an economy can be a source of great technological innovation—and high spiritual and cultural growth. Without frenetic intemperance, this balanced system, as it did before, could produce goods that would be diverse, ample, and, yes, even inexpensive. Above all, a return to a balanced order would address that spiritual dimension of consumption that is so often left unmet. It would restore those natural braking mechanisms that temper economy and prevent mass standardization. We would see production that enriches and delights the soul and which would be so contrary to what Tibor Scitovsky has called a "joyless economy" where basic human needs go unfilled and mass production produces spiritual impoverishment.[6]

6. See Scitovsky, *Joyless Economy*, 11.

CHAPTER 43

A Proportional Scale Economy

W e have criticized gigantism as a factor that leads to frenetic intemperance. If our model is to have any validity, we must address this important issue.

There are many who have correctly diagnosed the problems linked to gigantism, which leads them to call for a "human-scale" economy. But just as there are those who identify being "local" with proximity, there are others who mistakenly identify human scale with smallness. Some go to the point of imposing arbitrary limits upon industry or land ownership in the name of "human scale." We disagree with this perception, and, to avoid any confusion, we will use the term *proportional scale economy* to indicate an economy that corresponds to the wide variety of capacities of human nature.

This is because the problem with gigantism is its great disproportion and not the mere fact that it is big. We note that even smallness can be disproportional. Hence, we must address the problem of disproportion that causes disorientation and uneasiness in us.

The Varying Intensity of Our Instinct of Sociability

The cause of uneasiness towards disproportion comes from our instinct of sociability. We are social beings and therefore have a natural tendency to establish relationships and create environments that facilitate our knowing everything around us. Unknown or unknowable elements make us uneasy and make us feel like strangers in a foreign land.

Our powerful instinct of sociability asks of us that we know and be known with varying degrees of intensity. As a result, we naturally tend to know our families and relatives with great intimacy and ease. To a lesser degree, we know our neighbors or close friends who live nearby. This familiarity fans out in concentric circles until it reaches larger social groupings such as regions, nations, or areas of civilization. Depending upon one's role and projection in society, the need for all these relationships will vary; a diplomat, for example, will seek broader ties than that of a local farmer.

This desire for knowing also varies according to the circumstances. Sometimes this instinct is satisfied by intense relationships as in those of the family. At other times, it takes delight in familiarity shrouded in mystery. At times, even vague and distant ties—such as belonging to a great nation—can satisfy this instinct. It can even ask that we do not develop too-close relationships lest exaggerated intimacy breed contempt, as can be seen in certain very small towns that become dens of gossip and intrigue. In this case, smallness becomes ugly and disproportional.

What really makes this instinct very uneasy is having no point of reference. The mere knowledge that there exists something or someone nearby with which we cannot relate puts us ill at ease. That is why blindness is so traumatic; a person can never completely relate to the surrounding world.

Well-Being of the Medieval City

Pre-modern society naturally tended, almost unintentionally, to satisfy these varying degrees of familiarity. Medieval cities were examples of this balanced relationship with local surroundings since "every necessary institution, every friend, relative, associate, was in effect a close neighbor, within easy walking distance."[1]

Every resident felt fully a part of the city, yet each quarter was a world unto itself with its own church, local provision market, and water supply, all of which gave the whole city an intimate feeling full of warmth and proportion. The frequent contact between the country farmer and the consumer in the open marketplace added yet another element of familiarity with the rural surroundings. Furthermore, the town provided a window to the outside world by offering wares from outside merchants or news from passing travelers.

While we cannot return to the medieval city, we might imagine that even large cities like our own could develop distinctive neighborhoods with their own consumption patterns, fashions, and customs inside the general context of the city. This is so contrary to the cosmopolitan spirit

---

1. Mumford, *City in History*, 313.

of our day, which blends everything together and thus tends to frustrate the varying degrees of familiarity required by the instinct of sociability.

Town and Country

We might apply the same criteria of sociability to the relationship between urban and rural areas. In a city that corresponds to proportional scale, inhabitants would come to know the rural and economic context within which the city exists.

In fact, the immediate countryside used to supply the city with its food and raw materials. It was part of knowing one's surroundings that no city became so big as to prevent people from becoming a bit familiar with the sustaining countryside.[2]

That is also why in all great epochs there have always been country retreats in the form of chateaux, villas, dachas, country cottages, ranches, small farms, or little garden plots to which city people might repair and re-familiarize themselves with the countryside. On their part, the farmers in the country benefited from their periodic visits to the city where they had the opportunity to escape from the ruggedness of their daily life and enjoy the city's civilizing effect.

Today we obscure the difference between city and country to the point that most in their suburban retreats know neither one nor the other well. Again, we have taken away the proportional-scale points of reference that should help us understand the world. And we are left with a world without context where food and raw materials come from all over the globe, and it matters little who we are or where we live.

Formation of Human Types

Proportional scale relationships are also important in the formation of social groups and a personal identity. Our instinct of sociability leads us to engage in relationships with others, which leads us to develop our own identity. We do this by comparing ourselves with others and seeing and loving the legitimate similarities and differences that link us together with social groups.

Thus, for example, when a person named John Smith sees himself

---

2. The delicate balance between country and city was maintained by a pattern of "many small cities and subordinate villages in active association with their neighboring towns distributed widely over the landscape," not by huge concentrated industrialized cities (ibid., 314).

reflected in the large Smith family, he observes and develops certain qualities in himself supported by analogous qualities that he sees in other family members. From this elaboration, the human type is born. He is a Smith. He identifies himself with great pride with the way of being of the Smith family while maintaining his individuality.

When many families are related to each other as in a clan or small village, this same process repeats itself. The person observes more generic yet analogous qualities common to all and identifies himself with that group. Born of a legitimate instinct of sociability, this identification process continues up the scale to include regions and nations. All are proportional scale relationships since they make the person feel comfortable within that which is known.

This also explains the uneasiness caused by massive and disproportional immigration since it artificially introduces a situation that destroys points of reference and overwhelms the ability of a society to absorb new elements organically into a unified culture. A proportional immigration is always a healthy development in a society since it injects new life and qualities into a social body, which enriches the whole but does not destroy cultural points of reference.[3]

Local but Different Economy

Following the same principles, economy operates on a proportional scale when it facilitates our knowledge of that which is around us. Hence, the family, as the most primary economic unit, is the most intimate and most delightful of proportional scale economic relationships. Local production follows next in providing the comfort of familiar products adjusted to the tastes of the locality.

Advocates of "human-scale" economy usually tend to go no farther than the local area, thereby condemning a society to a stagnating smallness. We affirm that proportional scale economy also includes economic trade that increases our ability to know and enjoy our region, nation, or area of civilization.

Above all, trade should have a point of reference, and that is the great problem of gigantism—or even false localism. Neither serves to help us come to know our surroundings. Whether a gigantic industry or an individualist's isolated plot of land, both are without links to peo-

---

3. See Aquinas, *Summa Theologica*, I-II, q. 105 a.3.

ple or place, which then tends to make all places and consumers equal.

Big Is Also Beautiful

Our ability to know things beyond the local and the small leads us to affirm that there can also be proportion in bigness. We must, of course, reject monstrous proportions. Yet it cannot be denied that nature does give us as examples huge mountains, great plains, or immense oceans that convey the idea of a proportional vastness that delights yet does not disorient us.

Likewise, we must consider that economic endeavors can also convey the idea of greatness and grandeur without disorienting and disturbing an economy. We must reject the egalitarian notion that all men are equal in their abilities to deal with economy or governing and must therefore be limited to small economic or governing units. Some men have great capacity to deal with multitudes of people—as can be seen in the case of the popes or great rulers. Still others can manage big, and even very big, enterprises with ability and skill. Limiting such figures to small plots of property wastes their qualities and stifles their desires to perfect their nature. If they develop their abilities in due proportion and temperance, we do not hesitate to affirm that big can also be beautiful.

We have commented that a regime of a few large properties is easier for government to confiscate than that of a thousand smaller properties. We might also conclude that a regime of only small properties is equally vulnerable to be destroyed piecemeal, since none have the resources or leadership separately or collectively, like that of greater properties, to confront a large foe. The ideal arrangement is a proportional and harmonious representation of large, medium, and small holdings that form a unity that allows for mutual protection.

Optimum Size

The idea of proportional-scale economy is reinforced by some modern economists who maintain the theory of "optimum size," which rejects the notion that all firms must grow indefinitely to be profitable.[4] Rather, they hold that there are points where a firm can become too

---

4. See Lindenberg, *Free Market in a Christian Society*, 151-52.

small or too large for efficient operation.

Depending on the nature of the business, this theory postulates that firms naturally tend to attain and stay at a certain size at which efficiency is maximized. Companies often grow beyond this optimum size when they are favored by monopoly, semi-monopoly, privileged access to credit, or government favors, all of which are promoted in a regime of frenetic intemperance and tend to breed inefficient bureaucracies.

Thus we conclude that proportional scale depends on many more factors than just size. As long as there are points of reference that help us familiarize ourselves with our environment, we can say something has proportional scale. Thus, a person can identify with a small town, a great nation, or the universal Catholic Church—all are proportional scale *social* relationships. A person might manage a small farm, a local factory, or a large estate—all are proportional scale *economic* relationships. Proportional scale also varies due to the immense inequality among men, which makes it almost impossible to define proportional scale in precise terms given the great diversity of capacities.

Thus, the cultivation of proportional scale in society and economy is a matter that requires great balance and virtue. It asks of us an appreciation of varying degrees of size and familiarity that is only made possible by the practice of the cardinal virtues, especially temperance. It is to this proportional scale that we must return.

CHAPTER 44

A Missing Fortitude

W hile we have already discussed in depth the other three cardinal virtues, it is fitting that fortitude now be mentioned. Indeed, our search for temperance, prudence, and justice would be useless unless there be a firmness and vigor of character that will give us the courage to confront the present crisis and pursue our return to order.

The Need for Fortitude

Fortitude is the virtue by which the appetites and passions are guided by the rational soul with courage and constancy.[1] It helps us brave the greatest dangers and resist intense persecution and obstacles so that we might achieve our goals.

The virtue of fortitude is perfected by the gift of fortitude. This gift of the Holy Ghost is a supernatural habit that strengthens the soul and gives us a relentless vigor and superhuman energy in the practice of virtue. It awakens in us the unshakeable hope of final victory, enables us to suffer extreme pain with patience and joy and makes us heroes in things great and small. By this gift, we can completely overcome all lukewarmness in the service of God.

From fortitude comes magnanimity, which is the virtue that inclines one to perform great and splendid acts worthy of honor. Also part of fortitude is the virtue of magnificence which leads one to undertake splendid and great projects without being discouraged by their magnitude, difficulty, or expense. These are companion virtues that are incompatible with mediocrity and presuppose noble and lofty souls.

Given the great crisis we face, it is evident that we need fortitude to weather the coming storm.

---

1. Saint Thomas Aquinas cites Cicero (Rhet. ii), who affirms that "fortitude is the deliberate facing of dangers and bearing of toils" (*Summa Theologica*, II-II, q. 123, a. 9). "He will be called brave who is fearless in face of a noble death, and of all emergencies that involve death; and the emergencies of war are in the highest degree of this kind" (Aristotle, *Nichomachean Ethics,* trans. W. D. Ross, in *The Works of Aristotle: II*, vol. 9 of *Great Books of the Western World*, 361).

Acquiring This Necessary and Missing Fortitude

There are obstacles that prevent this. We believe that the chief obstacle to acquiring this necessary and missing fortitude is overcoming the cultural barriers that conspire against this essential virtue.

The first barrier is the notion of a technological utopia that may yet vanquish misfortune. We also encounter an obstacle in the rule of money, which proposes the fast and comfortable lifestyle of a material paradise that tries to exclude the idea of suffering, sin, and tragedy. This rule promotes the illusory and bubbly optimism that we can reach perfect happiness in this world without encountering any strife.

Alas, in this vale of tears, reality always contradicts these notions of an unlimited and perfectible world. The more we pretend that our lives are exempt from tragedy, the more sadness haunts us. For all our wishful thinking for an easy and happy ending to our problems, there is the reality that the only real solution is found by facing our problems head on—with fortitude.

Continually Engaged in the Struggle

Thus, the present crisis can well serve as the occasion for acquiring the virtue of fortitude since it rips off the veil of these modern illusions so often portrayed by Hollywood. It allows us to see that we must always be engaged in the struggle against misfortune, which is our lot due to Original Sin.

Moreover, we must also be continually engaged in the fight for a social and economic order since there will always be those who will oppose God's Law and work to the contrary by undermining the family, marriage, and all those other institutions that make up the heart and soul of an economy.

Like it or not, the minute we cease to fight for our Christian culture, we prepare ourselves for defeat. Unless society be permeated by the fortitude needed to confront this great struggle, all our efforts will come to nothing.

The Necessary Spirit of the Crusader

In general, medieval men understood the role of fortitude in maintaining their Christian culture. They had no illusions about their own weaknesses and vices. They understood the need to confront the dis-

A rendition of "The Credo Knight" by Emmanuel Frémiet (1824-1910).
An organic Christian society needs a spirit of self-sacrifice, fortitude, and
dedication like that found in knighthood and chivalry.

orders and evils that will always plague this vale of tears. Calling upon God, the faithful in varying degrees summoned from themselves the strength to confront sin, tragedy, and misfortune and defend the society they loved.

From this mentality logically came those who, by their spirit of self-sacrifice and dedication, took the practice of fortitude to the highest degree. This could be seen in the dedicated spirit of chivalry of the crusader who left everything to face suffering, separation from family, and even imprisonment or death to defend Christendom against the declared enemies of the Faith. We might also cite the members of monastic orders whose love of penance and prayer was such that it made of their lives a true spiritual crusade. Practicing fortitude were those representative figures in society—those *bourdon* souls—who made the great sacrifice of setting the tone and being role models for all society. Because these key figures practiced fortitude to a high degree, all society was permeated by this virtue, which in turn held up that organic order.

Fortitude was missing when frenetic intemperance entered into modern economy, and there was no courage to uphold traditional and moral restraint. Fortitude was needed to resist the harmful effects of those transformations wrought by the Industrial Revolution, which brought forth great production but also helped shape the mass man. Now more than ever we need fortitude as we face an economic crisis unlike any we have seen.

CHAPTER 45

Setting the Stage

W e have just described an organic order, its unifying principles, institutions, and economy. But a mere description—attractive though it might be—does not guarantee these elements will be adopted. The most difficult part of our exposition lies ahead. Amid the comfort and complacency of everyday life, we must convince modern man to go beyond self-interest and make the great sacrifice of returning to order.

Men act when outside circumstances force them to do so. This might be seen, for example, in the case of a person who is forced by a rainstorm to the nearest shelter. The storm serves as a catalyst to action. But this type of action has its dangers since it has no clear objective save that of moving energetically away from a problem.

We believe that in the present juncture of events, the force of outside circumstances is converging upon the nation and, like it or not, is setting the stage for some kind of major change that forces us to look at alternatives. There are three circumstances that could force this major change.

An Economic Collapse

The first circumstance is the very real danger of an economic collapse of massive proportions.

This grave perspective alone is already causing many to ponder their situation and rethink premises. When this crisis strikes with all its intensity, there is no doubt that it will force us to act with all urgency.

Based on the experience of times past, we know that America has risen to the occasion in the face of such great dangers—especially in time of war and crisis. We can hope that we will prove worthy of this challenge and look in the direction of those organic solutions we have discussed. Still, the danger of a collapse must also be a cause of great concern since, in our energetic movement away from the problem, we might be tempted to grab any socialist solution offered us in the hour of our affliction.

The Failure of Our Cooperative Union

A second circumstance is the fact that our cooperative union is now in crisis; it no longer provides its usual solutions. It forces us to look at alternatives.

Our cooperative union has been the framework by which we have always resolved our problems. As long as it flourished, no one seriously questioned its ability to meet our needs. We were content to enjoy the freedom to pursue and gratify our desires in an atmosphere of comfort and abundance.

As the situation worsens, this cooperative model falters and even works to our detriment. There is a great frustration in pursuing our customary material happiness. As a result, there is a great void that must be filled and moves us to action, which likewise raises both concerns and hopes.

An Internal Tension

Finally, a third circumstance setting the stage for change is the internal tension of the present polarization. This separation is reaching a point where the center no longer holds and we are faced with the grueling task of working out a new consensus amid times of tribulation.

We have observed—and many political analysts concur—that the country is divided into two Americas. One is defined by our faltering cooperative union; the other is formed around the willingness to sacrifice for God, family, and country. The outcome of this clash of mentalities depends upon the actions we will be forced to take.

The force of circumstances is upon us. Like it or not, we will be obliged to take action in the face of the present crisis. It is not a matter of *if* but *when* we will change and what our course will be.

As in all times of major change, the dangers posed are great. We must ask if our reaction will be well chosen. Our future course must not be based upon impulses where we grab onto anything when fleeing a situation. It should be based upon the deliberation of sound ideas and principles. It should be based upon an articulate vision of an organic order.

Now is the time to reflect and debate ideas as to the course we must choose. If we take this time to articulate those principles, ideas, and moral values around which we might rally, then we will be in much better conditions to weather the storm and return to order. Socialist alternatives make these considerations all the more urgent.

Such a vision of things requires the daring to transcend the "unheroic" standards of our materialism. It challenges us to envision new ways to go beyond the frenetic intemperance that has done so much harm to our economy. In this period of debate, our key task is to articulate a vision of life whereby we might thrash out those organic solutions that can serve to forge a new consensus upon which to build our future.

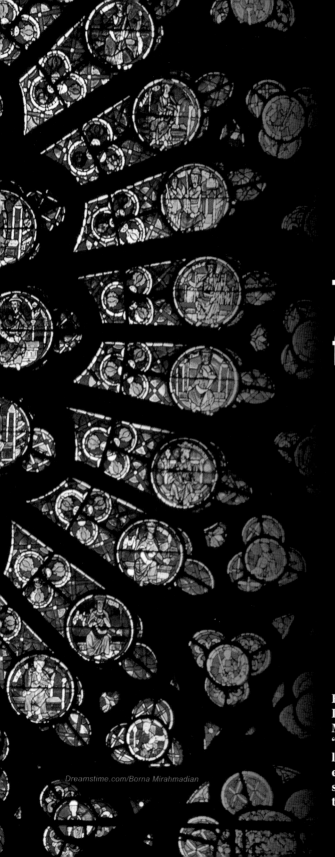

The Search
for Meaning

Dreamstime.com/Borna Mirahmadian

Rose window at Notre Dame Cathedral in Paris. Medieval man first built "cathedrals of ideas" that later found sublime expression in the stone buildings themselves.

Illuminated manuscript of Saint Mark writing the Gospel (from the Bedford Book of Hours). To return to order, we must return to the wellspring of our Christian culture based on the Gospel and surrounded by all that is beautiful, elevated, dignified, and noble.

CHAPTER 46

Returning to the Wellspring

As the stage is set for a great storm, our common peril forces us to look for a vision of life that will serve to unify the nation. We believe this vision will not be inspired by economic reforms, financial policies, or government programs. The question remains as to where we must go to find the ideas that will inspire our return to order.

In our times of crisis, we would do well to repair to the wellspring of our Christian culture in the hope of rediscovering those spiritual values that gave us birth. We should look beyond our materialistic vision and turn to what Johan Huizinga calls "more and higher values than the mere gratification of want and the desire for power. These values lie in the domain of the spiritual, the intellectual, the moral, and the aesthetic."[1]

In this spiritual quest, we must avoid the idealized inventions of great philosophers or the complex schemes of sociologists. We must reject the rigid ideologies of modern thinkers who have constructed ideal systems without any link to reality, much to the detriment of mankind. We must embrace instead those ideals, principles, and values that have always served to inspire and unify men. They are ideals that are connected to reality and manifest themselves in the diverse customs, traditions, and ways of life of a people.

Horizontal Vision of Society

By returning to the source of our values, we engage in a real search for meaning and unity. It is not the scattered modern vision of things that so characterizes our age of individualism. To employ a metaphor, we might say that the present socio-economic model resembles a horizontal line drawn on a piece of paper where the line scatters our attention with no single point of focus. This line extends outward; it is

---

1. Johan H. Huizinga, *In the Shadow of Tomorrow* (New York: W. W. Norton, 1936), 40-41.

flat with no hierarchy of interests.

Such a model corresponds to a horizontal vision of society. It is an image of a model that favors frenetic intemperance, expanding markets, and gigantist networks obsessed with outward progress and the horizontal expansion of finance or empire without any central focus. Lawrence Friedman writes that "urban, industrial, mass-media society" is a "horizontal society" full of superficial links among equals.[2]

A Vertical Vision

Our return to the wellspring calls for a vertical perspective. It supposes a vertical vision of the universe where things are viewed through another prism. To extend our metaphor, we can liken the model we seek to a vertical line drawn on paper. This line draws our attention towards a single point as it progresses upward, much like the vertical lines of a church bell tower draw our gaze upward towards the cross at the top.

This vertical vision invites us to elevate our minds with singular purpose to transcendent values and ultimately to God. R. H. Tawney describes this vision as a "theory of a hierarchy of values, embracing all human interests and activities in a system of which the apex is religion" as opposed to the modern "conception of separate and parallel compartments, between which a due balance should be maintained, but which have no vital connection with each other."[3]

This vision confers a great unity of purpose upon a society. This unity, which might also be ours, could be seen in Christendom. "There have been periods in European history in which more rapid progress has been made in some directions, and in which there has been a greater variety of individual genius," writes R. W. Southern about the Middle Ages, "but there has never been a period which has displayed so great a variety of achievement in the service of a single aim."[4]

The Good, True, and Beautiful

The inspiration of this vision is found inside man himself. It corresponds to the most fundamental desires of the human heart. It comes from our constant search for all that is good, true, and beautiful. This

---

2. Friedman, *Horizontal Society*, 60.
3. Tawney, *Religion and the Rise of Capitalism*, 8.
4. R. W. Southern, *Western Society and the Church in the Middle Ages* (London: Penguin Books, 1970), 43.

impulse is something that occurs naturally in us and sets in motion powerful movements inside our souls that call us to sacrifice.

Aristotle speaks of what he calls *to kalon*, that is, our passionate concern for all that is elevated, dignified, and noble. It was something he recognized as universally present in the spiritual core of each human being. These highest aspirations of rational and free beings are "capable of dedication, devotion, and even sacrifice for the sake of causes perceived as just and as thereby partaking of transcendent or eternal value."[5]

Likewise, Saint Paul in Holy Scriptures calls upon us to look to these same ideals when he says, "Finally, brothers, whatever is true, whatever is honorable, whatever is just, whatever is pure, whatever is lovely, whatever is gracious, if there is any excellence and if there is anything worthy of praise, think about these things"(Phil 4:8).[6]

When men seek after these high standards of perfection, beauty, or excellence, it gives rise to a vision of life that inspires civilizations. We need only look to our Christian roots as a confirmation of their efficacy. History gives ample testimony to the selfless acts of saints, heroes, and martyrs who put Christian ideals before all else. Their influence permeated the culture, established a rule of honor, and gave birth to a whole civilization.

However, there is more.

"*Omne Delectamentum in se Habentem*"

When we search for that which is most elevated, dignified, and noble, we inevitably encounter the supernatural and divine, which is at the pinnacle of all beauty and the true wellspring of Christian civilization. *Omne delectamentum in se habentem*, says the liturgy for Benediction. We might say of this vision that it has "within it all sweetness."

By embracing the supernatural, we encounter God and His Divine grace, which communicates supernatural life to our souls and makes our ideals shine brighter. Grace perfects nature and opens up new possibilities for the realization of our ideals beyond that of the merely human. While we cannot quantify the action of grace in history, we

5. Thomas L. Pangle, *Leo Strauss: An Introduction to His Thought and Intellectual Legacy* (Baltimore: Johns Hopkins University Press, 2006), 93.
6. North American Bible Revised Edition.

can observe those selfless acts of virtue that brought about amazing transformations in society. We see, for example, the fruits of grace in the noble, dignified and elevated acts of those who bear suffering with joy and dignity, experience triumph with humility, and treat others with veneration and respect as brothers. We can observe the effects of grace, which enlightens reason, and, guided by the light of the Faith and an infallible Magisterium, creates the ideal cultural conditions for an organic society.

By returning to the wellspring of our Christian civilization, we avail ourselves of this Divine assistance and thus our efforts become proportional to the challenges from the impending storm.

In short, as increasing numbers abandon the failing materialist culture that adopted the common, useful, and ordinary as its "unheroic" standard, we must repair to this Christian wellspring to regenerate our culture. It is this search for meaning and unity that we will now explore. From this source, we will see its fruits reflected in the hearth and home, the public square, the marketplace, and the sanctuary.

CHAPTER 47

The Quest for the Sublime

B y returning to a transcendental and supernatural vision of society, we touch on issues that go to the very core of our modern afflictions. We address those desires for spiritual things long suppressed by the *acedia* of our materialistic culture. We engage in a search for meaning beyond the frustrations of self-interest and the great unhappiness that now mock us amid our prosperity.

Above all, this vision of society sets in motion a natural and dynamic driving force inside the human soul that captures the imagination and moves us to act.

A Quest for Plenitude

This driving force is found in our great desire for plenitude: that is, a sense of full satisfaction or completeness. Because of our composite nature, we are not satisfied with mere material security. In our quest for perfection, we naturally seek after spiritual satisfaction as well. Our souls are strongly attracted to that which moves us towards plenitude. We rejoice in this plenitude and never tire in seeking after it.

This can be seen in the senses. It is proper for our eyes to see, but we are most drawn to very beautiful objects. When we hear, we experience greater delight by listening to the most beautiful harmonies. The sense of smell finds great fulfillment in exquisite perfumes. Even infants in their primitive reactions shun the ordinary and go after that which dazzles and sparkles. We naturally tend to the most expressive plenitude of our legitimate desires.

The object of this surging universal human desire has a name: it is called the sublime.

Defining the Sublime

The sublime consists of those things of transcendent excellence that cause souls to be overawed by their magnificence. It provokes what

Edmund Burke rightly calls "the strongest emotion which the mind is capable of feeling."[1]

Throughout history, man has been drawn to extraordinary panoramas, works of art, music, ideas, or heroic feats that have rightly been called sublime. It is not the mere physical aspects of these things that inspire us. Rather, it is a rational appreciation of the spiritual qualities of incomparable magnificence, vastness, or grandeur that captivates the soul and speeds it on its quest towards plenitude.

Thus, it is an appreciation of things sublime that has served to inspire Christian civilization and which must now inspire us. A culture turned towards the sublime uplifts those who would otherwise detain themselves with the purely ordinary and common. It draws us outside ourselves in wonder, and so opposes the inward egoistic vices that drive us to disgrace.

Like musicians who dedicate themselves to sublime music, those who habitually and logically seek and love the sublime are capable of great abnegation and sacrifice in its service. From such dedication come the masterpieces and epic feats of history.

Sublime Civilizations

Like individuals, civilizations and cultures can also seek and appreciate the sublime. This happens when any social grouping subconsciously elaborates and appreciates together splendorous works such as art, architecture, political achievements, or religious devotions.

To the degree that members of social units appreciate the sublime together, the greater is the culture or civilization. We ignore the influence of the sublime at our own risk for, as Johan Huizinga notes, "History pays too little attention to the influence of these dreams of a sublime life on civilization itself and on the forms of social life."[2]

Not only is the sublime found in arts or objects; we find the greatest

---

1. Edmund Burke, "A Philosophical Inquiry into the Origins of Our Ideas on the Sublime and Beautiful," in *Works of Edmund Burke*, 1:48. Burke was one of the first modern authors to dwell upon the sublime. We would definitely disagree with him and others of his period who interpreted the overwhelming aspect of the sublime as that of a terrifying grandeur. We would argue that the sublime inspires admiration, wonder, and reverent love proper to Catholic devotion and not terror as reflected in Burke's severe perspective. Cf. *Encyclopædia Britannica 2009 Deluxe Edition*, s.v. "aesthetics."
2. Johan Huizinga, *The Waning of the Middle Ages: A Study of the Forms of Life, Thought and Art in France and the Netherlands in the XIVth and XVth Centuries* (Garden City, N.Y.: Doubleday Anchor Books, 1954), 39.

masterpieces of a culture in its great men and elites. The popular capacity to admire and produce sublime models and heroes represents a civilization's crowning achievement. "Whether in the *Iliad*, the *Aeneid*, or *Beowulf*," writes Robert Nisbet, "the hero's deeds represent the highest exemplification of the society's sacred values; he fulfills rather than transforms them."[3]

Supernatural Aspects

While the sublime can be considered from a purely natural and more metaphysical perspective, its highest expression is the supernatural. The concept of God naturally flows from a knowledge of sublime things. God created us with an appetite for sublime things because they are His masterpieces and speak most about Him. By knowing them, we are invited to know, love, and serve the sublime Being par excellence: God.[4]

That is to say, the great *élan* or driving force, which we naturally feel when we encounter the sublime in our lives, ultimately propels us towards a religious end. These sublime works are, in the words of Benedict XVI, "real highways to God, the supreme Beauty."[5] In this sense, loving the sublime on earth is a preparation for the sublime of Heaven and the Beatific Vision where we will have the true plenitude of our contemplative joy in the contemplation of God Himself.

The Search for Meaning

Christian civilization was not only turned towards those sublime things but also found meaning in them. Medieval man believed happiness came from a true understanding of the order of the universe. He saw the universe as a great lesson book that was understood above all by its symbolism and its hierarchical order.

Thus, with great practical sense born of observation and pondered leisure, people of those times sought out the symbolism and relation-

---

3. Nisbet, *Twilight of Authority*, 92-93.
4. The basis of this vision comes from the fact that God created a whole universe to reflect Himself since no one creature could sufficiently mirror Him. Each creature reflects something of the good, true, and beautiful existing in God. When we contemplate this great work of creation, we grasp better the perfection of God and experience the great spiritual joy of understanding the order and meaning of things. See Aquinas, *Summa Contra Gentiles*, II, 45; *Summa Theologica*, I, q. 47, a. 2.
5. Benedict XVI, General Audience, Aug. 31, 2011, accessed Oct. 16, 2012, http://www.vatican.va/holy_father/benedict_xvi/audiences/2011/documents/hf_ben-xvi_aud_20110831_en.html.

ships that gave meaning to the concrete things they saw in Creation. When considering, for example, fire, precious stones, or the ocean, they believed these beautiful things spoke of excellence and marvels that must be appreciated and fit into a harmonious order. From this, they constructed veritable cathedrals of harmonious ideas that were reflected in the actual structures that they later built for God's greater glory.

Ultimately, they desired Heaven. Yet it was an idea of Heaven based on all the earthly marvels that they thought could reflect Heaven's marvels. Hence, the real joy of life consisted in this metaphysical search for the absolute perfection in things, that is, a kind of tropism whereby one naturally seeks God or the likeness of God in all things.

"Thus all things raise the thoughts to the eternal," writes Johan Huizinga, "being thought of as symbols of the highest, in the constant gradation, they are all transfused by the glory of divine majesty."[6]

Born of Wonder and the Marvelous

This driving desire for the sublime also awakens in us a sense of wonder. Aristotle claims that wonder is the beginning of philosophy.

Saint Thomas teaches that wonder is the longing for knowledge, which comes when we first contemplate this order and then seek after its first cause, which is either unknown to us or surpasses our faculty of understanding.[7] A child, for example, contemplating the stars in the vast firmament, experiences wonder as to the cause of this great marvel. This unsatisfied desire for knowledge of the highest cause, far from frustrating us, awakens in us a joyful hope of obtaining that knowledge for which we so long. Josef Pieper notes that Saint Thomas held that "the first wonder one feels forms the first step on the path that leads to the beatific vision."[8]

An Intelligible Universe

The practical result of all this is the ordering of a society according to this transcendent order. The world becomes intelligible—bristling with meaning and purpose. From wonder and the sublime come those

6. Huizinga, *Waning of the Middle Ages*, 206.
7. See Aquinas, *Summa Theologica*, I-II, q. 32, a. 8.
8. Pieper, *Leisure*, 103.

philosophical—as well as religious and aesthetic—considerations that are the basis of civilization.

Thus, the search for the sublime cannot be restricted to pure speculation or contemplation. Medieval man acted upon this quest by trying to construct the world accordingly. Looking at things symbolically, his goal became not only arranging his material well-being but elaborating a marvelous culture, art, or civilization based on the consideration of these perfections. The result was a life with a certain happiness on this earth, a foretaste of eternal happiness in Heaven.

This explains the intense artistic sense and the appreciation for quality of those times. Because of his uprightness and innocence, medieval man experienced a disinterested joy in seeing anything perfect, beautiful, or well done—even in things not his own. He strove to make and create these things as a means of surrounding himself with earthly marvels from which he could imagine heavenly ones.

Medieval man also made this same search inside his own soul. He sought to discern the ideal of those qualities inside himself that he could develop and then reflect this order in his soul. He acted upon this discernment by constantly "constructing" his soul to make it ever more according to that ideal likeness of God that he felt compelled to reflect.

Giving Meaning to Religion

Such a vision naturally gives religion great meaning. It is not merely a teaching of dogmas or catechism, but a way of finding magnificence, meaning, and happiness already in this world. Contrary to those who believe religion only teaches resigned unhappiness in this life, medieval man found it incomprehensible that this world would not have a serious foretaste of the happiness to come.

However, this notion of happiness was of a spiritual and supernatural character reflected in some material aspects of this life and based on the joy of understanding the universe. It was not a materialistic notion from which comes the sadness and illusion of confiding in perishable things.

"One of the greatest achievements of the Middle Ages," writes Robert Southern, "was the detailed development of this idea of a universal human society as an integral part of a divinely ordered universe in time and in eternity, in nature and supernature, in practical politics and in the world of spiritual essences."[9]

Compensating for Our Weaknesses

The nature of this disinterested pleasure also comes from the fact that we all sense our own weaknesses and infirmities. This, in turn, awakens in us a desire to repose in the contemplation of something perfect and consequently sense a kind of completeness. In this way, rather than pleasure for pleasure's sake, we sense the metaphysical joy of being linked with an order of being that completes our own.

It is in this sense of completeness that the medieval man constructed his society and also imagined the joy of the Beatific Vision. In the latter, we will sense ourselves ordered according to what our own being asks of us. We will also sense ourselves integrated into the general and perfect order of being, as we proceed to contemplate and repose in that absolute Perfection, which is God Himself.

It might be asked of what use is the sublime in the midst of an economic crisis of grand proportions? How can our quest for the sublime help us find a solution?

We would answer that we have built a market economy on the premise of a colossal production that can never satisfy us. Purely material goods will always frustrate us since they cannot satisfy the demands of our spiritual nature; they cannot satisfy our longings for eternal goods, which ultimately find their plenitude in God Himself.

As a result, we impose the unlimited expectations of a spiritual order upon a limited material order. In such circumstances, we can never produce enough goods since we will always be on a frantic search for fulfillment through unbridled demand fragmented in a thousand different markets. These frustrated desires create the conditions for an economy of frenetic intemperance and our great unhappiness.

How much better it would be if we could base our economy on the premise of our quest for the sublime. Such an economy depends much

---

9. Southern, *Western Society and the Church*, 22.

more on the quality rather than the quantity of goods produced. It would seek to imbue our production with the beauty and perfection that our nature asks of us. It would give our economy unity, order, and purpose. It would awaken in us passionate yet temperate desires that aid us in our quest for plenitude.

There is no reason why this economy of the sublime could not also have abundant production and development. We differ from those who would propose downsizing or sub-consumerism as a "spiritual" solution to today's crisis. The very nature of an economy of the sublime tends towards the production of magnificent and grand things like the medieval cathedrals that inspire in us so much awe and wonder. At the same time, the sublime does not despise the little marvels of artisan crafts, for example, that delight the soul by their innocent simplicity.

Today's consumerism frustrates desires by drowning them in a sea of materialism. With a more focused production, the sublime could satisfy our desires by producing those things that fill us with wonder and expectation. Such an economy would incite within us the desire to sacrifice for higher ideals. It would turn us towards the eternal where we will feel ourselves ordered according to our nature and disposed to repose in the perfection of God Himself.

The Adoration of the Magi stained glass in St. Patrick's Cathedral, Harrisburg, Pa. When men dream in a practical and rational manner, marvels like Christendom's celebration and depiction of Christmas become possible.

CHAPTER 48

When Men Dream

The quest for the sublime enters into our daily lives because it makes of us men of great desires.[1] It awakens in us demands that need to be satisfied. Hence, we can affirm that sublime ideals are among the most practical things that exist. On the platform of these ideals, we are moved to set our dreams in motion.

By "dream," we mean the process by which we idealize our goals in society. For this to happen, two things are necessary: men must first unite together to form a consensus around higher values. Secondly, inside this new consensus, they must conceive new ways of expressing and manifesting these higher values in daily life.

Forming a Consensus

The best example of how a consensus is formed is the family. Amid the joys and sufferings of life together, the family is such a source of intense cohesion that even non-family members such as close friends can be assimilated into it with a high degree of adherence and affinity. The whole family is enriched by every addition that is treated as yet one more star in the family constellation.

Similar absorbing unity can be observed in other social units, especially those where individuals experience together the vicissitudes of life, such as in a religious vocation, profession, school, or military unit.

The Birth of Society from Unity

Thus, all stable human relations can give rise to these powerful links that call to mind the intense spirit of the family. To the degree that a social unit develops this bonding, it contributes firmness, resilience, and quality to the social fabric.

Moreover, when nurtured by the Commandments and evangelical

---

1. Cf. Praise of the Prophet Daniel (Dn 9:23).

counsels, this natural society acquires a supernatural brilliance not unlike one who is born and then baptized. It creates ideal conditions for a meshing of personalities which, over time, can acquire excellence, uprightness, and extraordinary cohesion.

Idealizing a Life Together

In this atmosphere of cohesiveness and especially that of grace, the members of a society begin to idealize their life together. Some authors have referred to this sense of imagined perfection together as the creation of "*utopias*." We feel this action is much better expressed in terms of how social units create their own *myths*, *legends*, or *dreams*.

All these terms refer to this indispensable capacity whereby families, social units, or peoples in their great unity, envision a future for themselves that considers both the practical means at hand and a higher ideal.

"We have no knowledge of any human community where men do fail to dream," writes Irving Kristol. "Which is to say, we know of no human community whose members do not have a vision of perfection—a vision in which the frustrations inherent in our human condition are annulled and transcended."[2]

"The ideal society is not outside of the real society; it is a part of it," writes Émile Durkheim. "Far from being divided between them as between two poles which mutually repel each other, we cannot hold to one without holding to the other."[3]

"Without the metaphysical dream it is impossible to think of men living together harmoniously over an extent of time," writes Richard Weaver. "The dream carries with it an evaluation, which is the bond of spiritual community."[4]

The same author speaks similarly of myths as "great symbolic structures which hold together the imaginations of a people and provide bases of harmonious thought and action." He points out how this world of value and meaning is a timeless structure, "always here and now," and from which "the least member of a culture can borrow something to dignify and give coherence to his life."[5] The legendary figure of George

---

2. Kristol, *Two Cheers for Capitalism*, 153.
3. Émile Durkheim, *The Elementary Forms of the Religious Life*, trans. Joseph Ward Swain (London: George Allen and Unwin, 1915), 422.
4. Weaver, *Ideas Have Consequences*, 18.
5. Weaver, *Visions of Order*, 34.

Washington, for example, serves as a point of unity for all those American values that he upheld. Any American at any time in our history can draw inspiration from his example. In a similar way, symbols and narratives can hold up a high ideal that imparts a style and tone to society that is found in fashion, manners, arts, architecture, and cuisine.

Practical Nature of These Dreams

If these terms sound too abstract and unattainable, historian Lewis Mumford clarifies the issue by emphasizing the extremely practical nature of our dreams and distinguishing them from idle fantasy.

He defines a dream very simply as an ideal vision whereby a social unit conceives "a reconstituted environment which is better adapted to the nature and aims of the human beings who dwell within it than the actual one."[6]

That is to say, as soon as a family or social unit by consensus begins to conceive its own way of being or doing things that will hopefully make life better or more perfect, it is on its way towards creating its own myth or dream. In fact, Mumford claims with Anatole France that these dreams constitute the very principle of all progress, without which we might still be living as savages in caves.[7]

Thus, a family might idealize a particular way of being charitable, another of being prudent, still another of being austere. Each seeks to satisfy that deep psychological need to idealize its own dreams and organize its life accordingly, since "the things we dream of tend consciously or unconsciously to work themselves out in the pattern of our daily lives."[8]

We should not fear that our dreams will not always be completely attainable. Rather, they should serve to guide us in a general direction. Like the magnetic needle of the compass that points us towards an ideal and unreachable "north," Mumford notes that our dreams serve as guides to help us navigate safely on our way.

If our age seems culturally impoverished, it is not the fault of our dreams but because we have not dreamed enough. We do not listen to our dreams.

---

6. Lewis Mumford, *The Story of Utopias* (New York: Viking Press, 1962), 21.
7. See ibid., 22.
8. Ibid., 25.

The Deception of Utopias

Someone might object that such concepts do not correspond to reality. Men often seek false "utopias," only to be disillusioned, a fact which gives foundation to the popular notion that all dreams are illusions or even dangerous fantasies.

We would not dispute such claims. Like all things linked to man's fallen nature and fertile imagination, our dreams can lead to spectacular failures, nationalist incarnations, and horrific aberrations. Left to himself, man might achieve some great things, but his unrestrained dreams, more often than not, run the risk of being bitter utopias—literally paths to "nowhere."

Necessary Presuppositions for Dreams

Such risks do not in any way diminish the enormous importance of dreams in society. Rather, they only underscore why we insist on our initial presupposition for their balanced realization: the atmosphere of intense cohesion in the social unit, especially when accompanied by the practice of the Commandments and the spirit of the evangelical counsels.

Dreams stop being "nowhere" utopias to the extent they exercise this unity around the practice of a religious ideal. It is then that, with the help of grace, they acquire the balance whereby the seemingly evident impossibility of our dreams becomes possible.

"The Most Audacious Dream Imaginable"

This type of dream sustained by grace is what the Church proposed and spread throughout Christendom. It is what Plinio Corrêa de Oliveira called the "most striking, indisputable, and audacious dream imaginable."[9]

The most patent example of this audacious dream is the celebration of Christmas. *Puer natus est nobis, Et filius datus est nobis*, chants the Church. "For a child is born to us, and a son is given to us"(Is 9:6).

On that ineffable night when our Savior was born to Mary Ever Virgin, an immense impossibility became possible: the God-man was born. From Heaven descended torrents of graces, which paved the

---

9. Plinio Corrêa de Oliveira, American Studies Commission meeting, Oct. 12, 1989, Corrêa de Oliveira Documents.

way for the most audacious of any humanly-conceived dream, since it opened up for us the immense possibilities that grace would later develop into Christendom. It made possible the practice of the Commandments and counsels inside an order that the pagan world judged impossible.

Atheists or rationalists may smirk at such considerations. Yet they do not realize that, by limiting themselves to their atheistic reasoning, they embrace at best the narrow and fallible "utopias" of their soulless and pragmatic world. They do not perceive that they lose the best of reality.

Everything changes once we reason in function of a world created by God, turned towards God, and where God Himself, His angels, and His saints actively intervene. This conviction makes one capable of extraordinary *élan*, where the spirit of faith can unite with practical achievements and lead to the attainment of dreams in this vale of tears, which are marvelous foretastes of Heaven.

Uniting the Idealist and the Pragmatist

Alas, there is a modern tendency to divide the world between the idealist and the pragmatist, the metaphysical and the physical, or the spiritual and material, as if we were dealing with two different realities.

In a society that pursues its dreams, this separation need not be made. Both the ideal and the practical can be turned into a single reality. In fact, true dreams make use of what we might call two great driving forces—two powerful impulses of enthusiasm—that move the human soul in this direction.

The first driving force is the very essence of our dreams. It is that strong impulse towards that which excites our sense of wonder, admiration, and the marvelous, giving us the capacity to conceive marvelous things and a consuming desire to bring them about.

Christian civilization gave ample examples of this capacity to conceive with its magnificent liturgy, literature, art, architecture, and so many other marvels that were fully integrated into the lives of the common people, allowing them to live their ordinary lives in extraordinary ways.

Common Sense

There is a second driving force that serves as a counterbalance to the first lest it degenerate into dangerous fantasy. It comes from realizing that this land of exile is not all marvelousness; we must adjust ourselves to the world that exists. Hence, there is born in balanced souls a veritable enthusiasm for common sense that helps us deal with concrete reality. This practical driving force tempers the imagination and the inordinate search for novelties. It calls for a realistic evaluation of the practical elements at hand to construct the future.

The Balance We Seek

Neither driving force excludes the other. Rather, each is inspired by the other. Only the harmonious union of both driving forces will produce that same higher vision and common sense that allowed the saints to resolve the most concrete problems with wisdom and meditate on the most sublime and lofty considerations with great humility.

In this way, we avoid the two extremes of fantasy worlds and socialist "paradises." Like the two wings of a bird, these two driving forces lifted Christian civilization to its greatest flight, keeping it in balance and functioning well. The key to authentic progress in history consists in keeping this delicate balance.[10]

"Certain it is that the Church combined in an amazing degree the spiritual and temporal, the ideal and the practical," writes James Westfall Thompson. "If its head was in heaven, it always kept its feet upon the ground."[11]

The Great Works of Men

Great dreams are born of those who unite around sublime ideals. When we forsake our dreams, we put ourselves in the hands of bureaucrats in a regime of mediocrity.

This is because these great dreams are never the work of social planners, but rather the joint effort of great men, true elites, and peoples. Each member of a community lives and shares together the same original dream that serves to unite them under the blessings of God.

Each enters with a contribution to the great work of constructing this collective yet highly practical dream of idealizing a better life to-

---

10. See Plinio Corrêa de Oliveira, American Studies Commission meeting, May 13, 1988, Corrêa de Oliveira Documents.
11. Thompson, *Economic and Social History*, 2:648.

gether. There must be something of robustness, vigor, and ruggedness of the common people. There must be the varying degrees of culture, discernment, and sophistication of the intermediary layers of society. Finally, there must be those elites who, far from imposing their views upon a populace, refine and interpret what comes from below as their contribution to this dream that belongs to all.

When a society is blessed with great men, we could say they become almost prophets of this movement towards a dream. To the degree that they have deep roots in the whole of society, they sense where society must go and steer it in that direction. At times, God sends genial souls, such as King Saint Louis IX, who appear almost as angels in human form and hover over the multitudes, influencing and giving impetus to society and its economy. Indeed, this is true governance.

Some might object that the natural conditions to reconstruct our metaphysical dreams no longer exist in our modern society. There is no longer that atmosphere of intense cohesion in the social unit. There is little attempt to practice the Commandments, much less the evangelical counsels. Standardization and massification have done much to rob us of our dreams and replace them with the bland uniformity of our days.

We can overcome these obstacles by embracing once again that "audacious dream" that so transformed the West. If we unite ourselves around that same supernatural ideal of a world turned towards God, it will serve to be the catalyst to recreate the conditions where an immense impossibility can once again be made possible. It is left for us to dream anew.

The Way of the Cross by José R. Dias Tavares. A marvelous civilization is only possible when linked with the reality of suffering and tragedy. It must take as its model Our Lord and His Way of the Cross.

CHAPTER 49

A "Way of the Cross" Society

L est we be accused of glorifying the past, any dream of an ideal society cannot exclude the reality of hardship and suffering that comes from God's punishment of our first parents: "With labor and toil shalt thou eat thereof all the days of thy life" (Gn 3:17). Dreams become nostalgic and romantic fantasies if they are not linked with the reality of suffering and tragedy. We must therefore take to heart the model of the Cross.

Just as consumer society presupposes the consumer, Christian civilization presupposed the Christian. The Christian was not just a religious label. Rather it was the development of "the human type that had been produced by ten centuries of spiritual discipline and intensive cultivation of the inner life."[1] He was and is "another Christ," inseparable from His Cross.

What characterized early medieval man was his understanding that once disordered passions were let loose, they would unleash a tyrannical rule upon everything. This applied to private life, but this could also be seen in the barbaric and unruly passions of invading peoples who wreaked such havoc on medieval Europe.

Thus, medieval man perceived that the fight against these unbridled passions must play a central role in his private life. He also understood that in society there must always be dedicated sectors on the front lines of this great battle that, inspired by the Faith, take an attitude of fighting to the death at any moment to defend society as a whole.[2] The medieval knight, for example, held this ideal literally, as the civilizing monks of the West did analogously in their interior martyrdom.

Making a Sacrifice

When these dedicated sectors flourished, the spirit of their constant

---

1. Dawson, *Religion and the Rise*, 9.
2. "The life of man upon earth is a warfare" (Jb 7:1).

personal self-sacrifice and restraint permeated and set the tone for all society and helped all to control and counter their disordered passions. It was by this spirit that the barbarians were gradually both restrained by force of arms and tamed by prayer and penance under the loving gaze of the Church.

Hence, Summerfield Ballwin succinctly writes that "it was the Way of the Cross . . . which preoccupied the minds and hearts of Christendom."[3] The sublime perfume of this spirit of abnegation permeated economy, art, and thought, and gave value, meaning, and beauty to all things human.

"Way of the Cross" Economy

The economic implications of this spirit were particularly reflected in a "Way of the Cross" economy, where the need for sacrifice and restraint in supplying human needs coincided with the consuming ideal of seeking the Cross of Christ. Medieval man looked for ways to offer up his sacrifices in the economic dealings of every day.

One immediate manner of doing this was by offering to God the best fruits of one's labor. The farmer, for example, planted his wheat thinking that his best grains might be turned into hosts for the Consecration. The vintner saw his wine being used for Mass as the highest honor. Builders gave their best to build magnificent churches to house Our Lord. Fine linens and silks adorned the altars. Members of the ancient guild of joiners and cabinetmakers under the patronage of Saint Anne "looked upon the making of tabernacles wherein God may dwell in our churches as their most choice work."[4] The first and best apple of an orchard might be put in the hand of the Virgin statue at the village church as a symbolic gesture of this sacrifice.

In this way, man "immolated" as an offering the best products of his hands in the service of the God Who immolated Himself for us.

Pursuit of Excellence

With Christ as the perfect model, this "Way of the Cross" economy also

---

3. Summerfield Ballwin, *Business in the Middle Ages* (New York: Cooper Square Publishers, 1968), 5.
4. Prosper Guéranger, *The Liturgical Year*, trans. Laurence Shepherd (Great Falls, Mont.: St. Bonaventure Publications, 2000), 13:192. If the Blessed Mother was the ciborium of Christ, Saint Anne was the tabernacle.

served God's glory by awakening in men a passionate pursuit of excellence for excellence's sake.

To medieval man, this pursuit of excellence was an arduous task, not unlike a Way of the Cross that ultimately led not to profits but to God. He believed he could give glory to God by making His creation even more excellent. By making beautiful things, the artisan's sacrifice taught all society to love excellent things as a way that they might know and love God more. In this way, even the most modest things in Christian civilization tended to have a certain splendor, so that all creation could better sing the glory of God and thereby elevate souls towards Him.

One could see this in the craftsman who set about his arduous tasks motivated by this higher ideal. "The laborer toiled not merely to win sustenance," writes Richard Weaver, "but to see this ideal embodied in his creation."[5] The perfume-maker, for example, was motivated by a desire to produce a most excellent perfume. It was with great metaphysical joy that he made more effort and accepted less money in this quest to leave mankind a better perfume.

Rewards of the Cross

When such a metaphysical spirit permeates everything, all society cannot but grow in quality and excellence. The lawyer presents a magnificent legal brief or a cobbler searches for a marvelous shoe for the sake of the beauty of their actions. The artist—so sensitive to such an outlook—produces his masterpiece and dies content even though he be not rich. Even the most modest of men, generally speaking, pursued their crafts as if they were arts and came to be great appreciators of beauty.

Indeed, writes Lewis Mumford, "The purpose of art has never been labor-saving but labor-loving, a deliberate elaboration of function, form, and symbolic ornament to enhance the interest of life itself."[6] And in the practice of this art, the act of labor becomes a veritable prayer.

Such an economy involved arduous effort, but God rewarded this sacrifice by conferring upon society the flowering of what we consider

---

5. Weaver, *Ideas Have Consequences*, 73.
6. Mumford, *Pentagon of Power*, 2:137.

the better things of life: education, books, art, music, charity, and culture. All these rewards, Ballwin claims, "were, in the Middle Ages, the very paving, so to speak, of the Way of the Cross."[7]

Such artistic production finds little resonance in an industrialized world based on frenetic intemperance and unbridled consumption. However, this spirit of immolation and abnegation, found in the Way of the Cross, is like the ballast of a ship or the brake of a car. It puts things in order and gives stability to economy. With this ballast, the "Way of the Cross" economy produced results beyond all expectations and gave value, meaning, and beauty to all things human. With God's grace, it could do so again.

---

7. Ballwin, *Business in the Middle Ages*, 68.

CHAPTER 50

The Secret of the Middle Ages

W hile an understanding of the high and sublime ideals that moved medieval society may help us in our search for economic solutions, such considerations tell only part of the story. Neither these ideals nor the dreams built upon them give an entirely adequate explanation for the flowering of the Middle Ages.

Even the austere and arduous Way of the Cross, which served as an inspiration for the fight against the disordered passions, would not in itself be enough to inspire a society to strive towards excellence since man naturally avoids suffering and great effort.

Yet there was a motivating factor that overcame all obstacles. That "secret" of the flowering of the Middle Ages was the fact that medieval man had a very lively, admiring, and loving notion of the person of Our Lord Jesus Christ. There was a very palpable and personal understanding of His perfections—His wisdom, His goodness, and His justice—that permeated and unified all society.

Our Lord as the Point of Reference

In fact, Our Lord was the point of reference for all things. "About the figure of the Divinity," writes Johan Huizinga, "a majestic system of correlated figures crystallizes, which all have reference to Him, because all things derive their meaning from Him."[1]

It was not just an abstract figure of the Divinity that so attracted medieval man. What touched him was the fact that the Word, the Second Person of the Most Holy Trinity, became flesh and dwelt among us. In a very personal way, the medieval man took to heart not only Who He is, but all that He taught and did.

As we have seen, we can still hear the faint echoes of this generalized perception in the grace of Christmas. Christmas Eve is still impreg-

---

1. Huizinga, *Waning of the Middle Ages*, 202.

nated with that medieval notion of the birth of Our Savior where, in that holy and silent night, one can sense the sweetness and perfection that emanates from the Divine Infant in the manger in Bethlehem.

This same tender sentiment was heartily and universally felt for the Passion, Death, Resurrection, and Ascension of Our Lord Jesus Christ, far surpassing any devotion that had come before and "obliterate[ing] the traces of an older severity and reticence" that were part of the developing spirituality of the early Church of the patristic age.[2]

"It is true that Augustine had an enormous love of God," writes historical scholar Henry Osborn Taylor. "It was fervently felt; it was powerfully reasoned; it impassioned his thought. Yet it did not contain that tender love of the divinely human Christ which trembles in the words of Bernard and makes the life of Francis a lyric poem."[3]

Expressions of Tenderness

The signs of this tender love could be seen everywhere as medieval man sought to express the infinite perfections of Christ through tangible symbols. Indeed, love seeks nothing except to give itself and to communicate the riches it enjoys.

Thus, Taylor observes, "And the same need of grasping the infinite and universal through symbols was the inspiration of medieval art: it built the cathedrals, painted their windows, filled their niches with statues, carving prophet types, carving the times and the seasons of God's providence, carving the vices and virtues of the soul and its eternal destiny, and at the same time augmenting the Liturgy with symbolic words and acts."[4]

Medieval Uprightness

To be like Our Lord Jesus Christ was the ideal that inspired the Middle Ages. Medieval man desired to be linked to Him in the most complete way possible; to lose himself in Him.

These sentiments were not only loving movements of admiration and

---

2. R. W. Southern, *The Making of the Middle Ages* (New Haven: Yale University Press, 1953), 233.
3. Henry Osborn Taylor, *The Medieval Mind: A History of the Development of Thought and Emotion in the Middle Ages* (New York: Macmillan, 1919), 1:360.
4. Ibid., 21. Henry Osborn Taylor sees this movement as a poetic development of what medieval man received from patristic Christianity: "So saint and poet and artist-craftsman join in that appropriation of Christianity which was vivifying whatever had come from the Latin Fathers, by pondering upon it, loving it, living it, imagining it, and making it into poetry and art" (ibid).

THE MEDIEVAL SPIRIT OF THE *ANIMA CHRISTI*

Although not from the medieval period, Saint Ignatius of Loyola's prayer *Anima Christi* conveys the same intense medieval desire of union with Christ. He implores:

Soul of Christ, sanctify me.
Body of Christ, save me.
Blood of Christ, inebriate me.
Water from Christ's side, wash me.
Passion of Christ, strengthen me.
O Good Jesus, hear me.
Within Thy wounds hide me.
Suffer me not to be separated from Thee.
From the malicious enemy defend me.
In the hour of my death call me.
And bid me come unto Thee,
That I may praise Thee with Thy Saints and with Thy Angels
Forever and ever. Amen.

awe. Medieval man took them to their final consequences, reasoning that Christ could have come to earth in all His glory, shining forth for all the nations. Yet He chose the hardest, saddest, and most terrifyingly difficult path to accomplish His mission for our salvation. Stirred by gentle compassion, the medieval mind was "saturated with the concepts of Christ and the cross."[5]

With inflexible uprightness, he noted how Our Lord foresaw His sufferings yet nevertheless embraced the Cross, accepting it even to the point of asking with touching supplication: "Father, if thou wilt, remove this chalice from me: But yet not my will, but thine be done" (Lk 22:42).

Accepting Suffering

Here we find the secret of the "Way of the Cross" society. With similar rectitude, medieval man logically embraced his own suffering, paying special attention to the hardest part of his situation. This is frequently represented in medieval pictures and stained glass where each is en-

---

5. Huizinga, *Waning of the Middle Ages,* 190.

gaged in his craft. All work diligently but without hurry, anxiety, or laziness. They carry their crosses, this hardest part of their lives, with joy and resignation since their model is Christ, Who suffered infinitely more for us.

"In this way all individual suffering is but the shadow of divine suffering, and all virtue is as a partial realization of absolute goodness,"[6] observes Huizinga. The result of this uprightness in suffering was that the person imagined for himself a way of imitating Christ that had perfection and sanctification as its goal. This perfection was well reflected in the quality of all his works, masterpieces, and monuments.

Alas, how such considerations differ from those of today! People seek fleeting and easy happiness. They flee hardship, lose themselves in frenetic laughter, and constantly seek to escape their responsibilities. In their blindness, they cannot see Christ in His Divine rectitude and follow Him on the dolorous Way of the Cross.

Yet it was this perspective that brought forth the flowering of the Middle Ages. The medieval man did not plan the Middle Ages; he merely desired to be like Jesus Christ. And from the realization of that desire, the Middle Ages was born and flowered.

This is the secret of the Middle Ages—and it is also our secret. If we could but have a similar, lively, and loving idea of Jesus Christ, we would want what they wanted and obtain what they received.

---

6. Ibid., 206.

CHAPTER 51

Applying the Principles of This Book

W e are a practical people. It is natural that after a lengthy theoretical discussion many are impelled to ask what is to be done. That admirable practicality, which is so much a part of our national character, calls for action. As we reach our conclusion, it seems logical, then, that we should present a list of concrete measures that must now be taken to avoid the impending collapse. There should also be urgent action items that suggest what might be done to establish the organic order we so ardently desire.

Ironically, the task asked of us runs contrary to the organic order we propose. As we have noted, the nature of organic remedies is to present principles of action and allow for the widest possible concrete application of those principles. Concrete measures depend on concrete circumstances, which differ widely according to time, place, and person. Nevertheless, we can point to some general guidelines that can serve as suggestions as to how we might apply what we have seen.

A Core Denunciation and Self-Examination

There are certain things that each of us can do personally to return to order.

Our core denunciation is aimed at a reckless spirit of frenetic intemperance, which is constantly throwing our economy out of balance by seeking to be rid of restraints and gratify disordered passions. We have likened this spirit to that of a great never-ending party on a cruise ship, which leads us to spend and consume with reckless abandon.

The first thing we must do is to observe where we have succumbed to frenetic intemperance in our own lives. It is up to each of us, for example, to see how we have engaged in the unbalanced consumerism, full of fads and fashions, which stirs up the markets and batters down the barriers of restraint and self-control. Each of us might look at our own participation in the debt-driven frenzied economy that fuels frenetic intemperance.

We should ask ourselves in what ways we have allowed ourselves to be "massified" by mass media, mass advertising, and mass markets by basing our consumption patterns and opinions on what we believe others think. We might also see how we have worshipped at the altar of speed with our rushed schedules and stress-filled lives. To what extent has the frenzy of technological gadgetry entered and dominated our lives and thought processes? How have we adopted the materialistic lifestyle of our Hollywood culture with its denial of suffering and tragedy?

Our self-examination should also look at the harsh rule of money, which promotes a way of looking at life where social, cultural, and moral values are put aside. Each of us can see where we have judged the rule of money more important than family, community, or religion. More concretely, we can ask ourselves to what extent we engage in frenzied business practices fraught with vulnerability and risk.

Our first task is to identify these and other areas where frenetic intemperance touches us personally and then have the courage to adjust our lives accordingly. We would do well to rid ourselves of those situations, investments, gadgets, and attitudes that favor frenetic intemperance in our personal lives. To put it succinctly, we must identify those things that turn our lives into one big party, and then look for original ways to declare that the party is over.

Exploring Organic Alternatives

We have also outlined the positive principles of an organic order that lend themselves to personal applications. Our second task consists in evaluating the extent to which we might apply these principles to our personal lives.

Organic remedies are accessible to all. Some of these involve very simple things that come naturally to man. We can cite, for example, any measure that encourages reflection and introspection as something that one can do as part of a return to order. There is also the practice of virtue, especially the cardinal virtues, since simple acts of virtue oppose the rule of "selfish vice" and contribute to an organic order and its passion for justice.

Any measure, no matter how small, that strengthens the worn social fabric of family, parish, community, or nation is a step towards this organic order. We must encourage any manner of leadership that expresses ties of mutual trust. We should think of concrete ways—by how we dress, speak, and lead—whereby we can truly be representative figures to those who look up to us. This would lead us to discover ways to embrace duty, responsibility, and sacrifice and reject a misguided and selfish individualism. Upon this social framework, an organic economy becomes possible.

As we have shown, an organic order leads to the fullest expression of a person's individuality, addressing both the material and spiritual needs of the person. Applying organic principles to this individual development means taking measures that favor the rule of honor and its set of values. Among these measures, we can list any concrete means by which we promote that which is excellent and lasting; the cultivation of wholesome intellectual development and debate; or the appreciation of beauty, art, and all things sublime.

We should ponder these personal avenues and then have the courage to adjust our lives accordingly.

Beyond Personal Avenues

These avenues, both positive and negative, are an extremely important part of any return to order. We can only applaud those who examine their lives and employ their imagination and creativity to make the most concrete applications of our general principles to their personal lives.[1]

However, such personal efforts will not be enough. We cannot limit ourselves to devising ways to withdraw from our frenetically intemperate world, or to live more ordered, organic, and virtuous lives. This cannot be done because we simply do not have the luxury of withdrawing from society.

The present crisis represents not merely the end of a party, but the approach of a great storm that threatens all with a massive economic collapse. We delude ourselves if we think we can escape misfortune by leaving the rowdy ballrooms of the cruise ship for the comfort of a well-ordered cabin. If the ship founders, even the most organic of lifestyles in the most complete isolation in steerage will not be spared from ruin.

Alone, none of us can do anything proportional to the crisis. The only proportional response is a great debate involving the whole nation

---

1. Suggestions and other resources can be accessed at www.ReturntoOrder.org.

on how we might return to order. Nothing short of a new national consensus will serve to unify Americans to face the storm. Either we agree among ourselves which course we as a nation must take, or we will not survive the storm.

Understanding the Crisis

Our third task is then to understand the crisis and engage in the debate over our future course. This debate is one we need not create, since it is already raging. Across the nation, people are confused and asking questions about why the largest economy in the history of the world—our great pride—is now faltering. There is doubt and uncertainty about the future of "capitalism" and what direction we should take. Alternatives (including many involving big government) are being proposed.

Return to Order and its corresponding campaign is our contribution to this debate. We present a historical perspective that allows us to understand the causes of this crisis, rethink our premises, and go beyond the models of frenetic intemperance that constantly carry within them the seeds of recurring crises. As a lighthouse amid the rocks, we seek to provide clarity amid this chaos. We join with other groups and individuals of the conservative movement in reassuring Americans that the Christian roots of our economic order are sound, and it is to these roots that we should return.

Our greatest contribution is to help Americans from all walks of life engage in the debate by inviting them to join a veritable crusade of ideas and principles for use wherever the crisis is being discussed, be it in the family, workplace, media, church, or university. It is our hope that those who join this crusade will use any and all peaceful means to get these ideas into the lifeblood of the nation so they can lead to a wholesome reaction.

An Appeal to Sacrifice

There is one final application of the principles of this book, and it is the most difficult. It is not enough to understand the crisis or even to engage in the debate. The future belongs to those who believe America is worth fighting for.

Ours is an appeal to sacrifice. It is an appeal to leave behind the party of frenetic intemperance that captivates so many with games, gadgets, and amusements—modern bread and circuses. At the same time, we ask Americans to forego their own legitimate self-interest and search for personal happiness. Now is the time to think of the imperiled ship.

To save the ship, two things are needed. The first is that there be those who rise to the occasion and bring together the elements to deal with the present crisis. While all should be involved in doing this, our appeal is especially directed to those representative characters, leaders at all levels in society, that naturally embody and unify the aspirations of their families, social groups, or communities. In this time of danger, we ask that they take to heart and use the organic principles in this book as a road map to restructure that America that we are called by Providence to be. It is our hope that these representative characters, as they have done in the past, might quickly bring together and inspire a nation of heroes proportional to the storm we face.

The second element is a rallying point of unity. One reason why the present crisis looms so large is that we no longer have the points of reference that once oriented our actions. As we have seen, a passion for justice, or the practice of the cardinal virtues, no longer orients economy. Diminished are so many of the landmark institutions of the heart and soul of economy—the family, community, Christian State, and Church. Without the rule of honor, there are no longer those norms of civility, manners, morals, and decency that facilitated the smooth running of societies and economies. In such conditions, is it any wonder that people are perplexed?

It is time to raise a standard to rally those who are confused by the impending storm. Let order—organic Christian order—be a rallying point. We believe this proven order, which so corresponds to the material and spiritual needs of our nature, can serve as a point of unity and reference in face of the present crisis. Such a standard can reassure countless concerned Americans that they are not alone in their belief that America is not a co-op but a nation worth fighting for.

The storm approaches. Each of us has a job to do. On a personal level, we should look for ways to rid ourselves of frenetic intemperance and adopt more organic and temperate lifestyles as a means of preparing for the coming crisis.

Yet more important is to go beyond our personal lives and consider the effect of the storm upon society in general. We should, therefore, endeavor to understand the nature of the storm and join the crusade of ideas and principles that will allow all of us to engage, in any way we can, in the great debate that will decide our course.

Most important of all is our willingness to sacrifice for our beloved nation and rally around the banner of a return to order in this hour of need. Trusting in Providence, we could well make our own the words of George Washington who, when facing a grave and unavoidable crisis, declared: "Let us raise a standard to which the wise and the honest can repair. The event is in the hand of God."[2]

WHAT WE CAN DO

1. Identify those areas where we are affected by frenetic intemperance and adjust our lives accordingly.
2. Explore those ways in which we can apply the principles of an organic order to our personal lives.
3. Understand the crisis and engage in the debate over the nation's future.
4. Rise to the occasion and rally around the standard of an organic Christian order.

---

2. Spalding and Garrity, *A Sacred Union of Citizens*, 27.

Grand Return Home

We have presented the specter of a great crisis that has as its immediate cause an impending economic crash that will trigger as its effect the breakdown of our national consensus and American way of life.

Although this crisis will wreak great material havoc upon us, its greatest damage will be spiritual. While we have presented some practical guidelines as to what we might do in face of the present crisis, it is in this spiritual sphere that the main remedy lies. Without a great moral conversion of some kind, we will not see the return to order we so desire.

Return of the Prodigal Son by Bartolomé Esteban Murillo (1617-1682). In these times of affliction and disorder, we should turn to a Father whose love overlooks our shortcomings and faults and welcomes us with a grand return home.

There must be a great reawakening that addresses the core spiritual issues that are at stake in our great debate. It avails us nothing if we survive the present storm and even implement our organic principles if it is done with the same restless spirit that brought us to our present plight. As long as we are inside the framework of frenetic intemperance, we will always carry within us the seeds of our own destruction. We must first move outside this framework. There must be a fundamental spiritual transformation that will change our mentalities and mend our ways.

Such a proposal cannot fail to suggest the figure of the Prodigal Son who, having left his father's house for the "frenetic intemperance" of a dissolute life, realizes the gravity of his error and longs to return. In looking for our solution, we believe we must follow a similar path.

We Have Erred

Like the Prodigal Son, our first step must be to realize that *we have erred*. We have followed a path to ruin amid the din of the great party of frenetic intemperance.

In the course of these considerations we have sought to show how we have erred. Our error was not the fact that we enjoyed the enormous bounty of our great land, but rather that it served to help our flight from temperance. We sought speed and agitation when we should have delighted in recollection and reflection. We have tried to build a materialist paradise while our nature yearns for the sublime. We trusted in the rule of money to provide us with comfort and merriment only to be afflicted by sadness, stress, and anxiety. The gods of the modern secular pantheon—individualism, materialism, and technological utopianism, among others—have failed us. As we approach our great crisis, we are left in a vacuum without clear direction or oracle.

Saint Luke tells us of the Prodigal Son (15:14): "And after he had spent all, there came a mighty famine in that country: and he began to be in want."

The present hour should give us pause to reflect. For we too have exhausted our resources on a party we thought would never end. We too find ourselves on the edge of an impending and "mighty" disaster. Looming on the horizon are radical ecological and socialistic solutions that threaten to throw us in the pigsties of abject misery. If in this grave hour we could but realize that we have sinned, it would serve to awaken in us humble and contrite hearts.

We Must Long for Our Father's House

If this is done, we can take the second step of the Prodigal Son: *He longed for his father's house.* That is to say, we cannot wallow in the perspective of great misery. We cannot engage in self-pity. We must look beyond the economic collapse and cultivate longings for our father's house.

We must remember our father's house—that rich Christian order from whence we came. That is why we have made such a great effort to describe that organic, virtuous, spontaneous, and providential order in all its calm and simple grandeur. We invoke the memory of those cohorts of legendary saints and leaders inside society from top to bottom that took upon themselves the arduous task of upholding the rule of honor. We dare to dream of an order where economy rests on honor; our laws upon the Commandments. We stress that our way must be the Way of the Cross and the point of our reference Our Lord Jesus Christ.

It is by this realistic, unromantic review of timeless Christian principles that we seek to awaken those intense chords of longings for our Father's house that should move us to action.

We Must Clash with a Misguided Culture

"And rising up, he came to his father." With these simple words, Saint Luke (15:20) outlines the Prodigal Son's plan of action, which must also be ours.

In our desire to leave the crisis, it is not enough to simply isolate ourselves, move away, or search for another frenetic party. We must rise up against the culture that has led us to ruin; we must leave behind and disengage ourselves from the rule of money, both as individuals and as a nation. With humble and contrite hearts, we can then search out the object of our longings.

As to the practical means by which the Prodigal Son rose up and returned to his father's house, the Gospel is curiously silent. Nor does it seem essential to the narrative. The longings of the son call forth the means just as organic solutions adapt themselves to circumstances. It is enough that this clash be born of a strong rejection and a great love for the adequate means to appear.

We Must Respond to the Father's Love

There is a final aspect in the Prodigal Son's grand return home that is often disregarded, but herein lies the key point. We are told that the son longed for his father, but it is clear that the father longed much more for his son. Indeed, the father watched from afar for news of his son and ran out to meet him.

Thus, in our longing for that Christian order, which is our Father's house, we must also consider the longings of God, Our Father, and respond to His love. Alas, such sentiments of disinterested goodness are so foreign in our age that only promotes self-interest and advantage!

We must include them in our plan.

We must be convinced that God desires our grand return home much more than we do. He watches from afar for the least sign of our cooperation to the graces that He so gratuitously bestows upon us. And when He finds effort on our part, He is not outdone in His generosity. He goes out to meet us and treats us as if we had never erred. He kills the fatted calf and orders a great celebration. Our return home becomes grand because of the Father to whom we return, not because of our own merits or efforts.

To the manly solicitude of a father, we must add the maternal affection of a mother who also intensely desires our good. It is not without reason that Christian civilization had as its cultural soul the devotion to the Blessed Virgin Mary. To her were directed the towering vaults of medieval cathedrals, the sublime Gregorian chant of monks, and even the best fruits of economic production. Around her we find united saint and sinner, rich and poor, old and young, learned and ignorant. To paraphrase the words of Saint Bernard, all "fled to her protection, implored her help and sought her intercession." Her overwhelming desire to help "left none unaided."

Throughout these considerations of a socio-economic nature, we have made reference to the need to cooperate with the grace of God by being sensitive to His loving providence, by responding to His calling, or by prophetically discerning His designs. Here, we affirm the need for a holy and sacred alliance with God and recourse to Our Lady.

> **THE PATH OF THE PRODIGAL SON**
> We have erred.
> We must long for Our Father's house.
> We must clash with our misguided culture.
> We must respond to Our Father's love.

No Illusions

We can have no illusions about this path. We will not deny that this conversion, like any major amendment of life, is radical in character.

Yet we note that, to the degree that the impending collapse approaches and the music of the band subsides, there will be those who will join the already large number of concerned Americans who clash with our culture and look in the direction of the father's house they never knew.

Common Cause

History records how crisis and adversity have the effect of uniting men in common cause. In fact, no greater bond is forged than when people suffer together, as can be seen in the wartime ties among soldiers, or in the struggle for education that unites alumni for life.

Common struggles often initiate changes that would normally take generations to effect. They can give rise to dynamic social, cultural, or religious movements capable of creating new identities, cementing bonds of solidarity, and forging strong reciprocal relationships. It is not unreasonable to expect that, in the face of the present crisis, similar solutions might emerge. Here we must rely upon the longings of a Father and the ardent supplications of a Mother to call us home.

The Factor of Grace

It is then that what seems impossible becomes possible.

"When men resolve to cooperate with the grace of God," writes Plinio Corrêa de Oliveira, "the marvels of history are worked: the conversion of the Roman Empire; the formation of the Middle Ages; the reconquest of Spain, starting from Covadonga; all the events that result from the great resurrection of soul of which peoples are also capable. These resurrections are invincible, because nothing can defeat a people that is virtuous and truly loves God."[1]

One might ask if the impending collapse can be avoided. We would answer that the course of history is not predetermined, although its lessons are often repeated. If we are to avoid the crisis, we must turn our efforts now to our grand return home.

As Catholic countrymen concerned with the future of our nation, we appeal to our fellow Americans as the gathering storm approaches. Let us recognize those errors of the past that have led us so far astray. Let us rue the frenetic intemperance that threw our society and economy out of balance. Let us cultivate longings for our Father's house and our Mother's embrace. Above all, let us fervently beseech Almighty

---

1. Corrêa de Oliveira, *Revolution and Counter-Revolution*, 104.

God to avert or mitigate the evils which our errors have brought upon us. And if this be not possible, and we are called to eat of the husks of the swine, then let us arise from our misfortunes like new Saint Pauls, humbled and chastened, to call our society back home, back to order.

This was how Christendom was born. The humbled Prodigal Son who entered his father's house in the hope of becoming a servant was exalted as a son beyond all expectations. So also we can expect a similar grand return home.

We end these considerations invoking Our Lady of Fatima. It was she who appeared in Portugal in 1917 and warned us of communism and other errors of our modern times. She also spoke of the coming crisis and completed her message with a marvelous promise in which she invited us to dwell in a Christian order where her Immaculate Heart would triumph.

ACKNOWLEDGMENTS

This is a book born of great desires amid adversity. It was the passion to see this project through that overcame all the trials and obstacles that seemed to conspire against its completion. As this book finally appears, it marks the culmination of the efforts of many who must in all justice be mentioned here since they have shared in that passion.

It is proper that I first recognize and thank Prof. Plinio Corrêa de Oliveira. It was he who many decades ago foresaw the economic crisis in the United States and the West. Though Brazilian, with touching solicitude for our nation, he invited me and others to study modern economy so that we might later address this crisis from a Catholic perspective. In 1986, he formed what was called the American Studies Commission (1986-1991) for this purpose. His great desire to see this project succeed led to regular meetings where he developed so many of the ideas and concepts that are interwoven into the narrative of this work.

My gratitude must also extend to that first American Studies Commission of TFP members whose dedication broke the ground for this work. Among that core group, I would like to make special mention of Julio Loredo de Izcue and Péricles Capanema Ferreira e Melo for their encouragement and support.

Gratitude is especially fitting during hard times. These studies were discontinued shortly before the death of Prof. Plinio Corrêa de Oliveira in 1995 and it seemed there was no light at the end of the tunnel. Despite several attempts to revive the commission, the obstacles seemed insurmountable. For this reason, I would like to thank in a very special way American TFP director, Luiz A. Fragelli, whose unflagging support during this time helped resurrect these studies and create the conditions to form another commission to bring this work to a conclusion. It was he who advised me to adopt a regime of intense study, and I thank him for this. I also benefited from the encouragement of Caio Xavier da Silveira, which I felt along the way.

It is with special affection and appreciation that I thank those American TFP members who joined with me to form the current American Studies Commission (2006-present)—Raymond E. Drake, Gary J. Isbell,

Richard A. Lyon, Michael M. Whitcraft, C. Michael Drake, and Benjamin A. Hiegert. Over the years, this extraordinary band of brothers has served as an essential sounding board of the book's theses. They have offered wise counsel, frank commentary, and lively encouragement.

I have also been privileged to tap into the vast reservoir of knowledge of veteran TFP members around the world who have reviewed this work with care and charity. Each brought his own expertise and life experience into the project. First among them I thank Prince Bertrand of Orleans-Braganza for his kind observations and advice. I further thank Dr. Adolpho Lindenberg (an author in his own right), Chilean economist Carlos del Campo, José A. Ureta Zañartu, António Borelli Machado, Fernando Antúnez Aldunate, Mathias von Gersdorff, Mario Navarro da Costa, C. Preston Noell III, John R. Spann, and the learned brothers, Gustavo and Luiz Solimeo.

Several academics and writers agreed to review versions of the manuscript and offer their suggestions. I was heartened by the early encouragement of Prof. Richard Stivers, whose books I admire and advice I treasure. I thank Forrest McDonald, Robert H. Knight; Lt. Col. Joseph J. Thomas (Leadership professor at the U.S. Naval Academy); Dr. Alejandro A. Chafuen of the Atlas Economic Research Foundation; Fr. Jerry Wooton; and Dr. Kevin Schmiesing from the Acton Institute, all of whom offered very penetrating and welcome suggestions. I also profited from the remarks of Prof. David Magalhães, from the University of Coimbra in Portugal. A special thanks to economist Gregor Hochreiter from Austria, with whom I frequently discussed economics and whose explanations made the "dismal science" a bit less dismal. All have improved upon the text and made its shortcomings, which are my own, less apparent.

American TFP director Robert E. Ritchie has been tireless in his efforts to spread the ideas of this book far and wide. There are so many others—researchers, editors, proofreaders, and reviewers—who joined to bring this book to light. I thank them all for their support, enthusiasm, and patience.

A most important word of thanks must be reserved for those outside the process of the writing of this book. I am humbled by the solicitude of the TFP members, supporters, and friends who, while not directly involved in this work, nevertheless followed its progress and who, by their commentaries, encouragement, and prayers, have played an enormous role in its completion. Their passion for the subjects broached in the book truly inspired me to keep going. Especially true in this regard was the moral support of my fellow TFP members, who helped me in so many ways. I cannot thank them enough.

I thank all who have shared the ardent desires and adversity that brought forth this book and pray that the timely ideas and principles it contains play their role in the debate over the future of our beloved nation.

John Horvat II
Spring Grove, Pennsylvania
December 8, 2012
Feast of the Immaculate Conception,
Patroness of the United States

**The publication of this book was made possible
through the generosity of TFP-America Needs Fatima
benefactors listed below:**

Mrs. Eveylyn Damigella
Mr. and Mrs. Sergio De Paz in memory of Sergio A. De Paz, Jr.
Mrs. Maria Ivusic
Rev. Fr. Joseph W. Grace
Mr. and Mrs. Edward Ritchie
Anonymous donors known to God for whom we pray

Acedia – a state whereby a person displays a weariness for holy and spiritual things, which causes depression, sadness, and even despair.

***Bourdon* souls** – those persons with special insights who orient, harmonize, and set the tone of those around them with advice, direction, and leadership.

Christian State – the political organization and ordering of the nation according to Christian principles and natural law with the role to safeguard the common good and facilitate virtuous life in common.

Cooperative union – a socio-economic model in which citizens see their nation as a kind of shareholding corporation to which they contribute and from which they expect benefits and entitlements.

Currency – any government-issued notes, paper money, and coins that serve as legal tender and a medium of exchange, and make up the physical money supply of a nation.

Divine Providence – the plan conceived in the mind of God according to which He provides for and directs all creatures to their proper end.

Feudal bond – any of a broad range of mutually-beneficial personal relationships within the rule of law that bind individuals together in society. It is usually characterized by one party that seeks protection and another that seeks service.

Frenetic intemperance – a restless, explosive, and relentless drive inside modern man that manifests itself in economy by 1) seeking to throw off legitimate restraints; and 2) gratifying disordered passions.

Gigantism – a tendency inside modern economy which favors an intemperate and consuming expansion of manufacturing and other sectors to gigantic proportions often made possible by unfair business practices or government benefits.

Guild – family-like trade associations that look after the spiritual and temporal interests of their members. They are organic self-governing bodies that make their own rules, regulate competition, and set quality standards for the products of their trades.

Intermediary bodies – associations such as guilds, universities, parishes, and communities which stand between the individual and the State and play a major role in the formation and development of members in society.

Individualism – a deformation of individuality by which man closes himself up in and makes himself the center of a world of personal self-interest that tends to disregard the social character of man and his role in community.

Mass standardization – an imbalance of the markets in which goods are produced on a large scale to the detriment of consumer satisfaction and individuality.

Materialism – an imbalance in the market in which production and consumption are dominated by an excessive fixation on pleasure, physical comfort, utility, or quantity. It does not address the spiritual or metaphysical side of human nature which tends towards the good, true, and beautiful.

Money – a convention established by law for the convenience of exchange, the storage of wealth, and as a measure of the value for all things salable.

Nation – a community of people who share a common language, culture, descent, or history and live under the same ruler and laws.

Natural law – an ethical system inherent in human nature and discoverable by reason that helps man to act correctly according to the finality of human acts. It is the same for all peoples, places, and times.

Organic society – a social order oriented toward the common good that naturally and spontaneously develops, allowing man to pursue the perfection of his essentially social nature through the family, intermediary groups, the State, and the Church.

Proportional scale economy – an order in which the sizes of commercial activity favor knowledge of one's surroundings and the establishment of points of reference. Such commercial relationships may be big, medium, or small and vary according to the abilities of those involved.

Representative character – a person who perceives the ideals, principles, and qualities that are desired and admired by a community or nation, and translates them into concrete programs of life and culture.

Revolution – term used by Catholic thinker Plinio Corrêa de Oliveira to describe a single historical process characterized by a spirit of revolt against the spiritual, religious, moral, and cultural values of Christianity. There are four phases of this process: 1) the Renaissance which prepared the way for the Protestant Revolution (1517); 2) the French Revolution (1789); 3) the Communist Revolution (1917); and 4) the Cultural Revolution of the Sixties (1968).

Rule of honor – a set of ruling values in society which gives rise to a lifestyle that naturally leads men to esteem and seek after those things that are excellent. This set of values includes quality, beauty, goodness, and charity.

Rule of law – a state of order in society in which human events generally conform to a legal code.

Rule of money – a misuse of money that turns it from a common means of exchange into the principal measure of all relationships and values. It installs a set of values in which utility, efficiency, and quantity dominate.

Scholastic School – an intellectual movement in Europe (1100-1500) which formulated a unified body of Catholic thought applicable to all areas of life. It made use of Aristotelian philosophy, Biblical texts, Patristic literature and Roman jurists. Saint Thomas Aquinas was its foremost writer. A later development (called the Late Scholastic School) was the School of Salamanca (1500-1650) in Spain which dealt with many economic matters.

Social capital – any social network that is governed by shared norms and values and is maintained by sanctions, and that creates conditions for trust, thereby enriching social, civic, and economic life.

Sublime, the – those things that are of such excellence that they provoke great emotion, causing men to be overawed by their magnificence or grandeur. The sublime might be found in extraordinary panoramas, works of art, ideas, virtuous acts, or the heroic feats of great men.

Subsidiarity, the principle of – a social principle that holds that a community of a higher order should not unduly interfere in the internal life of a community of a lower order. At the same time, a lower social unit should solve its own problems and only have recourse to a higher unit or authority in those matters it is unable to handle.

Temperance – the virtue whereby man governs his natural appetites and passions in accordance with the norms prescribed by reason and Faith.

"Ten Commandments" America – that part of the American public that has a great respect for a consensual moral code loosely based on the Ten Commandments and as a result still preserves a healthy attachment to moral values.

Upright spontaneity – a manner of acting in organic society according to principles, natural law, and the Gospel, which respects the unplanned development of life and fosters the exercise of free will, creativity, and adaptation.

Vital flux – that exuberant human vitality and dynamism found in a true people in which unlocked talents and qualities are exhibited with tremendous bursts of energy and enthusiasm, which can in turn be channeled and refined to useful purposes.

BIBLIOGRAPHY

Acquaviva, Sabino S. *The Decline of the Sacred in Industrial Society*. Translated by Patricia Lipscomb. Oxford: Basil Blackwell, 1979.

Adams, Walter and James W. Brock. *The Bigness Complex: Industry, Labor, and Government in the American Economy*. Stanford, Calif.: Stanford University Press, 2004.

Aquinas, Saint Thomas. *Commentary on Aristotle's Politics*. Translated by Richard J. Regan. Indianapolis: Hackett Publishing, 2007.

—. *The Summa Contra Gentiles*. Translated by the English Dominican Fathers. New York: Benzinger Brothers, n.d.

—. *Summa Theologica*. http://www.newadvent.org/summa/.

Aristotle, "Nicomachean Ethics." Translated by W. D. Ross. In *The Works of Aristotle: II*. Vol. 9 of *Great Books of the Western World*. Edited by Robert Maynard Hutchins, 339-436. Chicago: University of Chicago, 1952.

Artz, Frederick B. *The Mind of the Middle Ages, A.D. 200-1500: An Historical Survey*. Chicago: University of Chicago Press, 1980.

Augustine, Saint. *In epistulam Ioannis ad Parthos* (Homily 7 on the First Epistle of John). http://www.newadvent.org/fathers/170207.htm.

—. *Epist. 138 ad Marcellinum*. In *Opera Omnia*. Vol. 2, in J.P. Migne, *Patrologia Latina*.

Ballwin, Summerfield. *Business in the Middle Ages*. New York: Cooper Square Publishers, 1968.

Barrett, William. *Death of the Soul: From Descartes to the Computer*. New York: Doubleday Anchor Books, 1986.

Beard, Charles. *The Industrial Revolution*. Westport, Conn.: Greenwood Press Publishers, 1975.

Bell, Daniel. *The Cultural Contradictions of Capitalism*. New York: Basic Books, 1976.

Bellah, Robert N., Richard Madsen, William M. Sullivan, Ann Swidler, and Steven M. Tipton. *Habits of the Heart: Individualism and Commitment in American Life*. Berkeley: University of California Press, 1985.

Benedict XVI, General Audience, Aug. 31, 2011. http://www.vatican.va/holy_father/benedict_xvi/audiences/2011/documents/hf_ben-xvi_aud_20110831_en.html.

Berle, Adolph A. and Gardiner C. Means. *The Modern Corporation and Private Property*. New Brunswick, N.J.: Transaction, 2002.

Berman, Marshall. *All That Is Solid Melts into Air: The Experience of Moder-

nity. New York: Simon and Schuster, 1982.

Blackstone, Sir William. *Commentaries on the Laws of England*. Oxford: Clarendon Press, 1765.

Bloch, Marc. *The Growth of Ties of Dependence*. Translated by L. A. Manyoa. Vol. 1 of *Feudal Society*. Chicago: University of Chicago Press, 1961.

—. *Social Classes and Political Organization*. Translated by L. A. Manyoa. Vol. 2 of *Feudal Society*. Chicago: University of Chicago Press, 1961.

Bogle, John C. *The Battle for the Soul of Capitalism*. New Haven: Yale University Press, 2005.

Bookstaber, Richard. *A Demon of Our Own Design: Markets, Hedge Funds, and the Perils of Financial Innovation*. Hoboken, N.J.: John Wiley and Sons, 2007.

Brankin, Anthony J. "The Cult of Ugliness in America." *Crusade Magazine*, May-June 2001.

Braudel, Fernand. *Afterthoughts on Material Civilization and Capitalism*. Translated by Patricia M. Ranum. Baltimore: Johns Hopkins University Press, 1977.

—. *The Structures of Everyday Life, The Limits of the Possible*. Translated by Siân Reynolds. Vol. 1 of *Civilization and Capitalism 15th-18th Century*. Berkeley: University of California Press, 1992.

—. *The Wheels of Commerce*. Translated by Siân Reynolds. Vol. 2 of *Civilization and Capitalism 15th-18th Century*. Berkeley: University of California Press, 1992.

—. *The Perspective of the World*. Translated by Siân Reynolds. Vol. 3 of *Civilization and Capitalism 15th-18th Century*. New York: Harper and Row, 1984.

Brooks, David. *On Paradise Drive: How We Live Now (And Always Have) in the Future Tense*. New York: Simon and Schuster, 2004.

Burke, Edmund. "Reflections on the Revolution in France." In *The Works of Edmund Burke, With a Memoir*. New York: Harper and Brothers, 1846.

—. "Letter from Mr. Burke to a Member of the National Assembly; In Answer to Some Objections to His Book on French Affairs. 1791." In *The Works of Edmund Burke, With a Memoir*. New York: Harper and Brothers, 1846.

—. "A Philosophical Inquiry into the Origins of Our Ideas on the Sublime and Beautiful." In *The Works of Edmund Burke, With a Memoir*. New York: Harper and Brothers, 1846.

Carr, Nicholas. *The Shallows: What the Internet Is Doing to Our Brains.* New York: W. W. Norton, 2010.

Chafuen, Alejandro A. *Faith and Liberty: The Economic Thought of the Late Scholastics.* Lanham, Md.: Lexington Books, 2003.

Chancellor, Edward. *Devil Take the Hindmost: A History of Financial Speculation.* New York: Plume, 2000.

Cipolla, Carlo M. *Before the Industrial Revolution: European Society and Economy, 1000-1700.* New York: W. W. Norton, 1976.

—. "The Italian and Iberian Peninsulas." In *Economic Organization and Policies in the Middle Ages.* Vol. 3 of *The Cambridge Economic History of Europe.* Edited by M. M. Postan. London: Cambridge University Press, 1953.

Corrêa de Oliveira, Plinio. *Nobility and Analogous Traditional Elites in the Allocutions of Pius XII: A Theme Illuminating American Social History.* York, Pa.: The American Society for the Defense of Tradition, Family and Property, 1993.

—. *Revolution and Counter-Revolution.* 3rd ed. York, Pa.: The American Society for the Defense of Tradition, Family and Property, 1993.

—. "Money Is Not the Supreme Value." In *Folha de São Paulo*, May 9, 1971.

—. 73 meetings with the American Studies Commission (1986-1991) and meetings on Aug. 21, 1986 and Mar. 12, 1991. Plinio Corrêa de Oliveira Documents. (Consisting of transcribed audio recording.) American TFP Research Library, Spring Grove, Pennsylvania.

Cox, Harvey. *The Secular City: Secularization and Urbanization in Theological Perspective.* New York: Macmillan, 1966.

Dawson, Christopher. *Religion and the Rise of Western Culture.* New York: Sheed and Ward, 1950.

Delassus, Henri. *L'Ésprit Familial dans la Famille, dans la Cité, et dans l'État.* Cadillac, France: Éditions Saint-Remi, 2007.

Dempsey, Bernard W. *The Functional Economy: The Bases of Economic Organization.* Englewood Cliffs, N.J.: Prentice-Hall, 1958.

—. *Interest and Usury.* London: Dennis Dobson, 1948.

de Roover, Raymond. *San Bernardino of Siena and Sant'Antonino of Florence: The Two Great Economic Thinkers of the Middle Ages.* Cambridge: Harvard University Printing Office, 1967.

—. *The Rise and Decline of the Medici Bank 1397-1494.* New York: W. W. Norton, 1966.

Duby, Georges, ed. *Revelations of the Medieval World*. Translated by Arthur Goldhammer.Vol. 2 of *A History of Private Life*. Cambridge: Harvard University Press, Belknap Press, 1988.

Durkheim, Émile. *The Elementary Forms of the Religious Life*. Translated by Joseph Ward Swain. London: George Allen and Unwin, 1964.

Evans, M. Stanton. *The Theme Is Freedom: Religion, Politics, and the American Tradition*. Washington, D.C.: Regnery Publishing, 1994.

Federer, William J. *The Ten Commandments & Their Influence on American Law: A Study in History*. St. Louis: Amerisearch, 2003.

Friedman, Lawrence M. *The Horizontal Society*. New Haven: Yale University Press, 1999.

Friedman, Milton. *A Program for Monetary Stability*. New York: Fordham University Press, 1960.

Friedman, Thomas L. *The World Is Flat: A Brief History of the Twenty-first Century*. New York: Picador, 2005.

Funck-Brentano, Franz. *The Middle Ages*. Translated by Elizabeth O'Neill. New York: G. P. Putnam and Sons, 1923.

Gaughan, William Thomas. *Social Theories of Saint Antoninus from His Summa Theologica*. Washington, D.C.: Catholic University of America Press, 1950.

Gautier, Léon. *Chivalry*. Translated by Henry Frith. New York: Crescent Books, 1989.

Gilby, Thomas. *The Political Thought of Thomas Aquinas*. Chicago: University of Chicago Press, 1958.

Gimpel, Jean. *The Medieval Machine: The Industrial Revolution of the Middle Ages*. New York: Penguin Books, 1977.

Goldwater, Barry. *The Conscience of a Conservative*. N.p.: Bottom of the Hill Publishing, 2010.

Gray, Sir Alexander. *The Development of Economic Doctrine*. New York: John Wiley and Sons, 1965.

Greenspan, Alan. "Remarks at the Annual Dinner and Francis Boyer Lecture of The American Enterprise Institute for Public Policy Research," Washington, D.C., Dec. 5, 1996. Accessed Oct. 14, 2012. http://www.federalreserve.gov/boarddocs/speeches/1996/19961205.htm.

Guéranger, Prosper. *The Liturgical Year*. Translated by Laurence Shepherd. Great Falls, Mont.: St. Bonaventure Publications, 2000.

Halpern, David. *Social Capital*. Cambridge: Polity Press, 2005.

Hayek, F.A. "The Road to Serfdom." In *The Road to Serfdom: Texts and Documents, The Definitive Edition.* Vol. 2 of *The Collected Works of F. A. Hayek.* Edited by Bruce Caldwell. London: University of Chicago Press, 2007.

Heer, Friedrich. *The Medieval World, Europe 1100-1350.* Translated by Janet Sondheimer. New York: Praeger Publishers, 1969.

Heilbroner, Robert. *The Nature and Logic of Capitalism.* New York: W. W. Norton, 1985.

Henry, Patrick. "'And I Don't Care What It Is': The Tradition-History of a Civil Religion Proof-Text." *Journal of the American Academy of Religion,* 49:1 (Mar. 1981): 35-49.

Herlihy, David. *The History of Feudalism.* New York: Walker, 1971.

Hobbes, Thomas. "Leviathan." In *Machiavelli, Hobbes.* Vol. 23 of *Great Books of the Western World.* Edited by Robert Maynard Hutchins, 39-283. Chicago: The University of Chicago, 1952.

Huizinga, Johan H. *In the Shadow of Tomorrow.* New York: W. W. Norton, 1936.

—. *The Waning of the Middle Ages: A Study of the Forms of Life, Thought and Art in France and the Netherlands in the XIVth and XVth Centuries.* Garden City, N.Y.: Doubleday Anchor Books, 1954.

Innes, A. M. "What Is Money?" *Banking Law Journal* (May 1913): 377-408.

John Paul II. Encyclical *Centesimus Annus.* 1991. Washington, D.C.: United States Catholic Conference, 1991.

Kennedy, Anthony M. *Lawrence v. Texas* 539 U.S. 558 (2003).

—. *Planned Parenthood of Southeastern Pennsylvania v. Casey* 505 U. S. 833 (1992).

Kern, Fritz. *Kingship and Law in the Middle Ages: The Divine Right of Kings and the Right of Resistance in the Early Middle Ages; Law and Constitution in the Middle Ages.* Translated by S. B. Chrimes. Oxford: Basil Blackwell, 1968.

Keynes, John Maynard. *The General Theory of Employment, Interest and Money.* Amherst, N.Y.: Prometheus Books, 1997.

Kindleberger, Charles P. and Robert Aliber. *Manias, Panics, and Crashes: A History of Financial Crises.* Hoboken, N.J.: John Wiley and Sons, 2005.

King, Mervyn. "Banking—from Bagehot to Basel, and back again." *BIS Review* 140 (2010): 1.

Kirk, Russell. *The Roots of American Order.* 3rd ed. Washington, D.C.: Regnery Gateway, 1991.

—. *Enemies of the Permanent Things: Observations of Abnormity in Litera-*

ture and Politics. New Rochelle, N.Y.: Arlington House, 1969.

Kirshner, Julius, ed., *Business, Banking and Economic Thought in Late Medieval and Early Modern Europe: Selected Studies of Raymond de Roover.* Chicago: University of Chicago Press, 1976.

Klugewicz, Stephen M. and Lenore T. Ealy, eds. *History, on Proper Principles: Essays in Honor of Forrest McDonald.* Wilmington, Del.: ISI Books, 2010.

Kriedte, Peter, Hans Medick, and Jurgen Schlumbohm. *Industrialization before Industrialization: Rural Industry in the Genesis of Capitalism.* Translated by Beate Schempp. Cambridge: Cambridge University Press, 1981.

Kristol, Irving. *Two Cheers for Capitalism.* New York: Basic Books, 1978.

Lane, Robert E. *The Loss of Happiness in Market Democracies.* New Haven: Yale University Press, 2000.

Langholm, Odd. *Economics in the Medieval Schools: Wealth, Exchange, Value, Money and Usury According to the Paris Theological Tradition 1200-1350.* Leiden: E. J. Brill, 1992.

—. *The Legacy of Scholasticism in Economic Thought: Antecedents of Choice and Power.* Cambridge: Cambridge University Press, 1998.

—. *The Merchant in the Confessional: Trade and Price in the Pre-Reformation Penitential Handbooks.* Leiden: Brill, 2003.

Lasch, Christopher. *The Revolt of the Elites and the Betrayal of Democracy.* New York: W. W. Norton, 1996.

Laslett, Peter. *The World We Have Lost—Further Explored.* 3rd ed. London: Routledge, 1983.

Lemoyne, Giovanni Battista. Vol. 1 of *The Biographical Memoirs of St. John Bosco.* Edited by Diego Borgatello. New Rochelle, N.Y.: Salesiana Publishers, 1965.

Leo XIII. Encyclical *Immortale Dei.* 1885.

—. Encyclical *Libertas.* 1888. In vol. 2 of *The Papal Encyclicals.* Edited by Claudia Carlen. Raleigh, N.C.: McGrath, 1981.

—. Encyclical *Quod Apostolici Muneris.* 1878. In vol. 2 of *The Papal Encyclicals.* Edited by Claudia Carlen. Raleigh, N.C.: McGrath, 1981.

—. Encyclical *Sapientiae Christianae.* 1890. In vol. 2 of *The Papal Encyclicals.* Edited by Claudia Carlen. Raleigh, N.C.: McGrath, 1981.

Lester, Richard A. "Currency Issues to Overcome Depressions in Pennsylvania, 1723 and 1729." *Journal of Political Economy* 46:3 (June 1938): 324-75.

Lichtenstein, Nelson, ed. *Wal-Mart: The Face of Twenty-First Century Capitalism*. New York: The New Press, 2006.

Lilley, Samuel. "Technological Progress and the Industrial Revolution 1700-1914." In *The Industrial Revolution 1700-1914*. Edited by Carlo M. Cipolla, 187-254. New York: Harvester Press, Barnes and Noble, 1976.

Lindenberg, Adolpho. *The Free Market in a Christian Society*. Translated by Donna H. Sandin. Washington, D.C.: St. Antoninus Institute for Catholic Education in Business, 1999.

Locke, John. "An Essay Concerning Human Understanding." In *Locke, Berkeley, Hume*. Vol. 35 of *Great Books of the Western World*. Edited by Robert Maynard Hutchins, 83-395. Chicago: University of Chicago, 1952.

—. "Concerning Civil Government, Second Essay." In *Locke, Berkeley, Hume*. Vol. 35 of *Great Books of the Western World*. Edited by Robert Maynard Hutchins, 25-82. Chicago: University of Chicago, 1952.

Long, D. Stephen. *Divine Economy: Theology and the Market*. New York: Routledge, 2000.

MacIntyre, Alasdair. *After Virtue: A Study of Moral Theory*. 3rd ed. Notre Dame, Ind.: University of Notre Dame Press, 2007.

Marche, Stephen. "Is Facebook Making Us Lonely?" *The Atlantic*. May 2012.

Marx, Karl. "Capital." Edited by Friedrich Engels. In *Marx*. Vol. 50 of *Great Books of the Western World*. Edited by Robert Maynard Hutchins, 1-411. Chicago: University of Chicago, 1952.

Marx, Karl and Friedrich Engels. "Manifesto of the Communist Party." In *Marx*. Vol. 50 of *Great Books of the Western World*. Edited by Robert Maynard Hutchins, 413-34. Chicago: University of Chicago, 1952.

Matthews, Richard K. and Elric M. Kline. "Jefferson Un-Locked: The Rousseauan Moment in American Political Thought." In *History, on Proper Principles: Essays in Honor of Forrest McDonald*. Edited by Stephen M. Klugewicz and Lenore T. Ealy, 133-165. Wilmington, Del.: ISI Books, 2010.

McDonald, Forrest. "The Founding Fathers and the Economic Order." In *History, on Proper Principles: Essays in Honor of Forrest McDonald*. Edited by Stephen M. Klugewicz and Lenore T. Ealy, 263-69. Wilmington, Del.: ISI Books, 2010.

Minsky, Hyman P. *Stabilizing an Unstable Economy*. New York: McGraw Hill, 2008.

Mises, Ludwig von. *Bureaucracy*. New Haven: Yale University Press, 1944.

Mokyr, Joel. *The Lever of Riches: Technological Creativity and Economic Progress*. New York: Oxford University Press, 1992.

Mousnier, Roland. *Society and State*. Translated by Brian Pearce. Vol. 1 of *The Institutions of France under the Absolute Monarchy 1598-1789*. Chicago: University of Chicago Press, 1979.

—. *The Origins of State and Society*. Translated by Brian Pearce. Vol. 2 of *The Institutions of France under the Absolute Monarchy 1598-1789*. Chicago: University of Chicago Press, 1979.

Mumford, Lewis. *Technics and Human Development*. Vol. 1 of *The Myth of the Machine*. New York: Harcourt, Brace, Jovanovich. 1967.

—. *The Pentagon of Power*. Vol. 2 of *The Myth of the Machine*. New York: Harcourt, Brace, Jovanovich, 1970.

—. *The City in History: Its Origins, Its Transformations, and Its Prospects*. New York: Harcourt, Brace, Jovanovich, 1961.

—. *The Story of Utopias*. New York: The Viking Press, 1972.

Nisbet, Robert A. *The Quest for Community: A Study in the Ethics of Order and Freedom*. San Francisco: ICS Press, 1990.

—. *The Social Bond: An Introduction to the Study of Society*. New York: Alfred A. Knopf, 1970.

—. *Twilight of Authority*. Indianapolis: Liberty Fund, 2000.

Noonan, John T., Jr. *The Scholastic Analysis of Usury*. Cambridge: Harvard University Press, 1957.

Novak, Michael. *The Spirit of Democratic Capitalism*. New York: Touchstone, 1983.

Owst, G. R. *Literature and Pulpit in Medieval England: A Neglected Chapter in the History of English Letters & of the English People*. 2nd ed. Oxford: Basil Blackwell, 1961.

Pangle, Thomas L. *Leo Strauss: An Introduction to His Thought and Intellectual Legacy*. Baltimore: Johns Hopkins University Press, 2006.

Parente, Pietro, Antonio Piolanti, and Salvatore Garofalo. *Dictionary of Dogmatic Theology*. Milwaukee: Bruce Publishing, 1951.

Paul VI. Allocution *Resistite Fortes in Fide* (June 29, 1972). In *Insegnamenti di Paolo VI*. 10: 707-9.

Pieper, Josef. *Leisure: The Basis of Culture*. Translated by Gerald Malsbary. South Bend, Ind.: St. Augustine Press, 1998.

Pirenne, Henri. *Medieval Cities: Their Origins and the Revival of Trade*. Translated by Frank D. Halsey. Princeton: Princeton University Press, 1952.

Pius X. Motu Proprio *Fin Dalla Prima Nostra*. 1903. *American Catholic Quarterly Review* 29 (1904): 234-39.

Pius XI. Encyclical *Quadragesimo Anno*. 1931. In vol. 3 of *The Papal Encyclicals*. Edited by Claudia Carlen. Raleigh, N.C.: McGrath, 1981.

Pius XII. "1941 Allocution to the Roman Patriciate and Nobility." In *Discorsi e Radiomessaggi di Sua Santità Pio XII*. Vatican: Tipografia Poliglotta Vaticana, 1940-1958.

—. "1944 Christmas Message." In *Christmas Messages*. Vol. 2 of *The Major Addresses of Pope Pius XII*. Edited by Vincent A. Yzermans. St. Paul, Minn.: North Central, 1961.

Polanyi, Karl. *The Great Transformation: The Political and Economic Origins of Our Times*. 2nd ed. Boston: Beacon Press, 2001.

Postman, Neil. *Technopoly: The Surrender of Culture to Technology*. New York: Vintage Books, 1993.

Putnam, Robert D. *Bowling Alone: The Collapse and Revival of American Community*. New York: Simon and Schuster, 2000.

Ratzinger, Joseph Cardinal and Vittorio Messori. *The Ratzinger Report: An Exclusive Interview on the State of the Church*. Translated by Salvator Attanasio and Graham Harrison. San Francisco: Ignatius Press, 1986.

Reich, Charles A. *The Greening of America*. New York: Crown Trade Paperbacks, 1970.

Reinhart, Carmen M. and Kenneth S. Rogoff. *This Time Is Different: Eight Centuries of Financial Folly*. Princeton: Princeton University Press, 2009.

Riesman, David, Nathan Glazer, and Reuel Denney. *The Lonely Crowd: A Study of the Changing American Character*. New Haven: Yale University Press, 1989.

Ritzer, George. *The McDonaldization of Society 5*. Los Angeles: Pine Forge Press, 2008.

Roberts, James A. *Shiny Objects: Why We Spend Money We Don't Have in Search of Happiness We Can't Buy*. New York: HarperOne, 2011.

Rommen, Heinrich A. *The State in Catholic Thought: A Treatise in Political Philosophy*. St. Louis: B. Herder, 1947.

Röpke, Wilhelm. *A Humane Economy: The Social Framework of the Free Market*. Chicago: Henry Regnery, 1960.

Rothkopf, David. *Superclass: The Global Power Elite and the World They Are Making*. New York: Farrar, Straus and Giroux, 2008.

Roubini, Nouriel and Stephen Mihm. *Crisis Economics: A Crash Course in the Future of Finance.* New York: Penguin Books, 2010.

Rousseau, Jean Jacques. "The Social Contract or Principles of Political Right." In *Montesquieu, Rousseau.* Vol. 38 of *Great Books of the Western World.* Edited by Robert Maynard Hutchins, 387-439. Chicago: University of Chicago, 1952.

Russell, Bertrand. "A Free Man's Worship." In *Mysticism and Logic and Other Essays.* London: George Allen and Unwin, 1959.

Sandoz, Ellis. *A Government of Laws: Political Theory, Religion, and the American Founding.* Baton Rouge: Louisiana State University Press, 1990.

Schor, Juliet B. *The Overworked American: The Unexpected Decline of Leisure.* New York: Basic Books, 1991.

Schumpeter, Joseph A. *Capitalism, Socialism and Democracy.* New York: Harper Perennial Modern Thought Edition, 2008.

—. *History of Economic Analysis.* Edited by Elizabeth Boody Schumpeter. New York: Oxford University Press, 1986.

Schwarz, Barry. *The Paradox of Choice: Why More Is Less.* New York: Harper Perennial, 2004.

Schwer, Wilhelm. *Catholic Social Theory.* Translated by Bartholomew Landheer. St. Louis: B. Herder, 1940.

Scitovsky, Tibor. *The Joyless Economy: An Inquiry into Human Satisfaction and Consumer Dissatisfaction.* New York: Oxford University Press, 1976.

Simmel, Georg. *The Philosophy of Money.* Translated by Tom Bottomore and David Frisby. 2nd ed. New York: Routledge, 1990.

Smith, Adam. "An Inquiry into the Nature and Causes of the Wealth of Nations." In *Adam Smith.* Vol. 39 of *Great Books of the Western World.* Edited by Robert Maynard Hutchins. Chicago: University of Chicago, 1952.

Southern, R. W. *The Making of the Middle Ages.* New Haven: Yale University Press, 1953.

—. *Western Society and the Church in the Middle Ages.* London: Penguin Books, 1970.

Spalding, Matthew and Patrick J. Garrity. *A Sacred Union of Citizens: George Washington's Farewell Address and the American Character.* Lanham, Md.: Rowman and Littlefield, 1996.

Stark, Rodney. *The Victory of Reason: How Christianity Led to Freedom, Capitalism, and Western Success.* New York: Random House, 2005.

Stewart, Matthew. *The Management Myth: Why the Experts Keep Getting it*

Wrong. New York: W. W. Norton, 2009.

Stivers, Richard. *Shades of Loneliness: Pathologies of a Technological Society.* Lanham, Md.: Rowman and Littlefield, 2004.

—. *Technology as Magic: The Triumph of the Irrational.* New York: Continuum Publishing, 2001.

—. *The Culture of Cynicism: American Morality in Decline.* Cambridge, Mass.: Blackwell, 1994.

—. *The Illusion of Freedom and Equality.* Albany: State University of New York Press, 2008.

Strauss, Leo. *Natural Right and History.* Chicago: University of Chicago Press, 1953.

Strayer, Joseph R. *On the Medieval Origins of the Modern State.* Princeton: Princeton University Press, 1973.

—. *Western Europe in the Middle Ages: A Short History.* New York: Appleton-Century-Crofts, 1955.

Tawney, R. H. *Religion and the Rise of Capitalism.* New York: Harcourt, Brace, 1926.

Taylor, Henry Osborn. *The Medieval Mind: A History of the Development of Thought and Emotion in the Middle Ages.* New York: Macmillan, 1919.

TFP Committee on American Issues. *I Have Weathered Other Storms: A Response to the Scandals and Democratic Reforms That Threaten the Catholic Church.* York, Pa.: Western Hemisphere Cultural Society, 2002.

Thirsk, Joan. "The Rural Economy." In *Our Forgotten Past: Seven Centuries of Life on the Land.* Edited by Jerome Blum, 81-108. London: Thames and Hudson, 1982.

Thompson, C. Bradley. "The Revolutionary Origins of American Constitutionalism." In *History, on Proper Principles: Essays in Honor of Forrest McDonald.* Edited by Stephen M. Klugewicz and Lenore T. Ealy, 1-27. Wilmington, Del.: ISI Books, 2010.

Thompson, James Westfall. *Economic and Social History of the Middle Ages: 300-1300.* New York: Frederick Ungar, 1959.

Tocqueville, Alexis de. *Democracy in America.* Translated by Henry Reeve. Cambridge: Sever and Francis, 1863.

Turkle, Sherry. *Alone Together: Why We Expect More from Technology and Less from Each Other.* New York: Basic Books, 2011.

Walsh, James J. *The Thirteenth, Greatest of Centuries.* New York: Fordham University Press, 1946.

Washington, George. "Farewell Address." In vol. 1 of *A Compilation of the Messages and Papers of the Presidents.* Edited by James D. Richardson. New York: Bureau of National Literature, 1897.

Weaver, Richard. *Ideas Have Consequences.* Chicago: University of Chicago Press, 1984.

—. *Visions of Order: The Cultural Crisis of Our Time.* Wilmington, Del.: Intercollegiate Studies Institute, 1995.

Weber, Max. *The Protestant Ethic and the Spirit of Capitalism.* Translated by Talcott Parsons. New York: Charles Scribner's Sons, 1958.

White, Lynn, Jr. *Machina Ex Deo: Essays in the Dynamism of Western Culture.* Cambridge: MIT Press, 1968.

Whitehead, Alfred North. *Science and the Modern World.* New York: Free Press, 1967.

Wood, Diana. *Medieval Economic Thought.* Cambridge: Cambridge University Press, 2002.

Wynne, John J., S.J., ed. *The Great Encyclical Letters of Pope Leo XIII.* New York: Benziger Brothers, 1903.

Yzermans, Vincent A., ed. *The Major Addresses of Pope Pius XII.* St. Paul, Minn.: North Central, 1961.

INDEX